DIGITAL LABOR

Digital Labor calls on the reader to examine the shifting sites of labor markets to the Internet through the lens of their political, technological, and historical making. Internet users currently create most of the content that makes up the web: they search, link, tweet, and post updates—leaving their "deep" data exposed. Meanwhile, governments listen in, and big corporations track, analyze, and predict users' interests and habits.

This unique collection of essays provides a wide-ranging account of the dark side of the Internet. It claims that the divide between leisure time and work has vanished so that every aspect of life drives the digital economy. The book reveals the anatomy of *playbor* (play/labor), the lure of exploitation and the potential for empowerment. Ultimately, the 14 thought-provoking chapters in this volume ask how users can politicize their troubled complicity, create public alternatives to the centralized social web, and thrive online.

Trebor Scholz is Associate Professor of Culture and Media at The New School.

DIGITAL LABOR

The Internet as Playground and Factory

Edited by Trebor Scholz

Routledge
Taylor & Francis Group

NEW YORK AND LONDON

First published 2013
by Routledge
711 Third Avenue, New York, NY 10017

Simultaneously published in the UK
by Routledge
2 Park Square, Milton Park, Abingdon, Oxon OX14 4RN

Routledge is an imprint of the Taylor & Francis Group, an informa business

© 2013 Taylor & Francis

Library of Congress Cataloging-in-Publication Data
Digital labor : the Internet as playground and factory / edited by Trebor Scholz.
p. cm.
Includes bibliographical references and index.
1. Internet–Social aspects.   2. Information society.
I. Scholz, Trebor.
HM851.D538 2013
302.23'1–dc23   2012012133

ISBN: 978-0-415-89694-8 (hbk)
ISBN: 978-0-415-89695-5 (pbk)
ISBN: 978-0-203-14579-1 (ebk)

Typeset in ApexBembo
by Apex CoVantage, LLC

CONTENTS

ACKNOWLEDGMENTS

Many thanks go to a great many people. I am indebted to my colleagues at The New School, a university in New York City, who have generously and enthusiastically supported my work, specifically The Politics of Digital Culture conference series that I started there in 2009.

Nearly three years have passed since I convened The Internet as Playground and Factory conference that led to the publication of this book. I wish to recognize and thank the participants of this conference who have contributed chapters to this book.

I would like to particularly thank my colleague McKenzie Wark for his intellectual fire and many helpful critical comments. Also working with Erica Wetter at Routledge has been a pleasure.

I would like to thank the following friends and colleagues, for thought-provoking debates, challenging and constructive comments, practical help with the conference, and putting this book together: Frank Pasquale, Neil Gordon, Gabriella Coleman, Shannon Mattern, Laura De Nardis, Mark Greif, Sven Travis, Joel Towers, Jenny Perlin and the students in my spring 2012 seminar "Play and Toil in the Digital Sweatshop."

In addition, I would also like to thank the members of the mailing list of the Institute for Distributed Creativity for the six-month-long pre-conference discussion on the commercial geographies of unsung digital labor, value, and the fight for fairness and economic democracy.

I dedicate this book to the memory of my grandmother Herta Fritzsche, who was born in 1917 and labored as a home worker most of her life.

R. Trebor Scholz

INTRODUCTION

Why Does Digital Labor Matter Now?

Trebor Scholz

In 2009, the Internet as Playground and Factory conference at The New School, a university in New York City with a rich history of critical theory and student activism, asked whether Marxist labor theory, with its concept of exploitation of labor, is still applicable to emerging modes of value capture on the Internet. This book is a result of this international conference that I convened.

What does it mean to be a digital worker today? The Internet has become a simple-to-join, anyone-can-play system where the sites and practices of work and play increasingly wield people as a resource for economic amelioration by a handful of oligarchic owners. Social life on the Internet has become the "standing reserve," the site for the creation of value through ever more inscrutable channels of commercial surveillance. This inquiry has important ramifications for struggles around privacy, intellectual property rights, youth culture, and media literacy.

To this collection of essays the authors bring a common commitment to understanding the complex implications of new forms of waged and unwaged digital labor. Throughout this publication, you will find the consistent analysis of digital labor as a continuation of the social relations surrounding the traditional workplace. While also exploring discontinuities, shifts of labor markets to the Internet are described as an intensification of traditional economies of unpaid work.

Over the past six years, web-based work environments have emerged that are devoid of the worker protections of even the most precarious working-class jobs. Amazon.com's Mechanical Turk is only one example. These are new forms of labor but old forms of exploitation. There are no minimum wages or health insurance, and so far federal and state regulators have not intervened. Digital labor matters; such underpaid, waged occupations must not be ignored when thinking about cognitive capitalism.

But several authors in this book are also thinking about unwaged labor, the activation of our behavior on the social web as monetizable labor. This argument is frequently challenged because in opposition to traditional labor, casual digital labor looks merely like the expenditure of cognitive surplus, the act of being a speaker within communication systems. It doesn't feel, look, or smell like labor at all. This digital labor is much akin to those less visible, unsung forms of traditional women's labor such as child care, housework, and surrogacy.

In 2011, the value of Facebook was pegged at $100 billion, which can be linked to vast financial speculation but also the company's collection of user data over a seven-year time span. Intimate forms of human sociability are being rendered profitable for Facebook, which makes it such a big-ticket company. Facebook sells its user data to its customers, which are mostly third-party advertisers. The social web appears to be free for us to use, but there are hefty social costs; oligarchs capture and financialize our productive expression and take flight with our data. We, the "users," are sold as the product. The loss of our privacy, with all its psychological and political consequences, buys us the convenience of "free," innovative services. All of life is put to work, unfairly harnessing implicit participation for wild profits.

But can we really understand labor as a value-producing activity that is based on sharing creative expression? Harry Potter fans produce fan fiction and give their creative work away for free in exchange for being ignored by the corporation that owns the original content. Such unpaid labor practices also include "game modding" and the submission of "captchas." Does it really make sense to think of these activities or the updating and "liking" of status updates as labor? Many contemporary discussions on productivity take as a starting point the ubiquity of pleasure online and relate this to the eroding distinction between work and play. Alexander Galloway writes that it is impossible to differentiate cleanly between nonproductive leisure activity existing within the sphere of play and productive activity existing within the field of the workplace.

On whichever side of this argument you may fall as a reader, the topic of digital labor is an invitation to dust off arguments about the perilous state of privacy, unequal wealth distribution, and the private exploitation of the public Internet.

One significant event in this debate occurred in 1867, when Karl Marx distinguished between necessary labor time and surplus labor time. The former is labor that is entirely aimed at the worker's survival, while the latter is meant to describe any additional labor time. In 1966, Norbert Wiener warned that responsive machines would intensify the exploitation of workers and even replace them altogether. In 1981, Dallas Smythe suggested that audiences are produced and sold to advertisers as a commodity. The audience, Smythe wrote, commits unpaid time and in return can watch a program along with ads. Twenty years later, Maurizio Lazzarato defined such immaterial labor as an activity that produces the cultural content of the commodity. Already in 2000, Tiziana Terranova examined new forms of capitalist exploitation of unwaged free labor, thinking about the viewers of broadcast media and the burgeoning Internet.

Audience manufacture, a salient topic in the digital labor discussion, reached a first height in the 1920s, when radio started to establish commonalities among suburbanites across the United States. Communities that were previously connected through national newspapers started to bond over radio and, starting in the late 1940s and 1950s, over broadcast television. Also cinema played a significant role in the capture of the masses and the creation of a common culture. Now, in the overdeveloped world, people are leaving behind their television sets—gradually but increasingly—in favor of communion with and through digital networks.

Beyond this historical context, *Digital Labor: The Internet as Playground and Factory* also contains the voices of those who are cautious of a discussion of digital labor altogether. Jonathan Beller and others remarked that we can fall victim to a technocratic fetishization of the Internet that takes away from a full acknowledgment of the "real" places of exploitation—namely the slums of economic developing countries. Digital labor in the overdeveloped world is contingent upon the sweat of exploited labor in countries such as China.[1]

The focus on the Internet and the attendant issues of time theft and addiction may distract us from perhaps the most important issues of our time. Bluntly put, time spent on Facebook stops us from giving love and affection to others or from furthering projects that undermine capitalism. What's more, many people still labor on farms and in factories, and let's not forget the working poor, undocumented workers, and youth in rural areas for whom access to the Internet is not a given.

"The digital" does not sum up our entire condition. The essence of technology is not solely technological. But without falling for the fallacious rhetoric of "Twitter revolutions," digital media have also been instrumental for social movements worldwide. It is time to rethink well-worn conceptions of the digital divide by acknowledging the unprecedented global turn in online sociability. While the 2 billion Internet users are indeed a global minority, the 5 billion people and their families who use cell phones are not. Facebook is becoming available on cell phones all across Africa, and it should be understood that digital labor is not just a predicament for the privileged few. Our silence will not save us from the tyranny of digital labor.

About the Organization of This Book

Following the structure of the Internet as Playground and Factory conference, this book is arranged in four parts. The first part, "The Shifting Sites of Labor Markets," introduces the broadest issues in the debate. The second part, "Interrogating Modes of Digital Labor," provides examples and case studies of emerging digital work environments. The third part, "The Violence of Participation," focuses on questions of exploitation. The fourth part, "Organized Networks in an Age of Vulnerable Publics," reflects on near-future scenarios, including peer-to-peer alternatives.

In the first part, Andrew Ross provides a wide-ranging and sobering overview of the implications of digital technologies and monetizable labor. He states that the profits of the owners of Google or Facebook are evidence of the current rent extraction boom. Ross also thinks through the class action suit against Huffington Post. The question is whether HuffPo had a contractual obligation to share the spoils of the sale to AOL with the bloggers who created the content for the site.

The entire fabric of our everyday lives, rather than merely our workplace toil, becomes the raw material for capital accumulation. Ross points to the fact that corporate America enjoys a $2 billion annual subsidy from largely unpaid or underpaid internships alone. Ross also asks us to consider that the vast majority of human labor, historically and to this day, is performed without remuneration—only 7% of India's workforce, for example, enjoys regular wages and salaries. Digital technology, to be sure, didn't give birth to free labor, but it has proven highly efficient as an enabler of dicey work arrangements.

In her chapter "Free Labor," Tiziana Terranova discusses what she calls free labor as work that is not based on employment, work that is unpaid and freely given. For companies it is very clear that the new source of added value in the digital economy is user participation. Terranova states that, "in 1996, at the peak of the volunteer moment [in AOL chat room moderation], over 30,000 'community leaders' were helping AOL to generate at least $7 million a month."

Sean Cubitt continues this line of thought by describing how social networking commercializes the gift of labor, not as individual activity but as aberrations from the average, which can be read as tendencies and exploited as such. He writes that the battle for the Internet is not yet over, but in critical strategic and tactical fields such as codecs and HTML5, capital is winning. Technological rule-making directly determines civil liberties online. Technical standards such as MP3, mpg, and Bluetooth are increasingly determined by private or hybrid private/public institutions, which become points of control over global information architectures.[2] While design decisions can have serious consequences for our freedom, it is only a small group of people that has control over the entire Internet. There are significant battles on this level. Victims of Hurricane Katrina, for example, couldn't register for federal emergency help unless they used the Internet Explorer browser. Technical standards are politics by other means.

McKenzie Wark states that the vectoral class, a term that he developed in *Hacker Manifesto,* has less and less interest in the viability of national spaces of production and consumption; it can do without factories. Wark also cautions against the rhetoric of "gamification," because it could be conceived of as getting people to do things without paying in exchange for symbolic rewards.

In the second part, "Interrogating Modes of Digital Labor," Patricia Ticineto Clough addresses labor metrics and affect. She wonders if it is possible that labor is not measurable on the parasitic platforms of the social web. Clough suggests that in financial capitalism, wealth is produced external to capital's organization of labor or external to the accumulation of capital through production. She writes that philosophy is registering the ongoing reconfiguring of labor, measure, and affect accompanying the effort to make productive the micro affects of matter itself.

Ayhan Aytes, in his chapter, poses that if the digital network is the assembly line of cognitive labor, then the Mechanical Turk is its model apparatus. Crowdsourcing, for Aytes, is a hybrid concept that merges the neoliberal outsourcing paradigm with the crowds on the digital networks. He continues that the unregulated nature of the emerging global cognitive labor market evokes the *Gastarbeiter* (guest worker) program of the economic wonder years of postwar Germany. This German *Gastarbeiter* program has been a prominent model for establishing a legislative immigration system without rights.

Abigail De Kosnik investigates the work of fan moderators, writers, and artists who post and comment on YouTube, Facebook, Twitter, and other social media sites. Their number is in the millions, and their free labor activities contribute to far more massive corporate revenues than the $7 million monthly garnered by AOL, mentioned also in Tiziana Terranova's chapter. The abundant contributions of fans to the Internet can be regarded as labor, she writes. Fan labor can ramp up the buzz and reputation of a product, and fans are booted into this emerging labor market. De Kosnik concludes that corporations should value fan labor as a new form of publicity and advertising. They should compensate fans who could understand their work as the first rung on the reputation ladder for aspiring creative professionals.

Jodi Dean contemplates blogging. As bloggers, she writes, we expose ourselves, our feelings and experiences, loves and hates, desires and aversions, but we need to be reminded of our exposure, our visibility, vulnerability, and ultimate lack of control. Access to my friend is a way of getting access to me, Jodi Dean notes. For Dean, publicity is the ideology of communicative capitalism, which suggests work without work (work without pay or work that is fun) and play without play (play for which one is paid and play for which one pays with enjoyment). Convenience trumps commitment. Dean concludes that in this economy, a lucky few will get nearly everything, but most will get very little, almost nothing.

In the third part, "The Violence of Participation," Mark Andrejevic reports from the new frontiers of data mining. He makes the case that the commercial appropriation of information meets an abstract definition of exploitation. Andrejevic argues that it is indeed the sign of a certain kind of material luxury to be able to be exploited online—to have the leisure time and resources to engage in the activities that are monitored and tracked. Google tracks its 1 billion unremunerated users and sells their data to advertising clients, who consequently target users with ads. The intertwining of labor, leisure, consumption, production, and play complicates the understanding of exploitation, but Andrejevic remarked that the potential usefulness of an exploitation-based critique of online monitoring is that it invites us to reframe questions of individual choice and personal pleasure in terms of social relations.

Andrejevic also discusses peer pressure and the obligation to network online, which is becoming institutionalized, and the fruits of this labor are recognized as a source of value. Commercial surveillance has become a crucial component of our communicative infrastructure, he observes. Exploitation, however, does not mean that workers don't take pleasure in the success of a collaborative effort. There are moments of pleasure despite the fact that we are losing control of our productive and creative activities. While his critique of exploitation does not disparage the pleasures of workers, it also does not nullify exploitative social relations.

Jonathan Beller argues that there is no easy distinction between financialization and digitization. For him, the Arab Spring, Los Indignados in Spain, and the worldwide protests of 2011 all transmit a radical disaffection with the capitalist organization of representation and assert the living history and potential of insurrection.

Lisa Nakamura's chapter examines the racialization of digital labor by Chinese gold farmers in the massively multiplayer online role-playing game World of Warcraft. These "farmers" produce and sell virtual goods such as weapons, garments, animals, and even their own avatars to other players for actual dollars. Asian gold farmers are constructed as unwanted guest workers within the culture of World of Warcraft. While on guard when it comes to explicit references to racial conflict in the real world, the game is premised upon a racial battle in a virtual environment.

The fourth and concluding part of this book, "Organized Networks in an Age of Vulnerable Publics," discusses alternatives to the logic of the network. Which tangible and imaginative suggestions can we offer that some of us could implement, today, after putting down this book?

For users, the web signals a double bind between the benefits of weak ties, the real possibilities of getting a job, and an awareness that their participation greases the wheels of the corporate Internet. How much power should society allocate to the major sites on the Internet? Shouldn't critically important digital platforms be regulated or even nationalized? What are the temptations of dominance? Should Google be able to dictate who has access to Google Books and perhaps only give full access to the highest bidder?

According to Mark Zuckerberg, "sharing and connecting are core human needs."[3] For him, consumer-communication is at the heart of the service that he offers. But self-disclosure is misunderstood if we talk about it in terms of basic needs. We don't always get what we want. Is it really self-disclosure when we vote thumbs-up or thumbs-down? Seeking praise and peer acknowledgment, hundreds of millions of post-job workers are flocking to the social web like moths to the light, trying to get noticed by transforming themselves into something quite generic. Instead of projecting identities that conform with what employers might expect, is there not an opportunity for collective self-becoming?

If class consciousness across social networks is an unrealistic proposal, maybe a call for political consciousness could lead to a fight against mindless individualism or the power imbalance between intermediaries and users.

Michel Bauwens argues that in conditions of social strife, capitalist corporations can be transformed into worker-owned, self-managed entities that create their own commons of shared knowledge, code, and design. The task of movements of cognitive forms of labor, he writes, is to try to create a new hegemony and a new commons-based alliance for social change, which challenges the domination of capital.

Ned Rossiter and Soenke Zehle explain the current transformation of networks into autonomous political and cultural "networks of networks." Zehle and Rossiter emphasize that in order to affect politics of the universal on its computational terrain, we have to take the condition of variational territories and topologies of code seriously. Such an action intervenes on the algorithmic level, they write.

How do we carve out autonomous spaces for creative resistance when frictionless sharing of network interaction undermines our privacy and when digital infrastructures of control invisibly capture value from all areas of our lives? Which practices and instruments provide us with true social power—the power to act collectively and form publics of common concern?

Are we willing to sit at the table and negotiate future scenarios with intermediaries, or is the end of capitalism a precondition to kick-start our actions? Christian Fuchs calls for a different world today. He demands that the communicative commons of society should not be privately owned or controlled. The commons should be available to all, without payment or other access requirements. A more pragmatic, near-future approach would be the establishment of legal jurisdiction that imposes restrictions on outsourcing services online, providing workers with some basic rights.

Digg.com's Digital Boston Tea Party or the so-called Facebook riots about the newsfeed, Beacon and the various other privacy hiccups are referenced frequently. The social web does empower consumers in their negotiation of the rules of their own consumptive activities by these "spectacles of democracy," as I call them, but do not give license to citizens in their struggle for meaningful social change. Instead of riots, what we witness are just-in-time user feedback loops.

Apart from such rebellions, further considerations include the building of actual alternatives—technical and social infrastructures—and the possibility of refusal of or withdrawal from the Internet.

There are a few nonproprietary social networking services, but at this point, they do not reach considerable membership. I hope that one day a mass exodus from Facebook will happen. The social networking service Diaspora is designed for that purpose.[4] Other initiatives include the independent citizen media project Crabgrass, which is especially designed to meet the needs of bottom-up grassroots organizing.[5] We can think of sites like Craigslist, which, despite recent controversies, is a good example of an online business that is not focused on profit maximization but rather on user satisfaction.

But the Internet is so intensely subjugated to corporate interests that even if you jump ship, if you abandon the Facebook Titanic today, chances are that you are jumping on to the next life raft that is likely just as profit oriented. Wikipedia,

Crabgrass, Diaspora, and Craigslist are exceptions; they are not practical models for the entire Internet. On the Internet, even peer-to-peer sharing practices, the exchange of the "gift" that almost always takes place on corporate turf, creates capital for those from whom we rent those platforms. In the age of friendship marketing, we rent the product of our own labor, as McKenzie Wark puts it.

Those who called for an all-out refusal of the sunless digital cycles of capitalist production and reproduction need to acknowledge the rare privilege of such position and need to understand that the engagement of users is not entirely voluntary. The violence of participation is about data mining on the one hand and the personal and professional price they would pay for their refusal of mainstream social media services on the other. Refusal would be tantamount to social isolation. Furthermore, in *Convergence Culture,* Henry Jenkins accurately points out that the debate keeps getting framed as if the only true alternative is to opt out of media altogether and live in the woods, eating acorns and lizards (Jenkins, 248–9). Instead, we can produce real counterpublics, support civil disobedience actions, and create networks of solidarity by diversifying/hybridizing our social media practices.

On the social web, we are getting used, we are using each other, and we can act together. Which social practices make it easier for us to be powerful together? Which political stance do we take by aligning ourselves with a particular network or service? Surely, we will want to question all those dear friends who only care about the bottom line instead of really doing something magnificent with these emerging online platforms. And if you think about it, well, wouldn't you like to stir up some serious havoc in the playground that is the factory?

Notes

1 Recent reports about Foxconn showed the atrocious working conditions under which iPads are produced. Nick Wingfield, "Apple's Suppliers Pressed to Improve Workers' Lot," *New York Times,* April 1, 2012. Web. June 13, 2012.

2 For an excellent discussion of network governance, see Laura Denardis's two recent books, *Protocol Politics: The Globalization of Internet Governance.* Cambridge, MA: The MIT Press, 2009; and *Opening Standards: The Global Politics of Interoperability.* 1st ed. Cambridge, MA: The MIT Press, 2011.

3 Justin Smith, "Exclusive: Discussing the Future of Facebook with CEO Mark Zuckerberg," *Inside Facebook,* June 13, 2012, http://www.insidefacebook.com/2009/06/03/exclusive-discussing-the-future-of-facebook-with-ceo-mark-zuckerberg/.

4 "Diaspora★," *Diaspora★,* June 13, 2012, https://joindiaspora.com/.

5 "All about Crabgrass—Groups," https://we.riseup.net/crabgrass/about.

References

Galloway, Alexander. 2007. "We Are All Goldfarmers." *Culture and Communication.* http://cultureandcommunication.org/galloway/interview_barcelona_sept07.txt.

Jenkins, Henry. 2008. *Convergence Culture: Where Old and New Media Collide.* Revised. New York: NYU Press.

Lazzarato, Maurizio. 1997. "Immaterial Labor." *Generation Online.* http://www.generation-online.org/c/fcimmateriallabour3.htm.

Marx, Karl. 1867. *Capital.Vol. 1: A critique of Political Economy.* Trans. Ben Fowkes. London: Penguin, reprint 1992.

Smythe, Dallas W. 1981/2006. On the Audience Commodity and Its Work. In *Media and Cultural Studies,* eds. Meenakshi G. Durham and Douglas M. Kellner, 230–56. Malden, MA: Blackwell.

Wiener, Norbert. 1954. *The Human Use of Human Beings: Cybernetics and Society.* Jackson, TN: Da Capo Press.

PART I

The Shifting Sites of Labor Markets

1

IN SEARCH OF THE LOST PAYCHECK

Andrew Ross

When the Huffington Post was sold to AOL in February 2011, fair labor advocates finally had a high-profile vehicle for their fight against exploiters of free online content provision. Legions of bloggers who had polished the site's reputation over the years were passed over when owner Arianna Huffington collected a cool $315 million from the sale of the site. Regular HuffPo contributors from ArtScene and Visual Art Source announced a boycott that burgeoned into a full-blown e-strike after Huffington ridiculed the action of the unpaid writers. "Go ahead, go on strike," she scoffed, opining that no one would notice, or care. In March, the 26,000-member Newspaper Guild threw its weight behind the strike, as did the National Writers Union (NWU)/UAW Local 1981), and an electronic picket line was thrown up.[1] Progressives who crossed the line to write for HuffPo drew heated protests, and some were labeled scabs for putting their bylines above the calls for professional solidarity. In April, a class action suit, claiming $105 million on behalf of the uncompensated bloggers, was filed by media labor activist Jonathan Tasini, who described the plaintiffs as "modern-day slaves on Arianna Huffington's plantation." Tasini had a good track record. Previously, in 2001, he won a milestone victory when the U.S. Supreme Court ruled (in *New York Times Co. Inc. et al. v. Tasini et al.*) that publishing companies must obtain permission from freelance writers before reusing their works in electronic databases.

By any measures, the practical impact of the boycott was limited, and, from the outset, the prospects for the lawsuit were not bright. But Huffington's let-them-eat-cake posture, amplified by her public renown as a left-leaning pundit, helped to push the affair into the limelight. Arguments about fair compensation for digital content got a good airing, along with some elements of the debate about free labor, which had been nurtured by the coterie of cybercritics for the last decade. The volume of the hubbub far exceeded the low-key grumbling that had accompanied previous sales of social web properties such as YouTube (to Google), Flickr (to Yahoo), and Bebo (to AOL itself).

Apologists for the "attention economy" played up all of the nonmonetary benefits that page-view exposure delivers to freelance strivers, piloting their do-it-yourself careers through the turbulence of the blogosphere. According to this view, the value of free promotion on a wide platform outweighs any benefits to be gotten from the surety of a professional pay scale. It was also argued that the publisher's relationship with her bloggers simply reflected the already-established norms of the digital information landscape, which seem to demand an initial donation of services as a customary price of entry. In any event, it was concluded that the owner was under no contractual obligation to share the spoils with those who had volunteered their labor up front. On the other side of the debate, supporters of the boycott played up the continuity of the case with traditional forms of capitalist expropriation. The lucre extracted by Huffington was not different in kind from that enjoyed by brick-and-mortar owners who profit from shortchanging their workers. Talk about the benefits of self-promotion is the sort of deceptive practice touted by employers who are in a position to take advantage of an oversupply of market labor. As for the publisher's debt to the bloggers, it was argued that she had a moral obligation, at the very least. But Tasini's class action suit went further, alleging "unjust enrichment" on Huffington's part—a legal claim that did not depend on whether writers had agreed up front to write for free.

Increasingly thrown on the defensive, Huffington insisted that, in her new position as AOL's head of content, she was pushing for the hiring of hundreds of professional journalists to staff the bureaus the company had opened as part of its Patch.com local news operation. That was a valid argument. But closer examination suggested that these new recruits would be servicing operations that are difficult to distinguish from what is known as a content farm—a site with shallow, non-original stories written specifically to trigger popular search queries and to game Google algorithms into placing the site on the first page of search results. Leading content farms such as Demand Media and Associated Media churn out low-quality articles and video in the field of online advice, paying a measly piece rate to their free agent creatives. As Dan Roth reported in his original 2009 *Wired* article on the topic, "pieces are not dreamed up by trained editors nor commissioned based on submitted questions. Instead they are assigned by an algorithm, which mines nearly a terabyte of search data, Internet traffic patterns, and keyword rates to determine what users want to know and how much advertisers will pay to appear next to the answers." As a gauge to the fast growth of this spam-like sector, Roth estimated that Demand Media alone would soon be publishing "the equivalent of four English-language Wikipedias a year."[2]

Just as these sites are ushering in a fast food revolution in content, they are engaged in a race to the bottom when it comes to remunerating employees. The filmmaker featured in Roth's 2009 article was paid $20 per clip for each how-to video he shot on location, edited at home on Final Cut Pro, and then uploaded to Demand Media. Given the growth rate of this sector, that $20 piece rate has undoubtedly come down in the intervening years. AOL's own business model for its big push into online content proved to be one of the factors driving the wage depreciation. The AOL Way, the company's expansion plan that was leaked in February 2011, revealed how it would pay a pittance to in-house writers who were expected to pen up to 10 blog articles per day, each prepped for search engine friendliness and for maximum ad exposure.[3]

Creatives who have been knocked to the ground by the recent Great Recession feel pressured to sign up with this kind of word factory when, increasingly, it is the only game in town that pays. After all, the alternative to churning out junk product for a content farm is to play the reputation game by posting for free, like the Huffington Post bloggers. The former option involves the kind of routine toil that is anathema to aspiring creative professionals. The latter option promises the kind of unalienated expression of thought that is closer to their ideal. Yet only one of these will guarantee food on the table.

On the face of it, this does not appear to be a new dilemma. Creatives have been facing this kind of choice since the eighteenth century, when the onset of commercial culture markets offered them the choice of eking out a living with the scribblers on Pope's Grub Street or of building a name-recognition relationship with the fickle public. Literary agents, unions, and other professional organizations sprang up or evolved in order to protect their livelihoods from the rough justice of the marketplace, and while the explosive growth of new media has outpaced and outsmarted the traditional agents of bargaining and regulation (such as the press unions), ever-fresher versions are likely to emerge. The Freelancers Union, for example, was founded in 2001 specifically to respond to the needs of the self-employed, and it has been the fastest-growing union in the United States in recent years. Its members are learning how to acquire an ever-larger share of social insurance and political clout while surfing each new wave that washes over the ever-mutating creative/digital landscape. Beginning in the 1990s, WashTech pioneered the business of labor protection for permatemps in the tech industry, and other Communications Workers of America (CWA) locals are following suit in their efforts to recruit independent contractors.

But it would be wrong to conclude that in the realm of digital labor there is nothing new under the sun. On the contrary, each rollout of online tools has offered ever more ingenious ways of extracting cheaper, discount work from users and participants. The transition from web 1.0 to social web was a quantum leap in this regard. The youthful zeal that went into the first generation of web designs was bought with cappuccinos and beaming admiration from clueless elders. Building the pioneer environment of the web was like a massive barn raising, largely dependent on uncoordinated volunteer effort. Its successor also trades on the openness of youth, but the sophisticated operations of its hidden labor economy bear as much resemblance to the block-building of web 1.0 as the exotic derivatives of today's Wall Street do to the origins of pork belly trading on the Chicago Mercantile Exchange. The social platforms, web crawlers, personalized algorithms, and other data mining techniques of recent years are engineered to suck valuable, or monetizable, information out of almost every one of our online activities. Whether all this activity can or should be classified as labor according to any traditional criteria of political economy is a case in point, and one of the themes of this book. To address the question more fully, as I will do in the pages that follow, involves delving far below the visible surface of the digital landscape on which the Huffington affair was exposed.

From the outset, however, let us bear in mind that new media are not determining agents. Like any other technology, they are facilitators, not causes, of changing social forces. So, too, as Marx and many others have noted, technologies are not simply weapons of class war, designed to control and deskill workers, they also harbor the potential to eliminate wage labor, socialize production, and free up our time. Whether they are deployed for the latter purpose depends not so much on their technical development as on what Marx called the "relations of production"—that is, the state of our socioeconomic relationship to capital, property, and governance. Reverse engineering begins with technology, but unless it is also taken up as a social challenge, the chances are that the outcome will only benefit tech-savvy elites.

Formerly Known as Employment

In the heyday of the labor movement, it was commonly observed that the bosses needed workers but that workers didn't need bosses. Yet in the third and fourth quarters of 2010, corporate America posted record profits at a time when the U.S. Bureau of Labor Statistics reported the real unemployment rate at 17%. Does this yawning disjunct between profits and joblessness mean that the bosses have learned how to get by without workers? Not exactly, no, but the statistics, which can be dissected a hundred ways, might suggest that a sea change is occurring in the world of work.

Two of the reasons for the high earnings seem to be beyond dispute. Corporations are moving more and more of their operations offshore, especially jobs in high-skilled sectors, where the largest savings in labor costs can be gotten. So they still need workers, but not expensive ones in the North. A second explanation rests on what business economists call increased productivity. Roughly translated, this means that employees have been pressed, by the stiff threat of redundancies, either to work harder and longer for the same paycheck or to take a cut. In any downturn, employers will push their advantage in this way, but in a soul-sucking recession like this one, there is no quarter; the assault comes from all sides, whether in the form of pay freezes, concessions, furloughs, layoffs, or further casualization. A third reason—and this is the unfamiliar quantum—is the growing reliance on new kinds of free labor to boost the balance sheet of companies that are canny enough to harvest it. Hard evidence for this footprint is not so easy to muster, but the strong anecdotal record suggests it is large enough to be statistically significant.

Free, or token-wage, labor is increasingly available though a variety of channels: crowdsourcing; data mining or other sophisticated digital techniques for extracting rents from users/participants; expanded prison labor programs; the explosion of unpaid, near-obligatory internships in every white-collar sector; and the whole gamut of contestant volunteering that has transformed so much of our commerce in culture into an amateur talent show, with jackpot stakes for a few winners and hard-luck swag for everyone else. The web-enabled developments have attracted the most media attention, not least because the tidal surge of free online content directly threatens the livelihoods of professional writers and artists. After all, the widespread shuttering of newspapers, magazines, and overseas news bureaus has seen a generation of union jobs scattered to the winds. Professional pay scales are reduced to dust as the online content aggregators sweep all before them, and resistance was few and far between until the Huffington affair came along. In most corners of the information landscape, working for nothing has become normative, and largely because it is not experienced as exploitation.

From the early days of the Great Recession, business press pundits have wondered how far firms could go in taking advantage of new sources of free labor in order to stay afloat and improve their market positions. How can we take advantage of all the free time (or "cognitive surplus," as net evangelist Clay Shirky puts it) that people have, especially the newly unemployed? Since many of the latter will be spending their newly free time online, how can we exploit their willingness to explore any avenue in search of the possibility of employment? Can we take advantage of their inclination to take on tasks that feel like fun? Or, more ominously, how can we harness their habitual need to participate in something that feels like work, in the absence of paid work and just to keep their hand in? Advocates for this line of thinking have seen it as a viable business strategy. They have also made overblown bonanza-scale claims for the potential windfall, inspired no doubt by the high valuations of social media firms. Inevitably, it has been suggested that social networking is the oil of the twenty-first century; yet, so far at least, it looks as if oil is still the oil of the twenty-first century.

Even so, the financial profile of these companies is remarkable. In 2011, Facebook took in an estimated $4.3 billion in revenue, and almost $1 billion of that was net profit. Leaving aside its pre-IPO valuation at more than $100 billion, these numbers are big enough, especially if you consider that the firm only had not many more than 2,000 employees on payroll. This ratio of employees to revenue is unusual by any historical standards, but it is typical of firms that dominate the upper stratosphere of information services. In 2011, Google, for example, had around 30,000 employees, but it pulled in an estimated $35 billion in revenue for a $13 billion profit. The other fast-growing social media companies—Twitter, Groupon, Zynga, LinkedIn, and Tumblr—are in the same boat.

For the rapidly shrinking population that are not Facebook users, Aaron Sorkin's film *The Social Network* must have presented a conundrum. On the one hand, the story of creative conception that it presents is reasonably familiar. Take a hothouse Ivy League environment where collegiate values are easily trumped by the predatory marketplace ethos already incubating on the campus and add a cast of recognizable characters: a socially challenged white male engineer; a brainy white girlfriend who challenges him even further through humiliation; a socially desirable male entrepreneur; assorted and primarily Asian female groupies who are irresistibly attracted to Jewish men; and a neo-bohemian start-up crew working 24/7 to make a market breakthrough. These are all updated components of the standard Hollywood template for myth making in the field of technical invention. This is how national champions labor to bring dazzling innovations and lustrous wealth into existence.

On the other hand, there is no actual social networking depicted in the film, and so uninformed viewers could plausibly conclude that the firm's huge financial success rests on the subscription base of Facebook's half a billion users. Yet these users are not consumers in any traditional sense of paying customers. Rather, the variety of activities they perform (technically known as click signals) is the source of valuable data that is sold to the true customers—advertisers or behavior market vendors such as Bluekai, TargusInfo, and Acxiom. According to Eli Pariser, "Acxiom alone has accumulated an average of 1500 pieces of data on each person in its database, which includes 96% of Americans."[4] Some of these customers pay to advertise on the site, though most use the information to follow users around the web with personalized spot advertising. The trade-off for users, of course, is free access to the platform and the software, but, from the company's perspective, the cost of hosting and maintenance is dwarfed by the tradeable value of the information it can extract from the daily churn on its site. By far the majority of social network users are unaware of how the platform owners profit from the volunteer content of their communications, or indeed how they themselves are generating monetizable product for the owners. But as Andrew Lewis has succinctly put it, "If you're not paying for something, you're not the customer, you're the product being sold."[5]

The 1960s futurist Alvin Toffler coined the term "prosumers" to describe the class of consumers who had evolved beyond a passive acceptance of marketplace choice. But he could hardly have imagined how the term would come to be used, as it is today, to denote the mass of Internet users whose devoted efforts to build relationships and polish their online social identity are the raw material for tidy profits enjoyed by others. Nor could any of the other sunny 1970s prognosticators of postindustrial society such as Daniel Bell have imagined the new order being driven by an attention economy, or that it would be sustained not by the gainful labor of cognitive workers but by the self-promotion of ordinary, unpaid individuals. Moreover, the rewards that underpin this economy are, in some respects, redolent of the kinds of assets that secured social standing in an era that preceded industrialization, when the careful and laborious nurturing of relationships with wealthy and powerful names were sources of considerable worth.

Today, we can see the resurgence of such a culture based on the cultivation of social capital, whether for those in search of breakthrough or blockbuster attention in the reputation stakes (in Twitter trending and top viral links) or in the more low-hanging circuits of Internet self-exposure. In some quarters, this affective currency has replaced the wages of industrialization, especially for professionals who used to earn a structured living from paid content and who now disseminate their bylines far and wide in hopes of securing a niche livelihood from name recognition. But by far the most substantial rewards are allocated, on an industrial basis, to those who build and maintain the technologies of extraction, who hold the system's intellectual property, and who can trade the aggregate output of personal expression as if it were some bulk commodity like grain or beets.[6] The real spoils, in other words, do not go to the aspiring stars, ranked and rated by the battery of metrics that measure Internet sentiment and opinion, but to behind-the-scenes content hosts and data miners, who utilize these and other metrics to guarantee their profits. The outcome, for this latter group, is a virtually wage-free proposition. When all is said and done, the informal contract that underpins this kind of economy is a profoundly asymmetrical deal.

The art of producing gratis media content by showcasing the vox populi has a long history; its origins could arguably be traced to the establishment of letters to the editor columns in print publications. Since these contributions were selected, edited, and, in many cases, fabricated in order to support the editorial line of newspapers and magazines, they offer a good illustration of how supposedly unsolicited public opinion can be generated, shaped, or even ventriloquized. Websites that depend on user input, whether for the main action or in the form of comments posted in response to a featured item, are in direct linear descent from these first letters to the editor. More raw and unfiltered by far, they build on the popularity and cost-effectiveness of their print antecedents.

In recent years, as the open comments sections ("Comment Is Free") have lengthened and proliferated, more and more online newspaper versions have turned to crowdsourcing appeals for readers to generate free columns, images, videos, designs, fact checking, and other information supplies.[7] The principle underlying these appeals is that readers will be gratified to participate and that the results will be more authentic, especially if they are drawing on skills and knowledge unavailable to a commissioned reporter. Outside of the mainstream media, this principle also applies to the widespread uptake of crowdsourcing as a semi-industrial technique for extracting ideas, opinions, designs, and intelligence with little or no compensation for the provider other than name recognition. Informal evidence suggests that as long as a task can be advertised as fun or cool, there is a good chance you can get it done for free, or for a pittance from the seemingly ever-obliging crowd. Moreover, if some of the input seems to be very professional, that is because either the crowdsourcing call is specifically crafted to appeal to professionals on their downtime, or else because it quite probably comes from someone who used to be a professional employee and has been cast into the amateur demimonde of the volunteer content provider.

At the other end of the spectrum are more routine tasks, such as those put out for bid on programs like Amazon's Mechanical Turk. The bids are accepted in return for a minimal fee set by the requester and are assigned to tasks that may take no more than a few minutes to perform.[8] The registered taskers of the Mechanical Turk and other e-lance operations would not be thought of as remotely resembling temporary employees any more than the uncompensated creatives who respond to the more skill-intensive kinds of crowdsourcing. They leave no trace of their employment, and certainly nothing to implicate an employer in any legal or regulated network of obligations. What they do, however, is bring the definition of a job much closer to its etymological source—a discrete lump, or piece, of work that exists only for the duration of its fulfillment.

Distributed Workplaces

Distributed labor has been suggested as a way of describing the use of the Internet to mobilize the spare processing power of a widely dispersed crowd of discrete individuals. This should not be confused with an older use of this term to describe the business process outsourcing business model for coordinating geographically dispersed workplaces, whether from telecommuting or from distant nodes on a global production chain. That model was especially critical to the wave of white-collar offshore outsourcing in the first half of the last decade, and it depended on sophisticated work-flow platform technologies to slice up, allocate, and recombine work. So, too, the new model should be distinguished from the distributed workplace known today as the mobile office. Business strategists advocate on behalf of the benefits to employee morale of allowing high-wage corporate talent to work anytime, anywhere, and on any device. But it is the boost to efficiency and productivity that commands the most attention in their reports. Untold revenue can be extracted from the steady erosion of the boundary between work and leisure time—a long-held dream of employers—which results from putting employees on an unforgiving 24/7 leash.

The new kind of distributed labor does not need to be performed by payroll employees in far-flung branch locations, or by notebook toters in wired coffee shops, the default workplace for a generation of contract freelancers who forsake the privacy of their homes (Toffler's "electronic cottage") to work in public view, braving, or feeding off, the gregarious hum of society. Rather, it is done either by users who do not perceive their interactive input as work at all, or else it is contracted out online—through a growing number of e-lance service sites—to a multitude of taskers who piece together lumps of income from motley sources. As in the offshore outsourcing model, the dispersion of this labor is highly organized, but it is not dependent on physical relocation to cheap labor markets. Instead, the cost savings can be derived from either the latent talent of the crowd or the microdivision of labor into puzzles, stints, chores, and bits, which, if they amount to anything more than distractions, require only fitful bursts of concentration.

The devising and parceling out of these microtasks is arguably only the latest development in a lineage of work management that derives from Taylorism. Taskers are effectively deskilled, dispersed, and deprived of any knowledge about the nature of the product to which their labor contributes. The coordinating manager, by contrast, is in complete control of the labor process. As for the donor labor of the crowd, that has a longer historical lineage since it owes a lot to the traditions of creative work, where sacrifices in monetary compensation are commonly made in return for job gratification or for the opportunity to test and advertise one's talent. This willingness to donate labor was referred to as self-exploitation when it first emerged as an industrial prototype in the formal employment offered by the New Economy or dot-com firms of the late 1990s. In the course of my own ethnographic research on these new media workplaces, for No-Collar, I recall that one of my interviewees told me her job offered "work you just couldn't help doing"—a description that seemed to sum up the mentality of passionate, or sacrificial, labor.[9] Subsequent ethnographic studies of knowledge and creative industry workplaces have shown that job gratification comes at a heavy cost—longer hours in pursuit of the satisfying finish, price discounts in return for aesthetic recognition, self-exploitation in response to the gift of autonomy, and dispensability in exchange for flexibility.[10]

One of the ways to contextualize the rise of the creative industries over the course of the last decade is to interpret it quite literally as an effort to industrialize creativity, aimed, of course, at the market prize of intellectual property.[11] Adapting the tempo of creative work to an industrial template is an acute managerial challenge, however, and, in a jackpot intellectual property economy, the costs of competing are considerable. The turn to crowdsourcing offers a more impersonal solution that slices costs and delivers owners from any employer-type obligations. The crowd is not only smarter than trained employees, you don't need to make social security contributions to take advantage of its wisdom or put up with the wayward personalities of the creatives on payroll.

Crowdsourcing and allied techniques are the progeny of strange bedfellows. On the one hand, there is a clear debt to the collaborative basis of the open-source movement, shareware, and the hacker ethic, which is profoundly proto-anarchistic in its embrace of the principle of the commons. The underlying spirit of mutuality, or what Trebor Scholz and Geert Lovink call "the art of free cooperation," has been surprisingly tenacious in the face of concerted efforts on the part of would-be monopolists to enclose, privatize, and commercialize the digital domain.[12] After all, a handful of corporate giants—Google, AOL, Facebook, Yahoo, and Microsoft—now account for the overwhelming majority of daily web traffic. On the other hand, the corporate race to the bottom in pursuit of cut-price labor costs is also drawing heavily on the same collaborative spirit. It is no surprise that entrepreneurs scouting around for a fresh, dressed-to-impress business model have seized on crowdsourcing as a technique that unleashes the latent, or native, genius of Internet culture.

Many readers will no doubt conclude that this dual utilization is all part of some big-picture trade-off. After all, the social web has opened up a whole new universe of information-rich public goods—including the potential for anticapitalist organizing; really, really free markets; peer-to-peer common value creation; public access culture; cyberprotest; and alternative economies of all sorts (and, if you believe any of the cyberhype about the Twitter revolution, it is even the key to overthrowing authoritarian rulers in Middle Eastern and North African states). On balance, then, it could be said that the role social web platforms are playing in new modes of capital accumulation is simply the price one pays for maintaining nonproprietary networks whose scope of activity is large and heterogeneous enough to escape the orbit of government or corporate surveillance. Though the enclosers are pushing hard, the balance, for the time being, is still in favor of the commons. From this point of view, all of the free labor that gets skimmed off can be seen as a kind of tithe we pay to the Internet as a whole so that the expropriators stay away from the parts of it we really cherish.

Computers Are Not to Blame

Participants in the free labor debate often come close to assuming that digital technology is its causal agent—responsible in and of itself for punching a colossal hole through the universe of employment norms. Yet blaming new media is a sorry instance of the fallacy of technological determinism at work. Among other things, it ignores the proliferation of unpaid labor in old media and other parts of the employment landscape over the last decade and a half.

There is no doubt that new media, which has the technical capacity to shrink the price of distribution to almost zero, is hosting the most fast-moving industrial efforts to harness the unpaid effort of participants. But old media has also seen heavy inroads from the volunteer or amateur economy. Nowhere is this more visible than in the rise of reality TV, which was recognized and nurtured as a degraded labor sector almost from the outset. Indeed, the first significant lurch in the direction of utilizing free content as a business model was in the TV industry of the late 1980s, when producers responded to the explosion of cable channels and the concomitant fragmentation of audiences by introducing genre formats that drove down production inputs and professional labor costs.[13] The cumulative outcome was an assault on entertainment unions. The response was a strike wave on the part of several of these media unions and craft guilds. The twenty-two-week-long 1988 strike by the Writers Guild of America was especially significant in the annals of reality TV, because it opened the door to the sector's longest-running show, *COPS*. Faced with an acute content shortage, and on the lookout for scab material, the Fox network green-lighted this unscripted show, which required no actors' salaries and boasted extra-low production costs. Indeed, much of the cinema verité feel of reality programming was pioneered by the use, in *COPS,* of handheld cameras to capture real-life police officers as they pursued their more action-oriented assignments.

Since 2001, with the jumbo success of *Survivor* and *Big Brother,* the programming share claimed by reality TV and amateur challenge game shows has ballooned. The production costs of these shows are a fraction of what producers pay for conventional, scripted drama, while the ratings and profits have been mercurial. Indeed, they are so cheap to make that virtually all the production costs are earned back from the first network showing; syndicated or overseas sales are pure profit. From the outset, owners have insisted that producers and editors are not so much writers, who pen scripts and dialogue, as editors, who patch together chunks of real life. Anyone who views raw footage of reality shows can see that the dialogue is carefully scripted and plotted and that the supposedly real-life scenes, usually shot in multiple takes, are highly constructed. Nonetheless, this fiction is used to keep the Writers Guild of America out of reality programming. So, too, networks have begun to categorize game shows as reality programming in order to produce them without contracts.

Not surprisingly, the nonunionized reality sector teems with substandard conditions. Below-the-line workers, such as production assistants, loggers, assistant editors, drivers, and other technical crew, are often asked to work eighteen-hour days, with no meal breaks and no health or other benefits, and they face employer coercion to turn in time cards early. Wage rates are generally half of what employees on scripted shows are paid, and most overtime goes unpaid.[14] Writers, pressured to produce by just-in-time network schedules, are also faced with the same roster of wage and hours violations, and, since they are usually hired at-will, suffer chronic job instability.[15]

Nor are the amateur contestants much better off. They are not considered actors and so do not enjoy the rights and protections that an actors' union would afford. Yet, as befits a jackpot economy, talent on the top shows can make a bundle. Indeed, some are paid handsome fees for each episode, though most of their remuneration comes from aftermarket revenue in the form of endorsements. However, the majority receive trifling stipends, if anything, and the price for their shot at exposure is to endure conditions—deprived of sleep and plied with hard alcohol—that are designed to spark tension, conflict, and confrontation on screen.

The labor infractions in these old media sectors are conspicuous because they take place against the still heavily unionized backdrop of the entertainment industries. In the world of new media, where unions have no foothold whatsoever, the blurring of the lines between work and leisure and the widespread exploitation of amateur or user input has been normative from the outset. It would be more accurate to conclude, then, that while digital technology did not give birth to the model of free labor, it has proven to be a highly efficient enabler of nonstandard work arrangements.

Another illustration of the explosion of free labor is the white-collar or no-collar internship, arguably the fastest-growing job category of recent years for a large slice of educated youth trying to gain entry into workplaces that are leaner and meaner by the day. Entrants now go to extreme lengths (including paying outright for positions in the internship marketplace) to secure an unpaid internship (often the first of many) that might help them build a resumé and win a foot in the door, or a leg up in the skilled labor market. The biggest beneficiary of this galloping trade, of course, is the employer. In Ross Perlin's book on the internship explosion, he estimates that corporate America enjoys a $2 billion annual subsidy from internships alone, and this sum does not include the massive tax dodges that many firms execute though employer misclassification.[16] Perlin confirms that the Great Recession has seen a generation of full-time jobs converted into internships, while formerly paid internships have rapidly morphed into unpaid ones. An estimated 50% of U.S. internships are now unpaid or below minimum wage, 51% in Germany, and 37% in the United Kingdom.

If interning really were a rational career investment with a guaranteed payoff, then the ethics of this form of employment would be more transparent. But the conversion rates that Perlin cites—recording how many interns move into permanent positions—are not very impressive. In good times, and at some companies, the rate used to be as high as 50%, but in recent years, it has taken a nosedive, all across the board. Indeed, the figures are trending toward the sweepstakes pattern that has become so emblematic of late neoliberalism. Interning, in other words, will only win you the equivalent of a lottery ticket in the white-collar job economy if things continue along this path.

Given these stingy odds, why are more youth not turning toward the blue-collar forerunner of the internship, an apprenticeship in the skilled trades? Apprenticeships still offer a solid pathway—albeit after a lengthy probationary term—to distinct livelihoods in as many as a thousand trades. Some of these occupations die off as technologies and markets mutate, but most of them are relatively safe from offshoring—plumber and electrician jobs are not sent overseas. So, too, their association with manual craft evokes the kind of artisanal autonomy that excites the moralists among us—witness the overheated reception of Matthew Crawford's book *Shop Class as Soulcraft*. No doubt, the stigma of manual work is still the biggest factor in steering educated youth away from considering trade apprenticeships. But most of the trades in question remain male strongholds, an inconvenient fact that stymied Crawford's effort to exalt his own beloved art of motorcycle maintenance and its kindred occupational spirits. While less than 10% of registered apprentices are female, women tend to dominate the most precarious sectors of white-collar and no-collar employment, and it is no surprise that they are assigned the majority of unpaid internships—77% according to one survey.[17]

Can we conclude that the intern economy is yet another reflection of what sociologists call the feminization of work? If so, then it is not just because it involves women in the majority, doing a lot of unpaid work. Internship labor also blurs the line between task and contract, between duty and opportunity, and between affective and instrumental work. Women are disproportionately burdened when these kinds of boundaries are eliminated. The sacrifices, trade-offs, and humiliations entailed in interning are more redolent of traditional kinds of women's work, whether at home or in what used to be called the secondary labor market (to distinguish it from the family wage generated by the primary market).

The internship is particularly relevant to our overall discussion because most interns do not see themselves as hard done by. In this respect, it is one more example of the twisted mentality of self-exploitation that has marched on to the killing fields of employment. Today, there is fairly broad agreement on what constitutes fair labor in the waged workplace of industry, or, to be more accurate, there are limits to the range of disagreement on the topic. People understand, more or less, what a sweatshop is, and also recognize that its conditions are unfair. By contrast, we have very few yardsticks for judging fairness in the salaried or freelancing sectors of the new, deregulated jobs economy, where any effort to draw a crisp line around work and pay (not to mention work and play) seems to be increasingly ineffectual.

Marx or Not?

Capital owners have long sought to transfer work from the producer to the consumer or user, or from the formal site of production to decentralized points of consumption. Michael Palm's account of the rise of self-service (a major component of this history of work transfer) begins with Bell's elimination of telephone operators in favor of customer dialing. Persuading phone customers to take on the additional work of dialing for themselves required a great deal of cajoling, not to mention practical education.[18] In retrospect, of course, dialing for ourselves is very small beer compared to the much more challenging tasks we have taken over from producers in the intervening century. Think of the massive amount of buyer's time and energy that goes into researching and assembling consumer products, or the growing volume of user input that is considered mandatory for customer services of all sorts. Because these time soaks are palpable, especially those involving customer service, they are the ones that irritate us most, and so we end up venting our anger on robo-voices or on hapless call center employees in Bangalore.

But these burdens are only the most tangible evidence of what Italian *operaismo* theorists such as Mario Tronti called the "social factory." According to this thesis, the work discipline of the factory is exported far beyond its bounded walls, and a large share of the work of production is subsequently and increasingly performed, without remuneration, in our daily social doings. Consequently, the entire content of our everyday lives—our net subjectivity—and not just our workplace toil, becomes raw material for capital accumulation. In the mid-1970s when this thesis was put forth, it was an avant-garde analysis of the efforts of capital owners to liberate themselves from factory-bound conflicts with unionized and often militant workers organizations. The transfer of work outside of the traditional sites of production was only part of capital's response. Another was to relocate to cheaper, union-free locations, and a third was to casualize workforces wherever possible. Today, offshore outsourcing is a fait accompli, and the forced march of temping into most professions seems to be unstoppable. Nor is there anything avant-garde about the concept of social factory, at least not when business strategies to extract rents through social web platforms and crowdsourcing techniques are openly discussed and urged in the pages of *Businessweek*.[19]

One of the salient questions at The Internet as Playground and Factory conference was whether the Marxist labor theory of value is still applicable to the new modes of capital accumulation exemplified by Facebook. The new profile of gladsome work—sometimes referred to as play-labor or "playbor"[20]—does not seem to fit neatly into Marx's classic analysis of how surplus value is generated from socially necessary, waged labor. On the other hand, some commentators in the Italian school have suggested that Marx, in a few prescient passages in the *Grundrisse*, predicted the increasing dependence of capitalism on the "general intellect" or "social brain"—the vast network of cooperative knowledge that is the source and agent of the cognitive mode of production.[21] On the face of it, this theory does seem capable of accommodating or explaining the exploitative use of donated or passionate effort that is part and parcel of immaterial labor.

In response to the first debate about the relevance of Marx, it is worth noting that waged labor is not the only, or the best, lens through which to view work under capitalist conditions. Michael Denning has argued that, for Marx, the accumulation of labor was just as significant a feature of capitalism as the accumulation of capital.[22] In that regard, the proliferation of unwaged (and thus less measurable) work may be a better analytical standpoint for understanding global economic life. After all, the template of the bounded, waged workday (and five-day workweek), with its formal wraparound of mutually observed rules, obligations, and expectations, was a highly artificial product of bargaining in the advanced economies during the temporary postwar truce between capital and labor. Though it was adopted and referred to as standard employment in those decades, there was nothing natural about its norms, and it applied almost exclusively to the primary employment of unionized male industrial workers. Indeed, this closely contested arrangement floated upon an ocean of unpaid work in the home, and it coexisted with casualized work in the secondary employment sector and wageless work in the informal sector, both of which have swelled in the last quarter century.

In addition, and this hardly goes without saying, the vast majority of human labor, historically and to this day, is wageless—only 7% of India's workforce, for example, enjoys regular wages and salaries, and that number is on the decrease. The chances are that waged labor in a legally limited workday may soon come to be seen as the short-lived norm for a small minority, and most of them employed in the world's increasingly besieged public sectors.[23] The upsurge of precarious work in the private sector—whether in low-wage services or in the high-wage knowledge and creative industries, where a self-employed or gig-based profile is more and more normative—may be seen as the degradation of the formal model, but it is viewed quite differently by those who were excluded from standard employment in the first place. The under-40 workforce, who have known nothing but precarious underemployment, have their own understanding of what counts as fair or unfair labor, and it is highly contextual and subject to continual readjustment.

Are they not the arbiters of their own exploitation? To argue otherwise is to come close to charging them with "false consciousness."

On the question of the general intellect, there is little dispute that some high-growth industrial sectors are increasingly dependent on ideas and creative talent, and that capital has had to grant some concessions in order to guarantee a supply of cognitive skills. As long as their control over intellectual property is assured, capital owners have been willing to cede some ground over labor discipline; the creative work landscape now hosts multiple forms of autonomy and self-organization, at a far remove from the Taylorist rules of standardization and deskilling. Yet the copy-fight over intellectual property is a fraught terrain, featuring running skirmishes with the commons-loving hacker fractions of the cognitive class over the policing of digital rights management. So, too, the exposure of capital to open knowledge networks for sources of profit carries its own risks; investments in technically specific business models can go south rapidly when access to the same knowledge is widely available at no cost. In the case of free inputs, the hand that gives is also the hand that takes.

The least we can say, then, about capital's dependence on the general intellect is that the outcome is a field of engagement within which contests can crop up virtually anywhere. In this respect, we are far beyond the confrontation at the factory gates—the customary location of the wage earner's efforts to negotiate the sale of labor power—or the bargaining of a wage contract—which is the legal or symbolic effort to limit this confrontation. Indeed, as Angela McRobbie has recently pointed out, the cognitives or creatives who quarry the general intellect are often less consumed by struggles over compensation than by other political causes. They often invest more of their time and energy in fights over schooling, community development, food sovereignty, racism, sexism, and homophobia on the information landscape or other issues affected by unfair distribution.[24]

It would be naive, however, to conclude, as some advocates of immaterial labor do, that capital has been weakened or outsmarted by the need to forage far and wide, and on especially uncertain and hostile terrain, for cognitive inputs and surpluses. The evidence from the current rent-extraction boom is that profits from new markets are far from soft, whether for jumbo monopolists like Google and Facebook or rapidly expanding content farms like Demand Media and Associated Content or for the army of smaller content aggregators. Moreover, their business models are highly quantitative and are very precisely tied to the measurable value of inputs from users or contributors. In this regard, it is by no means clear that the increasingly sophisticated Internet metrics industry represents a significant departure from the gainful calculus of the labor theory of value. Far from transforming the conventions of worker productivity and rewards beyond recognition, the digital labor system, as Chris Lehman suggests, has "merely sent the rewards further down the fee stream to unscrupulous collectors."[25]

Nor should the dizzying pace of development in the information sector lead us to conclude that factory gates are no longer important flashpoints. Virtually all of the technological infrastructure for this sector is manufactured in the workshops of the world in East Asia, where harsh factory conditions give rise to high-intensity labor conflicts on a regular basis. Where the creative use, say, of a notebook computer involves a highly customized work experience, emblematic of the fluid, flexible, self-organized profile of post-Fordism, the conditions of its manufacture could not be more different. Factories employing hundreds of thousands of workers are more and more common in the electronics production chain, and the most recent tendency in the industry is to integrate all the component operations under one roof, as opposed to contracting out to suppliers in different parts of the world. The result looks something like Fordism on steroids.

The giant Taiwanese original design manufacturer notebook makers like Quanta, Compal, Wistron, and Inventec grew to monopolize global production by building a component supply chain that snaked all over East Asia and by utilizing cheap Chinese labor to integrate and assemble the finished products. Yet this contracting model is currently undergoing a sea change as a result of the 2009 entry into the notebook sector of another Taiwanese heavyweight called Hon Hai Precision Industry Co., better known to the world as Foxconn. Foxconn's rise to industrial prominence threatens to revolutionize manufacture in the way that Walmart changed the retail industry. According to what passes for humor among its executives: "In 20 years, there will be only two companies; everything will be made by Foxconn and sold by Walmart."[26] Until recently, the company was itself a supplier of the Taiwanese notebook kingpins. Because its profit margin from making components was much larger than the margins it enjoyed from computer assembly, Foxconn was able to take them on by integrating all the parts manufacture and lowering its own margin on the final assembly work. Now that it is the largest private employer in China, with more than one million workers, Foxconn has the market power to force these former customers to adopt its vertical production methods by merging with its other component suppliers. Moreover, as part of the megafirm's bid to become an original design manufacturer, it is developing its own design capacity, aimed ultimately at taking on the top brands that it currently supplies: Dell, Hewlett-Packard, Apple, Acer, and Sony.

Foxconn is the same company that has earned a toxic reputation for the militaristic labor discipline in its gargantuan factories. In 2010, a string of worker suicides focused international scrutiny on its Longhua factory campus in Shenzhen, which houses and employs an army of 400,000, mostly migrant, youth from China's hinterland. The deaths—eighteen in all, and dozens of others narrowly averted—were widely interpreted as an existential response to the brutality of factory labor conditions, heightened by an oppressive speed-up brought on by the sharp market demand for Apple's iPad. After the twelfth jump from the dormitory windows, a worker blog carried this poignant post: "Perhaps for the Foxconn employees and employees like us... the use of death is simply to testify that we were ever alive at all, and that while we lived, we had only despair."

Foxconn's CEO, Terry Gou, launched an extensive public relations crusade in response to the outcry and promised to raise wages. The most telling response to the suicides, however, has been to move production inland to the western provinces; to Chongqing, 1,000 miles up the Yangtze River, to the Sichuanese capital of Chengdu, and to Zhengzhou, the capital of a province, Henan, that is home to one-fifth of Foxconn's workforce. The firm has a lot of company. In the biggest restructuring since the migration across the Taiwan Straits a decade ago, the entire PC industry looks to be moving lock, stock, and barrel to Chongqing and Chengdu to take advantage of the much cheaper labor, generous government subsidies (the result of fierce bidding among inland provinces), and locations that are farther removed from the scrutiny of labor and human rights groups. But this time, Foxconn is at the head of the pack, and its methods of labor discipline and vertical production models are setting the pace.[27]

Foxconn's move to integrate production may seem like a throwback to the IBM model of the 1960s, when the original computer giant made everything in-house. So, too, Foxconn's vast, ruthlessly marshaled workforces are redolent of the Taylorism of the early twentieth-century assembly lines. Both of these industrial models are supposed to be gathering dust, irredeemably associated with the bygone era of mass society. Yet here they are, thriving at the profitable heart of one of the world's most advanced manufacturing sectors. For the best part of two decades, anti-sweatshop activists have tried to force consumers in the global North to confront the human costs that lie behind their clothing purchases. Whether the same moral crusade can be applied to information technology products remains to be seen. Apparel never had the air of magical production that sustains the aura of high-tech. For their part, Foxconn's Longhua workers used the most extreme means at their disposal to generate public attention—"To die is the only way to testify that we ever lived." Through their suicides, they spelled out the literal implications of the "dead labor" precept used by Marx to explain the process of capitalist production. Nor are they likely to be the last to publicize their alienation in this way.

Two Ends of the Chain Gang

In Marx's well-known analysis, "living labor" is needed to reanimate the "dead labor" embodied in factory machinery. As a result of the surplus generated (Marx described this as a vampiric act), capital is able to roam, zombie-like, wherever it pleases, until its profiteers are forced, under communism, to dig their own graves in an act of self-administered exorcism.

In the case of the new generation of work technologies, especially the mobile ones, the living labor is also allowed to range freely, choosing when and where to clock in, and whether to play along the way. In return for this rare permission, though not exactly out of gratitude, we seem to be offering up more and more of our work for free, or at a tidy discount. Mobile workers—whether they are banging away in a coffee shop, a teleworker "hotel," or on a beach—appear to be at a far remove from the sweaty precincts of the industrial age. But their *par-cours* digital feats depend on the uniform regimentation of mass workforces at the other end of the production chain, some of them larger in scale and more strictly controlled than anything dreamed of by Henry Ford. As fast as we can dream of ever more personal tools and applications, those individual desires get mined and harvested into industrial demands that are serviced by the most impersonal forms of manpower that modernity has seen.

In these low-wage manufacturing locations, work is feminized not because it involved a blurring between the factory and the traditionally feminine house-hold sphere, but because the workforce is disproportionately composed of the most vulnerable segment of the population: rural teenage girls. It's worth not-ing the female dominance of this factory labor pool has come into being at the same time as young women have disproportionately entered the precarious world of self-employment and creative labor at the other end of the produc-tion chain, moving, as McRobbie has put it, "from the reserve army of labor" to the very "heartland of new forms of work."[28] The women in the first kind of workforce are firmly disciplined according to traditional gender roles at the same time as they have access, for the first time, to some disposable income and to the feel of urban freedoms. The women in the second—the so-called crea-tive industries—enjoy full equality of access and unprecedented control over the scheduling of their lives at the same time as their gendered skills and aptitudes around networking, multitasking, and social finessing of a whole range of work-leisure overlaps have made them ideal workers for the most neoliberal forms of flexible accumulation.

These creative workers operate in the do-it-yourself economy, where skilled entrants fashion their own livelihoods by piecing together disparate lumps of work and income. Yet this defiantly postindustrial world of custom-built workers does not subsist on its own ethereal, cyberspace foundation. It is tied, as I have shown, to conditions of production that have much in common with the early stages of industrialization. The workers that service either end of the chain are drawn from quite different strata—one is educated and urban, the other underresourced and migrant—but they share the existential condition of radical uncertainty that intermittent work begets. Whether they labor in the increasingly thin regulation state of reform China or in the hothouse creative capitals of the world, they find themselves isolated from any protective framework of social insurance, marooned in the crowded ether of selfhood.

Notes

1 This debate was initiated by Tiziana Terranova in "Free Labor: Producing Culture for the Digital Economy," *Social Text* 63, Vol. 18, No. 2 (summer 2000): 33–58, and it entered mainstream public discussion with the publications of Andrew Keen, *The Cult of the Amateur: How Blogs, MySpace, YouTube, and the Rest of Today's User-Generated Media*

are Destroying Our Economy, Our Culture, and Our Values (New York: Crown, 2007) and Chris Anderson, *Free: The Future of a Radical Price* (New York: Hyperion, 2009). The contributors to a special issue of *ephemera* touch on various elements of the debate. See Jonathan Burston, Nick Dyer-Witheford, and Alison Hearn, eds., "Digital Labour: Workers, Authors, Citizens," *ephemera: theory & politics in organization* 10, no. 3/4 (August 2010): 214–21, http://www.ephemeraweb.org/journal/10-3/10-3index.htm.

2 Daniel Roth, "The Answer Factory: Demand Media and the Fast, Disposable, and Profitable as Hell Media Model," *Wired,* October 19, 2009.

3 See "The AOL Way: Content, Product, Media Engineering, and Revenue Management," http://www.businessinsider.com/the-aol-way#-1.

4 Eli Pariser, *The Filter Bubble: What the Internet Is Hiding from You* (New York: Penguin Press, 2001), 7, 43.

5 Quoted in Parisier, p. 21.

6 See Alison Hearn, "Structuring Feeling: Web 2.0, Online Ranking and Rating, and the Digital 'Reputation' Economy," *ephemera: theory & politics in organization* 10, no. 3/4 (August 2010): 421–38.

7 See Jeff Howe, *Crowdsourcing: Why the Power of the Crowd Is Driving the Future of Business* (New York: Crown, 2008).

8 Katharine Mieszkowski, "I Make $1.45 a Week and I Love It," *Salon,* July 24, 2006, http://www.salon.com/technology/feature/2006/07/24/turks, and Jonathan Zittrain, "Work the New Digital Sweatshops," *Newsweek,* December 8, 2009.

9 Andrew Ross, *No-Collar: The Humane Workplace and Its Hidden Costs* (New York: Basic Books, 2002).

10 Melissa Gregg, *Work's Intimacy* (Cambridge, England: Polity Press, 2010); Rosalind Gill, *Technobohemians or the New Cybertariat: New Media Work in Amsterdam a Decade After the Web* (Amsterdam: Institute of Network Cultures, 2007); David Hesmondhalgh and Sarah Baker, *Creative Labour: Media Work in Three Cultural Industries* (New York: Routledge, 2010); Sybille Reidl, Helene Schiffbanker, and Hubert Eichmann, "Creating a Sustainable Future: The Working Life of Creative Workers in Vienna," *Work, Organization, Labour & Globalization* 1, no. 1 (2006): 48–58; D. Perrons, "The New Economy and the Work Life Balance. A Case Study of the New Media Sector in Brighton and Hove," *Gender, Work and Organisation* 10, no. 1 (2003): 65–93; Ursula Huws, Jorg Flecker, Monique Ramioul, Karen Guerts, et al., WORKS Project, Work Organisation and Restructuring in the Knowledge Society (Leuven: Institute for Labor Studies, 2009), http://www.worksproject.be/.

11 The literature on the rise of the creative industries includes: Geert Lovink and Ned Rossiter, eds., *MyCreativity Reader: A Critique of Creative Industries* (Amsterdam: Institute of Network Cultures, 2007); John Hartley, ed., *Creative Industries* (Oxford: Blackwell, 2005); Ursula Huws, ed., "The Creative Spark in the Engine," special issue, *Work, Organization, Labour & Globalization* 1, no. 1 (2007); David Hesmondhalgh and Andy Pratt, eds., "The Cultural Industries and Cultural Policy," special issue, *International Journal of Cultural Policy* 11, no. 1 (2005); David Hesmondhalgh, *The Cultural Industries* (London: Sage, 2007); Mark Banks and John O'Connor, eds., Special Issue on "After the Creative Industries," *International Journal of Cultural Policy* 15, no. 4 (2009).

12 Geert Lovink and Trebor Scholz, eds., *The Art of Free Cooperation* (New York: Autonomedia, 2007).

13 Chad Raphael. "Political Economy of Reali-TV." *Jump Cut* 41 (1997): 102–9.

14 Robert Elisberg, "The Amazing Reality of 'Reality' TV." Huffington Post (2008), http://www.huffingtonpost.com/robert-j-elisberg/the-amazing-reality-of-re_b_118433.html.

15 Writers Guild of American West, *Harsh Reality: WGA Report on Standards in Reality Television* (2007), http://www.wga.org/uploadedfiles/news_and_events/press_release/harsh_reality.pdf.

16 Ross Perlin, *Intern Nation: How to Earn Nothing and Learn Little in the Brave New Economy* (New York: Verso, 2011), 124.

17 Ibid., 27.

18 Michael Palm, "Phoning It In: Self-Service Technology and the History of Consumer Labor" (PhD dissertation, New York University, 2010).

19 *Businessweek* articles on the strategy include Paul Boutin, "Crowdsourcing: Consumers as Creators," July 13, 2006; Jessi Hempel, "Tapping the Wisdom of the Crowd," January 18, 2007; Heather Green, "The Wisdom of the Business Crowd," September 18, 2008; Damian Joseph, "Pushing the Limits of Crowdsourcing," March 2, 2009; John Winsor, "Crowdsourcing: What It Means for Innovation," June 15, 2009.

20 Julian Kücklich, "FCJ-025 Precarious Playbour: Modders and the Digital Games Industry," *Fibreculture* 5 (2005).

21 Karl Marx, *Grundrisse: Foundations of the Critique of Political Economy* (1861), chap. 13, http://www.marxists.org/archive/marx/works/1857/grundrisse/ch13.htm#p694; Maurizio Lazzarato, "Immaterial Labor," in *Radical Thought in Italy,* eds. Paolo Virno and Michael Hardt (Minneapolis: University of Minnesota Press, 1996), 133–46; Michael Hardt and Antonio Negri, *Empire* (Cambridge, MA: Harvard University Press, 2000).

22 Michael Denning, "Wageless Life," *New Left Review* 66 (November–December 2010).

23 Brett Neilson and Ned Rossiter, "Precarity as a Political Concept, or Fordism as an Exception," *Theory Culture Society* 25, no. 7–8 (2008): 51–72.

24 Angela McRobbie, "Reflections on Feminism, Immaterial Labour and the Post-Fordist Regime," *New Formations* 70 (Winter 2011): 60–76.

25 Chris Lehmann, "An Accelerated Grimace," *The Nation,* March 21, 2011, 32.

26 Frederik Balfour and Tim Culpan, "The Man Who Makes Your iPhone," *Bloomberg Businessweek,* September 9, 2010.

27 The one labor rights group with access to the new factories, Hong Kong–based Students and Scholars against Corporate Misbehaviour (SACOM), reported that a year after Foxconn's initial response to the suicides, most of the company's promises regarding increased wages, reduced overtime, improved worker-management communication, and internship regulation remained unfulfilled. SACOM, "Foxconn and Apple Fail to Fulfill Promises: Predicaments of Workers after the Suicides," May 6, 2011, http://sacom.hk/wp-content/uploads/2011/05/2011-05-06_foxconn-and-apple-fail-to-fulfill-promises1.pdf.

28 Angela McRobbie, "Reflections on Feminism, Immaterial Labour and the Post-Fordist Regime," *New Formations* 70, no. 1 (2011).

2

FREE LABOR

Tiziana Terranova

The real not-capital is labor.

—Karl Marx, *Grundrisse*

Working in the digital media industry was never as much fun as it is made out to be. Certainly, for the workers of the best-known and most highly valued companies, work might have been a brief experience of something that did not feel like work at all.[1] On the other hand, even during the dot-com boom, the "netslaves" of the homonymous webzine had always been vociferous about the shamelessly exploitative nature of the job, its punishing work rhythms, and its ruthless casualization.[2] They talked about "24-7 electronic sweatshops" and complained about the 90-hour week and the "moronic management of new media companies."[3] Antagonism in the new media industry also affected the legions of volunteers running well-known sites for the Internet giants. In early 1999, 7 of the 15,000 "volunteers" of America Online rocked the info–love boat by asking the Department of Labor to investigate whether AOL owed them back wages for their years of playing chat hosts for free. They used to work long hours and love it; but they also felt the pain of being burned by digital media.

These events point to an inevitable backlash against the glamorization of digital labor, which highlighted its continuities with the modern sweatshop and the increasing degradation of knowledge work. Yet the question of labor in a digital economy as an innovative development of the familiar logic of capitalist exploitation is not so easily dismissed. The netslaves are not simply a typical form of labor on the Internet; they also embody a complex relation to labor that is widespread in late capitalist societies.

In this chapter, I call this excessive activity that makes the Internet a thriving and hyperactive medium "free labor"—a feature of the cultural economy at large and an important, yet unacknowledged, source of value in advanced capitalist societies. By looking at the Internet as a specific instance of the fundamental role played by free labor, this chapter also highlights the connections between the digital economy and what the Italian autonomists have called the "social factory" (or "society-factory").[4] The society-factory describes a process whereby "work processes have shifted from the factory to society, thereby setting in motion a truly complex machine."[5] Simultaneously voluntarily given and unwaged, enjoyed and exploited, free labor on the net includes the activity of building websites, modifying software packages, reading and participating in mailing lists, and building virtual spaces. Far from being an unreal, empty space, the Internet is animated by cultural and technical labor through and through, a continuous production of value that is completely immanent to the flows of the network society at large.

Support for this argument, however, is immediately complicated by the recent history of Anglo-American cultural theory. How should we speak of labor, especially cultural and technical labor, after the demolition job carried out by 30 years of postmodernism? The postmodern socialist feminism of Donna Haraway's "Cyborg Manifesto" spelled out some of the reasons behind the antipathy of 1980s critical theory for Marxist analyses of labor. Haraway explicitly rejected the humanistic tendencies of theorists who see the latter as the "pre-eminently privileged category enabling the Marxist to overcome illusion and find that point of view which is necessary for changing the world."[6] Paul Gilroy similarly expressed his discontent at the inadequacy of Marxist analysis of labor to the descendants of slaves, who value artistic expression as "the means towards both individual self-fashioning and communal liberation."[7] If labor is "the humanizing activity that makes [white] man," then, surely, this humanizing labor does not really belong in the age of networked, posthuman intelligence.

However, the "informatics of domination" that Haraway describes in the manifesto is certainly preoccupied with the relation between cybernetics, labor, and capital. In the 20 years since its publication, this triangulation has become even more evident. The expansion of the Internet has given ideological and material support to contemporary trends toward increased flexibility of the workforce, continuous reskilling, freelance work, and the diffusion of practices such as "supplementing" (bringing supplementary work home from the conventional office).[8] Advertising campaigns and business manuals suggest that the Internet is not only a site of disintermediation (embodying the famous death of the middle man, from bookshops to travel agencies to computer stores), but also the means through which a flexible, collective intelligence has come into being.

This chapter does not seek to offer a judgment on the effects of the Internet on society. What I will rather do is map the way in which the Internet connects to the autonomist social factory. I will look at how the "outernet"—the network of social, cultural, and economic relationships that crisscrosses and exceeds the Internet—surrounds and connects the latter to larger flows of labor, culture, and power. It is fundamental to move beyond the notion that cyberspace is about escaping reality in order to understand how the reality of the Internet is deeply connected to the development of late postindustrial societies as a whole. It is related to phenomena that have been defined as "external economies" within theoretical perspectives (such as the theory of transaction costs), suggesting that "the production of value is increasingly involving the capture of productive elements and social wealth that are *outside* the direct productive process."[9] Cultural and technical work is central to the Internet but is also a widespread activity throughout advanced capitalist societies. Such labor is not exclusive to so-called knowledge workers but is a pervasive feature of the postindustrial economy. The pervasiveness of such production questions the legitimacy of a fixed distinction between production and consumption, labor and culture. It also undermines Gilroy's distinction between work as "servitude, misery and subordination" and artistic expression as the means to self-fashioning and communal liberation. The increasingly blurred territory between production and consumption, work and cultural expression, however, does not signal the recomposition of the alienated Marxist worker. The Internet does not automatically turn every user into an active producer and every worker into a creative subject. The process whereby production and consumption are reconfigured within the category of free labor signals the unfolding of another logic of value whose operations need careful analysis.[10]

The Digital Economy

The term *digital economy* emerged in the late 1990s as a way to summarize some of the processes described above. As a term, it seems to describe a formation that intersects on the one hand with the postmodern cultural economy (the media, the university, and the arts) and on the other hand with the information industry (the information and communication complex). Such an intersection of two different fields of production constitutes a challenge to a theoretical and practical engagement with the question of labor—a question that has become marginal for media studies as compared with questions of ownership (within political economy) and consumption (within cultural studies).

We will distinguish here between the New Economy—"a historical period marker [that] acknowledges its conventional association with Internet companies"[11]—and the digital economy—a less transient phenomenon based on key features of digitized information (its ease of copying and low or zero cost of sharing). In Richard Barbrook's definition, the digital economy is characterized by the emergence of new technologies (computer networks) and new types of workers (the digital artisans).[12] According to Barbrook, the digital economy is a mixed economy: it includes a public element (the state's funding of the original research that produced ARPANET, the financial support to academic activities that had a substantial role in shaping the culture of the Internet); a market-driven element (a latecomer that tries to appropriate the digital economy by reintroducing commodification); and a gift economy element (the true expression of the cutting edge of capitalist production that prepares its eventual overcoming into a future "anarcho-communism").

What Barbrook proposed was that the vision of politicians and corporate leaders who linked the future of capitalism to the informational commodity involved a basic misunderstanding. Pointing to the world of discussion groups, mailing lists, and the distributed learning of programmers, he suggested that the Internet was far from simply being a new way to sell commodities. The predominance of relationships of collaboration across distance and exchange without money suggested that this was a practiced relationship with a viable and alternative political and economic model.

> Unrestricted by physical distance, they collaborate with each other without the direct mediation of money and politics. Unconcerned about copyright, they give and receive information without thought of payment. In the absence of states or markets to mediate social bonds, network communities are instead formed through the mutual obligations created by gifts of time and ideas.[13]

Barbrook's vision of the informational commons was only reinforced by the subsequent explosion of peer-to-peer, file-sharing networks—a huge network phenomenon that had the music and film industries up in arms.

From a Marxist-Hegelian angle, Barbrook saw the high-tech gift economy as a process of overcoming capitalism from the inside. The high-tech gift economy is a pioneering moment that transcends both the purism of the New Left do-it-yourself culture and the neoliberalism of the free market ideologues: "money-commodity and gift relations are not just in conflict with each other, but also co-exist in symbiosis."[14] Participants in the gift economy are not reluctant to use market resources and government funding to pursue a potlatch economy of free exchange. However, the potlatch and the economy ultimately remain irreconcilable, and the market economy is always threatening to reprivatize the common enclaves of the gift economy. Commodification, the reimposition of a regime of property, is, in Barbrook's opinion, the main strategy through which capitalism tries to reabsorb the anarcho-communism of the net into its folds.

This early attempt to offer a polemical platform from which to think about the digital economy overemphasizes the autonomy of the high-tech gift economy from capitalism. The processes of exchange that characterize the Internet are not simply the reemergence of communism within the cutting edge of the economy, a repressed other that resurfaces just at the moment when communism seems defeated. It is important to remember that the gift economy, as part of a larger digital economy, is itself an important force within the reproduction of the labor force in late capitalism as a whole. The provision of free labor, as we shall see later, is a fundamental moment in the creation of value in the economy at large—beyond the digital economy of the Internet. As will be made clear, the conditions that make free labor an important element of the digital economy are based in a difficult, experimental compromise between the historically rooted cultural and affective desire for creative production (of the kind more commonly associated with Gilroy's emphasis on "individual self-fashioning and communal liberation") and the current capitalist emphasis on knowledge as the main source of added value.

The volunteers for America Online, the netslaves and the amateur web designers, did not work only because capital wanted them to, but they were acting out a desire for affective and cultural production, which was nonetheless real just because it was socially shaped. The cultural, technical, and creative work that supported the digital economy had been made possible by the development of capital beyond the early industrial and Fordist modes of production and therefore is particularly abundant in those areas where post-Fordism has been at work for a few decades. In the overdeveloped countries, the end of the factory has spelled out the obsolescence of the old working class, but it has also produced generations of workers who have been repeatedly addressed as active consumers of meaningful commodities. Free labor is the moment where this knowledgeable consumption of culture is translated into excess productive activities that are pleasurably embraced and at the same time often shamelessly exploited.

Management theory is also increasingly concerned with the question of knowledge work, that indefinable quality that is essential to the processes of stimulating innovation and achieving the goals of competitiveness. For example, Don Tapscott, in a classic example of New Economy managerial literature, *The Digital Economy,* wrote about a "new economy based on the networking of human intelligence."[15] Human intelligence provides the much-needed added value, which is essential to the economic health of the organization. Human intelligence, however, also poses a problem: it cannot be managed in quite the same way as more traditional types of labor. Knowledge workers need open organizational structures in order to produce, because the production of knowledge is rooted in collaboration; this is what Barbrook had defined as the "gift economy":

> The concept of supervision and management is changing to team-based structures. Anyone responsible for managing knowledge workers knows they cannot be "managed" in the traditional sense. Often they have specialized knowledge and skills that cannot be matched or even understood by management. A new challenge to management is first to attract and retain these assets by marketing the organization to them, and second to provide the creative and open communications environment where such workers can effectively apply and enhance their knowledge.[16]

For Tapscott, therefore, the digital economy magically resolves the contradictions of industrial societies, such as class struggle: whereas in the industrial economy, the "worker tried to achieve fulfillment through leisure [and] . . . was alienated from the means of production which were owned and controlled by someone else," in the digital economy, the worker achieves fulfillment through work and finds in her brain her own, unalienated means of production.[17] Such means of production need to be cultivated by encouraging the worker to participate in a culture of

exchange whose flows are mainly kept within the company but also need to involve an "outside," a contact with the fast-moving world of knowledge in general.
The convention, the exhibition, and the conference—the more traditional ways
of supporting this general exchange—are supplemented by network technologies both inside and outside the company. Although the traffic of these flows of
knowledge needs to be monitored (hence, the corporate concerns about the use
of intranets), the Internet effectively functions as a channel through which human
intelligence renews its capacity to produce.

Is it possible to look beyond the totalizing hype of the managerial literature but
also beyond some of the conceptual limits of Barbrook's gift economy model? We
will look at some possible explanation for the coexistence, within the debate about
the digital economy, of discourses that see it as an oppositional movement and
others that see it as a functional development to new mechanisms of extraction of
value. Is the end of Marxist alienation wished for by the manager guru the same
thing as the gift economy heralded by leftist discourse?

We can start undoing this deadlock by subtracting the label "digital economy" from its exclusive anchorage within advanced forms of labor (we can start
then by depioneering it). This chapter describes the digital economy as a specific
mechanism of internal capture of larger pools of social and cultural knowledge.
The digital economy is an important area of experimentation with value and
free cultural/affective labor. It is about specific forms of production (web design,
multimedia production, digital services, and so on), but it is also about forms of
labor we do not immediately recognize as such: chat, real-life stories, mailing lists,
amateur newsletters, and so on. These types of cultural and technical labor are not
produced by capitalism in any direct, cause-and-effect fashion; that is, they have
not developed simply as an answer to the economic needs of capital. However,
they have developed in relation to the expansion of the cultural industries and
are part of a process of economic experimentation with the creation of monetary
value out of knowledge/culture/affect.

This process is different from that described by popular, left-wing wisdom
about the incorporation of authentic cultural moments: it is not, then, about the
bad boys of capital moving in on underground subcultures or subordinate cultures
and incorporating the fruits of their production (styles, languages, music) into
the media food chain. This process is usually considered the end of a particular
cultural formation, or at least the end of its authentic phase. After incorporation,
local cultures are picked up and distributed globally, thus contributing to cultural
hybridization or cultural imperialism (depending on whom you listen to). Rather
than capital incorporating from the outside the authentic fruits of the collective
imagination, it seems more reasonable to think of cultural flows as originating
within a field that is always and already capitalism. Incorporation is not about capital descending on authentic culture but a more immanent process of channeling
collective labor (even as cultural labor) into monetary flows and its structuration
within capitalist business practices.

Subcultural movements have stuffed the pockets of multinational capitalism for decades. Nurtured by the consumption of earlier cultural moments, subcultures have provided the look, style, and sounds that sell clothes, CDs, video games, films, and advertising slots on television. This has often happened through the active participation of subcultural members in the production of cultural goods (e.g., independent labels in music, small designer shops in fashion).[18] This participation is, as the word suggests, a voluntary phenomenon, although it is regularly accompanied by cries of "Sell-out!" The fruits of collective cultural labor have been not simply appropriated, but voluntarily *channeled* and controversially *structured* within capitalist business practices. The relation between culture, the cultural industry, and labor in these movements is much more complex than the notion of incorporation suggests. In this sense, the digital economy is not a new phenomenon but simply a new phase of this longer history of experimentation.

Knowledge Class and Immaterial Labor

Despite the numerous, more or less disingenuous endorsements of the democratic potential of the Internet, its links with capitalism have always been a bit too tight for comfort to concerned political minds. It has been very tempting to counteract the naive technological utopianism by pointing out how computer networks are the material and ideological heart of informated capital. The Internet advertised on television and portrayed by print media seems not just the latest incarnation of capital's inexhaustible search for new markets, but also a full consensus-creating machine, which socializes the mass of proletarianized knowledge workers into the economy of continuous innovation.[19] After all, if we do not get online soon, the hype suggests, we will become obsolete, unnecessary, disposable. If we do, we are promised, we will become part of the "hive mind," the immaterial economy of networked, intelligent subjects in charge of speeding up the rhythms of capital's "incessant waves of branching innovations."[20] Multimedia artists, writers, journalists, software programmers, graphic designers, and activists together with small and large companies are at the core of this project. For some they are its cultural elite, for others a new form of proletarianized labor.[21] Accordingly, the digital workers are described as resisting or supporting the project of capital, often in direct relation to their positions in the networked, horizontal, and yet hierarchical world of knowledge work.

Any judgment on the political potential of the Internet, then, is tied not only to its much vaunted capacity to allow decentralized access to information, but also to the question of who uses the Internet and how. If the decentralized structure of the net is to count for anything at all, the argument goes, then we need to know about its constituent population (hence, the endless statistics about use, income, gender, and race of Internet users—the most polled, probed, and yet opaque survey material of the world). If this population of Internet users is largely made up of knowledge workers, then it matters whether these are seen as the owners of elitist cultural and economic power or the avant-garde of new configurations of labor that do not automatically guarantee elite status.

The question of who uses the Internet is both necessary and misleading. It is necessary because we have to ask who is participating in the digital economy before we can pass a judgment on the latter. It is misleading because it implies that all we need to know is how to locate the knowledge workers within a class, and knowing which class it is will give us an answer to the political potential of the net as a whole. If we can prove that knowledge workers are the avant-garde of labor, then the net becomes a site of resistance;[22] if we can prove that knowledge workers wield the power in informated societies, then the net is an extended gated community for the middle classes.[23] Even admitting that knowledge workers are indeed fragmented in terms of hierarchy and status won't help us that much; it will still lead to a simple system of categorization, where the net becomes a field of struggle between the diverse constituents of the knowledge class.

The question is further complicated by the stubborn resistance of knowledge to quantification: knowledge cannot be exclusively pinned down to specific social segments. Although the shift from factory to office work, from production to services is widely acknowledged, it just isn't clear why some people qualify and some others do not.[24] The knowledge worker is a very contested sociological category.

A more interesting move, however, is possible by not looking for the knowledge class within quantifiable parameters but by concentrating instead on labor. Although the notion of class retains a material value that is indispensable to make sense of the experience of concrete historical subjects, it also has its limits: for example, it freezes the subject, just like a substance within the chemical periodical table—one is born as a certain element (working-class metal) but then might become something else (middle-class silicon) if submitted to the proper alchemical processes (education and income). Such an understanding of class also freezes out the flows of culture and money that mobilize the labor force as a whole. In terms of Internet use, it gives rise to the generalized endorsements and condemnations that I have described above and does not explain or make sense of the heterogeneity and yet commonalities of Internet users. I have therefore found it more useful to think in terms of what the Italian autonomists, and especially Maurizio Lazzarato, have described as "immaterial labor." For Lazzarato, the concept of immaterial labor refers to two *different* aspects of labor:

> On the one hand, as regards the "informational content" of the commodity, it refers directly to the changes taking place in workers' labor processes . . . where the skills involved in direct labor are increasingly skills involving cybernetics and computer control (and horizontal and vertical communication). On the other hand, as regards the activity that produces the "cultural content" of the commodity, immaterial labor involves a series of activities that are not normally recognized as "work"—in other words, the kinds of activities involved in defining and fixing cultural and artistic

standards, fashions, tastes, consumer norms, and, more strategically, public opinion.[25]

Immaterial labor, unlike the knowledge worker, is not completely confined to a specific class formation. Lazzarato insists that this form of labor power is not limited to highly skilled workers but is a form of activity of every productive subject within postindustrial societies. In the highly skilled worker, these capacities are already there. However, in the young worker, the "precarious worker," and the unemployed youth, these capacities are "virtual"—that is, they are there but are still undetermined. This means that immaterial labor is a virtuality (an undetermined capacity) that belongs to the postindustrial productive subjectivity as a whole. For example, the obsessive emphasis on education of 1990s governments can be read as an attempt to stop this virtuality from disappearing or from being channeled into places that would not be as acceptable to the current power structures. Despite all the contradictions of advanced capital and its relation to structural unemployment, postmodern governments do not like the completely unemployable. The potentialities of work must be kept alive, the unemployed must undergo continuous training in order to be both monitored and kept alive as some kind of postindustrial reserve force. Nor can they be allowed to channel their energy into the experimental, nomadic, and antiproductive lifestyles, which, in Britain, have been so savagely attacked by the Criminal Justice Act in the mid-1990s.[26]

However, unlike the post-Fordists, and in accordance with his autonomist origins, Lazzarato does not conceive of immaterial labor as purely functional to a new historical phase of capitalism:

> The virtuality of this capacity is neither empty nor ahistoric; it is rather an opening and a potentiality, that have as their historical origins and antecedents the "struggle against work" of the Fordist worker and, in more recent times, the processes of socialization, educational formation, and cultural self-valorization.[27]

This dispersal of immaterial labor (as a virtuality and an actuality) problematizes the idea of the knowledge worker as a class in the industrial sense of the word. As a collective quality of the labor force, immaterial labor can be understood to pervade the social body with different degrees of intensity. This intensity is produced by the processes of "channeling of the capitalist formation which distributes value according to its logic of profit."[28] If knowledge is inherently collective, it is even more so in the case of the postmodern cultural economy: music, fashion, and information are all produced collectively but are selectively compensated. Only some companies are picked up by corporate distribution chains in the case of fashion and music; only a few sites are invested in by venture capital. However, it is a form of collective cultural labor that makes these products possible even as the profit is disproportionately appropriated by established corporations.

From this point of view, the well-known notion that the Internet materializes a collective intelligence is not completely off the mark. The Internet highlights the existence of networks of immaterial labor and speeds up their accretion into a collective entity. The productive capacities of immaterial labor on the Internet encompass the work of writing/reading/managing and participating in mailing lists/websites/chat lines. These activities fall outside the concept of "abstract labor," which Marx defined as the provision of time for the production of value regardless of the useful qualities of the product.[29] They witness an investment of desire into production of the kind cultural theorists have mainly theorized in relation to consumption.

This explosion of productive activities is undermined for various commentators by the minoritarian, gendered, and raced character of the Internet population. However, we might also argue that to recognize the existence of immaterial labor as a diffuse, collective quality of postindustrial labor in its entirety does not deny the existence of hierarchies of knowledge (both technical and cultural), which prestructure (but do not determine) the nature of such activities. These hierarchies shape the degrees to which such virtualities become actualities—that is, they go from being potential to being realized as processual, constituting moments of cultural, affective, and technical production. Neither capital nor living labor want a labor force that is permanently excluded from the possibilities of immaterial labor. But this is where their desires stop from coinciding. Capital wants to retain control over the unfolding of these virtualities and the processes of valorization. The relative abundance of cultural/technical/affective production on the net, then, does not exist as a free-floating postindustrial utopia but in full, mutually constituting interaction with late capitalism.

Collective Minds

The collective nature of networked, immaterial labor was exalted by the utopian statements of the cyberlibertarians. Kevin Kelly's popular thesis in *Out of Control,* for example, suggested that the Internet is a collective "hive mind." According to Kelly, the Internet is another manifestation of a principle of self-organization that is widespread throughout technical, natural, and social systems. The Internet is the material evidence of the existence of the self-organizing, infinitely productive activities of connected human minds.[30] From a different perspective, Pierre Levy drew on cognitive anthropology and poststructuralist philosophy to argue that computers and computer networks enable the emergence of a "collective intelligence." Levy, who is inspired by early computer pioneers such as Douglas Engelbart, argues for a new humanism "that incorporates and enlarges the scope of self knowledge and collective thought."[31] According to Levy, we are passing from a Cartesian model of thought based on the singular idea of *cogito* (I think) to a collective or plural *cogitamus* (we think).

What is collective intelligence? It is a form of universally distributed intelligence, constantly enhanced, coordinated in real time, and resulting in the effective mobilization of skills. . . . The basis and goal of collective intelligence is the mutual recognition and enrichment of individuals rather than the cult of fetishized or hypostatized communities.[32]

Like Kelly, Levy frames his argument within the common rhetoric of competition and flexibility that dominates the hegemonic discourse around digitalization: "The more we are able to form intelligent communities, as open-minded, cognitive subjects capable of initiative, imagination, and rapid response, the more we will be able to ensure our success in a highly competitive environment."[33] In Levy's view, the digital economy highlights the impossibility of absorbing intelligence within the process of automation: unlike the first wave of cybernetics, which displaced workers from the factory, computer networks highlight the unique value of human intelligence as the true creator of value in a knowledge economy. In his opinion, since the economy is increasingly reliant on the production of creative subjectivities, this production is highly likely to engender a new humanism, a new centrality of humans' creative potentials.

Especially in Kelly's case, it has been easy to dismiss the notions of a hive mind and a self-organizing Internet-as-free-market as Internet gold rush rhetoric, promptly demolished by more or less unexpected events of 2001 (dot-com crash, resurgence of international terrorism and imperialism). It was difficult to avoid a feeling of irritation at such willing oblivion of the realities of working in the high-tech industries, from the poisoning world of the silicon chips factories to the electronic sweatshops of America Online, where technical work is downgraded and worker obsolescence is high.[34] How can we hold on to the notion that cultural production and immaterial labor are collective on the net (both inner and outer) after the belated Y2K explosion in 2001 and without subscribing to the idealistic and teleological spirit of the wired revolution?

We could start with a simple observation: the self-organizing, collective intelligence of cybercultural thought captures the existence of networked immaterial labor, but was weal in its analysis of the operations of capital overall (including the coexistence of different capitalist lobbies and their relation to institutional governance). [Capital, after all, is the unnatural environment within which the collective intelligence materializes.] The collective dimension of networked intelligence needs to be understood historically, as part of a specific momentum of capitalist development. The Italian writers who are identified with the post-Gramscian Marxism of Autonomia Operaia have consistently engaged with this relationship by focusing on the mutation undergone by labor in the aftermath of the factory. The notion of a self-organizing collective intelligence looks uncannily like one of their central concepts, the "general intellect"—a notion that the autonomists extracted out of the spirit, if not the actual wording, of Marx's *Grundrisse*. The "collective intelligence" or "hive mind" captures some of the spirit of the general intellect but removes the autonomists' critical theorization of its relation to capital.

In the autonomists' favorite text, the *Grundrisse*, and especially in the "Fragment on Machines," Marx argues (as summarized by Paolo Virno) that

> knowledge—scientific knowledge in the first place, but not exclusively—tends to become precisely by virtue of its autonomy from production, nothing less than the principal productive force, thus relegating repetitive and compartmentalized labor to a residual position. Here one is dealing with knowledge..., which has become incarnate...in the automatic system of machines.[35]

In the vivid pages of the "Fragment," the "other" Marx of the *Grundrisse* (adopted by the social movements of the 1960s and 1970s against the more orthodox endorsement of *Capital*), describes the system of industrial machines as a horrific monster of metal and flesh:

> The production process has ceased to be a labor process in the sense of a process dominated by labor as its governing unity. Labor appears, rather, merely as a conscious organ, scattered among the individual living workers at numerous points of the mechanical system; subsumed under the total process of the machinery itself, as itself only a link of the system, whose unity exists not in the living workers, but rather in the living, (active) machinery, which confronts his individual, insignificant doings as a mighty organism.[36]

The Italian autonomists extracted from these pages the notion of the general intellect as "the ensemble of knowledge...which constitutes the epicenter of social production."[37] Unlike Marx's original formulation, however, the autonomists eschewed the modernist imagery of the general intellect as a hellish machine. They claimed that Marx completely identified the general intellect (or knowledge as the principal productive force) with fixed capital (the machine) and thus neglected to account for the fact that the general intellect cannot exist independently of the concrete subjects who mediate the articulation of the machines with each other. The general intellect is an articulation of fixed capital (machines) *and* living labor (the workers). If we see the Internet, and computer networks in general, as the latest machines—the latest manifestation of fixed capital—then it won't be difficult to imagine the general intellect as being well and alive today.

However the autonomists did not stop at describing the general intellect as an assemblage of humans and machines at the heart of postindustrial production. If this were the case, the Marxian monster of metal and flesh would just be updated to that of a world-spanning network where computers use human beings as a way to allow the system of machinery (and therefore capitalist production) to function. The visual power of the Marxian description is updated by the cyberpunk snapshots of the immobile bodies of the hackers, electrodes like umbilical cords connecting them to the matrix, appendixes to a living, all-powerful cyberspace. Beyond the special effects bonanza, the box-office success of *The Matrix* series validates the popularity of the paranoid interpretation of this mutation.

To the humanism implicit in this description, the autonomists have opposed the notion of a mass intellectuality, living labor in its function as the determining articulation of the general intellect. Mass intellectuality—as an ensemble, as a social body—"is the repository of the indivisible knowledges of living subjects and of their linguistic cooperation. . . . An important part of knowledge cannot be deposited in machines, but . . . it must come into being as the direct interaction of the labor force."[38] As Virno emphasizes, mass intellectuality is not about the various roles of the knowledge workers, but is a "quality and a distinctive sign of the *whole* social labor force in the post-Fordist era."[39]

The pervasiveness of the collective intelligence within both the managerial literature and Marxist theory could be seen as the result of a common intuition about the quality of labor in informated societies. Knowledge labor is inherently *collective;* it is always the result of a collective and social production of knowledge.[40] Capital's problem is how to extract as much value as possible (in the autonomists' jargon, to "valorize") out of this abundant, and yet slightly intractable, terrain.

Collective knowledge work, then, is not about those who work in the knowledge industry. But it is also not about employment. The mass layoffs in the dotcom sector have not stopped Internet content from growing or its technologies from mutating. The acknowledgment of the collective aspect of labor implies a rejection of the equivalence between labor and employment, which was already stated by Marx and further emphasized by feminism and the post-Gramscian autonomy.[41] Labor is not equivalent to waged labor. Such an understanding might help us to reject some of the hideous rhetoric of unemployment that turns the unemployed person into the object of much patronizing, pushing, and nudging from national governments in industrialized countries. (Accept any available work or else . . .) Often the unemployed are such only in name, in reality being the lifeblood of the difficult economy of under-the-table, badly paid work, some of which also goes into the new media industry.[42] To emphasize how labor is not equivalent to employment also means to acknowledge how important free affective and cultural labor is to the media industry, old and new.

Ephemeral Commodities and Free Labor

There is a continuity, and a break, between older media and new media in terms of their relationship to cultural and affective labor. The continuity seems to lie in their common reliance on their public/users as productive subjects. The difference lies both in the mode of production and in the ways in which power/knowledge works in the two types. Despite different national histories (some of which stress public service more than others), the television industry, for example, is relatively conservative: writers, producers, performers, managers, and technicians have definite roles within an industry still run by a few established players. The historical legacy of television as a technology for the construction of national identities also means that television is somehow always held more publicly accountable than the news media.

This does not mean that old media do not draw on free Labor. On the contrary, television and print media, for example, make abundant use of the free labor of their audiences/readers, but they also tend to structure the latter's contribution much more strictly, both in terms of economic organization and moralistic judgment. The price to pay for all those real-life-TV experiences is usually a heavy dose of moralistic scaremongering: criminals are running amok on the freeways and must be stopped by tough police action; wild teenagers lack self-esteem and need tough love; and selfish and two-faced reality TV contestants will eventually get their comeuppance. If this does not happen on the Internet, why is it, then, that the Internet is not the happy island of decentered, dispersed, and pleasurable cultural production that its apologists claimed it to be?

The most obvious answer to such questions came spontaneously to the early Internet users, who blamed it on the commercialization of the Internet. E-commerce and progressive privatization were blamed for disrupting the free economy of the Internet, an economy of exchange that Richard Barbrook described as a gift economy.[43] Indeed, maybe the Internet could have been a different place than what it is now. However, it is almost unthinkable that capitalism could stay forever outside of the network, a mode of communication that is fundamental to its own organizational structure.

The outcome of the explicit interface between capital and the Internet is a digital economy that manifests all the signs of an acceleration of the capitalist logic of production. It might be that the Internet has not stabilized yet, but it seems undeniable that the digital economy is the fastest and most visible zone of production within late capitalist societies. New products and new trends succeed each other at an anxiety-inducing pace. After all, this is a business where you need to replace your equipment/knowledges and possibly staff every year or so.

At some point, the speed of the digital economy, its accelerated rhythms of obsolescence, and its reliance on (mostly) immaterial products seemed to fit in with the postmodern intuition about the changed status of the commodities whose essence was said to be meaning (or lack of) rather than labor (as if the two could be separable).[44] The recurrent complaint that the Internet contributes to the disappearance of reality is then based *both* in humanistic concerns about real life *and* in the postmodern nihilism of the recombinant commodity.[45] Hyperreality confirms the humanist nightmare of a society without humanity, the culmination of a progressive taking over of the realm of representation. Commodities on the net are not material and are excessive (there is too much of it, too many websites, too much clutter and noise) with relation to the limits of real social needs.

It is possible, however, that the disappearance of the commodity is not a material disappearance but its visible subordination to the quality of labor behind it. In this sense, the commodity does not disappear as such; it rather becomes increasingly ephemeral, its duration becomes compressed, and it becomes more of a process than a finished product. The role of continuous, creative, innovative labor as the ground of market value is crucial to the digital economy. The process of valorization (the production of monetary value) happens by foregrounding the quality of the labor that literally animates the commodity.

The digital economy, then, challenged the postmodern assumption that labor disappears while the commodity takes on and dissolves all meaning. In particular, the Internet foregrounds the extraction of value out of continuous, updateable work, and it is extremely labor-intensive. It is not enough to produce a good website; you need to update it continuously to maintain interest in it and fight off obsolescence. Furthermore, you need updateable equipment (the general intellect is always an assemblage of humans and their machines), which is, in its turn, propelled by the intense collective labor of programmers, designers, and workers. It is as if the acceleration of production has pushed to the point where commodities, literally, turn into translucent objects. Commodities do not so much disappear as become more transparent, showing throughout their reliance on the labor that produces and sustains them. It is the labor of the designers and programmers that shows through a successful website, and it is the spectacle of that labor changing its product that keeps the users coming back. The commodity, then, is only as good as the labor that goes into it.

As a consequence, the sustainability of the Internet as a medium depends on massive amounts of labor (which is not equivalent to employment, as we said), only some of which is hypercompensated by the capricious logic of venture capitalism. Of the incredible amount of labor that sustains the Internet as a whole (from mailing list traffic to websites to infrastructural questions), we can guess that a substantial amount of it is still free labor.

Free labor, however, is not necessarily exploited labor. Within the early virtual communities, we are told, labor was really free: the labor of building a community was not compensated by great financial rewards (it was, therefore, free, unpaid), but it was also willingly conceded in exchange for the pleasures of communication and exchange (it was therefore free, pleasurable, not imposed). In answer to members' requests, information was quickly posted and shared with a lack of mediation that the early netizens did not fail to appreciate. Howard Rheingold's book, somehow unfairly accused of middle-class complacency, is the most well-known account of the good old times of the old Internet, before the net-tourist overcame the net-pioneer.[46]

The free labor that sustains the Internet is acknowledged within many different sections of the digital literature. Despite the volatile nature of the Internet economy (which yesterday was about community, today is about portals, and tomorrow who knows...?), the notion of users' labor maintains an ideological and material centrality that runs consistently throughout the turbulent succession of Internet fads. Commentators who would normally disagree, such as Howard Rheingold and Richard Hudson, concur on one thing: the best website, the best way to stay visible and thriving on the web, is to turn your site into a space that is not only accessed, but somehow built by its users.[47] Users keep a site alive through their labor, the cumulative hours of accessing the site (thus generating advertising), writing messages, participating in conversations, and sometimes making the jump to collaborators. Out of the 15,000 volunteers who kept AOL running, only a handful turned against it, while the others stayed on. Such a feature seems endemic to the Internet in ways that can be worked on by commercialization, but not substantially altered. The "open source" movement, which relies on the free labor of Internet tinkers, is further evidence of this structural trend within the digital economy.

It is an interesting feature of the Internet debate (and evidence, somehow, of its masculine bias) that users' labor has attracted more attention in the case of the open source movement than in that of mailing lists and websites. This betrays the persistence of an attachment to masculine understandings of labor within the digital economy: writing an operating system is still more worthy of attention than just chatting for free for AOL. This despite the fact that in 1996, at the peak of the volunteer moment, over 30,000 "community leaders" were helping AOL to generate at least $7 million per month.[48] Still, the open source movement has drawn much more positive attention than the more diffuse user labor described above. It is worth exploring because of the debates that it has provoked and its relation to the digital economy at large.

The open source movement is a variation of the old tradition of shareware and freeware software, which substantially contributed to the technical development of the Internet. Freeware software is freely distributed and does not even request a payment from its users. Shareware software is distributed freely, but incurs a moral obligation for the user to forward a small sum to the producer to sustain the shareware movement as an alternative economic model to the copyrighted software of giants such as Microsoft. Open source "refers to a model of software development in which the underlying code of a program—the source code, a.k.a. the crown jewels—is by definition made freely available to the general public for modification, alteration, and endless redistribution."[49]

Far from being an idealistic, minoritarian practice, the open source movement has attracted much media and financial attention. In 1999, Apache, an open source web server, became the "Web-server program of choice for more than half of all publicly accessible Web servers."[50] It has since then expanded to the point where Bavaria in Germany and the whole of China have recently announced a switchover to Apache. Open-source conventions are anxiously attended by venture capitalists, who have been informed by the digerati that the open source is a necessity "because you must go open-source to get access to the benefits of the open-source development community—the near-instantaneous bug fixes, the distributed intellectual resources of the Net, the increasingly large open-source code base."[51] Open-source companies such as Cygnus convinced the market that you do not need to be proprietary about source codes to make a profit: the code might be free, but tech support, packaging, installation software, regular upgrades, office applications, and hardware are not.

In 1998, when Netscape went open source and invited the computer tinkers and hobbyists to look at the code of its new browser, fix the bugs, improve the package, and redistribute it, specialized mailing lists exchanged opinions about its implications.[52] Netscape's move rekindled the debate about the peculiar nature of the digital economy. Was it to be read as being in the tradition of the Internet gift economy? Or was digital capital hijacking the open source movement exactly against that tradition? Richard Barbrook saluted Netscape's move as a sign of the power intrinsic in the architecture of the medium.[53] Others, such as John Horvarth, however, did not share this optimism. The "free stuff" offered around the Net, he argued,

> is either a product that gets you hooked on to another one or makes you just consume more time on the net. After all, the goal of the access people and telecoms is to have users spend as much time on the net as possible, regardless of what they are doing. The objective is to have you consume bandwidth.[54]

Far from proving the persistence of the Internet gift economy, Horvarth claimed that Netscape's move was a direct threat to those independent producers for whom shareware and freeware have been a way of surviving exactly those "big boys" that Netscape represents:

> Freeware and shareware are the means by which small producers, many of them individuals, were able to offset somewhat the bulldozing effects of the big boys. And now the bulldozers are headed straight for this arena. As for Netscape [sic], such a move makes good business sense and spells trouble for workers in the field of software development. The company had a poor last quarter in 1997 and was already hinting at job cuts. Well, what better way to shed staff by having your product taken further by the freeware people, having code-dabbling hobbyists fix and further develop your product? The question for Netscape now is how to tame the freeware beast so that profits are secured.[55]

Although it is tempting to stake the evidence of Netscape's layoffs against the optimism of Barbrook's gift economy, there might be more productive ways of looking at the increasingly tight relationship between an idealistic movement such as open source and the current venture mania for open source companies.[56] Rather than representing a moment of incorporation of a previously authentic moment, the open source question demonstrates the overreliance of the digital economy as such on free labor, both in the sense of not financially rewarded and willingly given. This includes AOL community leaders, the open source programmers, the amateur web designers, mailing list editors, and the netslaves willing to "work for cappuccinos" just for the excitement and the dubious promises of digital work.[57]

Such reliance, almost a dependency, is part of larger mechanisms of capitalist extraction of value that are fundamental to late capitalism as a whole. That is, such processes are not created outside capital and then reappropriated by capital, but are the results of a complex history where the relation between labor and capital is mutually constitutive, entangled, and crucially forged during the crisis of Fordism. Free labor is a desire of labor immanent to late capitalism, and late capitalism is the field that both sustains free labor and exhausts it. It exhausts it by subtracting selectively but widely the means through which that labor can reproduce itself: from the burnout syndromes of Internet start-ups to underretribution and exploitation in the cultural economy at large. Late capitalism does not appropriate anything: it nurtures, exploits, and exhausts its labor force and its cultural and affective production. In this sense, it is technically impossible to separate neatly the digital economy of the net from the larger network economy of late capitalism. Especially since 1994, the Internet has been always and simultaneously a gift economy *and* an advanced capitalist economy. The mistake of the neoliberalists (as exemplified by the *Wired* group), is to mistake this coexistence for a benign, unproblematic equivalence.

As stated before, these processes are far from confined to the most self-conscious laborers of the digital economy. They are part of a diffuse cultural economy that operates throughout the Internet and beyond. The passage from the pioneeristic days of the Internet to its venture and recession days does not seem to have affected these mechanisms, only intensified them. Nowhere is this more evident than on World Wide Web.

The Net and the Set

In the winter of 1999, in what sounds like another of its resounding, short-lived claims, *Wired* magazine announced that just after five years, the old web was dead:

> The Old Web was a place where the unemployed, the dreamy, and the iconoclastic went to reinvent themselves. . . . The New Web isn't about dabbling in what you don't know and failing—it's about preparing seriously for the day when television and Web content are delivered over the same digital networks.[58]

The new web was made of the big players, but also of new ways to make the audience work. In the new Web, after the pioneering days, television and the web converge in the one thing they have in common: their reliance on their audiences/users as providers of the cultural labor that goes under the label of "real-life stories." Gerry

Laybourne, executive of the web-based media company *Oxygen,* thinks of a hypothetical show called *What Are They Thinking?* a reality-based sketch comedy based on stories posted on the web, because "funny things happen in our lives everyday."[59] As Bayers also adds, "until it's produced, the line separating that concept from more puerile fare dismissed by Gerry, like *America's Funniest,* is hard to see."[60]

The difference between the puerile fare of *America's Funniest* and user-based content seems to lie not so much in the more serious nature of the new web as compared to the vilified output of television's people shows and reality television. From an abstract point of view, there is no difference between the ways in which people shows rely on the inventiveness of their audiences and the ways in which websites rely on users' input. People shows rely on the activity (even amid the most shocking sleaze) of their audience and willing participants to a much larger extent than any other television programs. In a sense, they manage the impossible; they create monetary value out of the most reluctant members of the postmodern cultural economy: those who do not produce marketable style, who are not qualified enough to enter the fast world of the knowledge economy, are converted into monetary value through their capacity to perform their misery.

When compared to the cultural and affective production on the Internet, people shows also seem to embody a different logic of relation between capitalism (the media conglomerates that produce and distribute such shows) and its labor force—the beguiled, dysfunctional citizens of the underdeveloped North. Within people shows and reality TV, the valorization of the audience as labor and spectacle always happens somehow within a power/knowledge nexus that does not allow the *immediate* valorization of the talk show participants: you cannot just put a Jerry Springer guest on TV on her own to tell her story with no mediation (indeed, that would look too much like the discredited access slots of public-service broadcasting). There is no real 24/7 access to reality TV, but increasing and decreasing levels of selective editing (according to the different modalities of a communication spectrum that goes from terrestrial to digital TV and the Internet). In the case of talk shows, various levels of knowledge intervene between the guest and the apparatus of valorization, which normalize the dysfunctional subjects through a moral or therapeutic discourse and a more traditional institutional organization of production. So after the performance, the guest must be advised, patronized, questioned, and often bullied by the audience and the host, all in the name of a perfunctory, normalizing morality. In reality television, psychologists and other experts are also brought in to provide an authoritative perspective through which what is often a sheer voyeuristic experience may be seen as a social experiment.

TV shows also belong to a different economy of scale: although there are more and more of them, they are still relatively few when compared to the millions of pages on the web. It is as if the centralized organization of the traditional media does not let them turn people's productions into pure monetary value. TV shows must have morals, even as those morals are shattered by the overflowing performances of their subjects.

Within the Internet, however, this process of channeling and adjudicating (responsibilities, duties, and rights) is dispersed to the point where practically anything is tolerated (sadomasochism, bestiality, fetishism, and plain nerdism are not targeted, at least within the Internet, as sites that need to be disciplined or explained away). The qualitative difference between people shows and a successful website, then, does not lie in the latter's democratic tendency as opposed to the former's exploitative nature. It lies in the operation, within people shows, of majoritarian discursive mechanisms of territorialization, the application of a morality that the excessive abundance of material on the Internet renders redundant and, even more, irrelevant. The digital economy cares only tangentially about morality. What it really cares about is an abundance of production, an immediate interface with cultural and technical labor whose result is a diffuse, nondialectical antagonism and a crisis in the capitalist modes of valorization as such.

A New Conclusion: The Liberation of Free Labor February 2012

"Free Labor" was written in the late 1990s as output of a funded research project about the future of the Internet and partially rewritten in the mid-2000s, after the crash of the dot-com bubble. It put forward two propositions. The first argued that the future of the Internet was going to be driven by the centrality of users' active participation. The second proposition argued that such process could be productively explained by means of the autonomist Marxists' thesis of the social factory and concurrent notions of immaterial labor and the social factory. Today, in the middle of chronic financial turbulence and a general slowing down or recession of the global economy, the digital economy of the social web seems to belong to a different universe, as numbers of users increase exponentially and the profits and market value of web 2.0 giants are exceptions to the general depressing economic climate. The idea that the value of such corporations is given by users' participation has become common business sense. The composition of labor producing the value of such companies shows a massive surplus of free labor as compared to a tiny percentage of actual waged labor. Furthermore, voluntary work, unpaid work, underpaid work, and a growing gap between the wealthy and everybody else have become salient features of contemporary economies at large. But what to make of the other thesis, put forward in the original article, that such activity could be considered as a form of labor and that such labor was being exploited?

Calling users' participation in the digital economy labor was not so much an empirical description of an undisputable social and economic reality, but a political choice. Subscribing to the autonomists' thesis of the social factory meant rejecting the separation between consumption and production and hence arguing that the production of value could no longer be confined to the spaces and times of waged work. This implies arguing that wages paid for work performed as such could no longer be considered an adequate way of distributing wealth socially generated in contemporary societies.

Within the economic limits of capitalist economies, then, living labor is doubly exploited. To the increasing exploitation clearly visible in the domain of waged digital work (decreasing autonomy and falling wages for increasing productivity), we have to add, then, a new kind of exploitation—that which concerns the immaterial commons of cultural and technical production. Such exploitation must be conceptualized differently than the one concerning waged work. It implies a privatization of the wealth produced by free labor that takes the shape of an impoverishment of potential users' appropriation of the fruits of such labor. This impoverishment can be understood in terms of the unilateral appropriation and hence accumulation of the wealth generated by users' interactions (both personal data, which become property of the company, and the general activity of sharing, posting, linking, commenting, etc.) but also in the actual quality of the participation to the digital economy constrained by the control unilaterally exercised by web giants on the technical configurations of social networking platforms. As the mechanisms of such expropriation are clearly embedded within forms of financialization that impoverish society as a whole, asking for the liberation of free labor means asking for two things: that such profits be returned to those who actually produce them—that is, to living labor—and that social networking platforms should be deprivatized—that is, that ownership of users' data should be returned to their rightful owners as the freedom to access and modify the protocols and diagrams that structure their participation.

These seem like simple conclusions, but their consequences are far reaching. Giving free labor access to the wealth that it generates cannot mean, as Michel Bauwens has argued, paying users individually. As the wealth generated by free labor is social, so should be the mode of its return. This means investing this wealth in the reproduction of the common—that is, in new forms of welfare (from the institution of basic guaranteed income to larger investments in housing, health, education, knowledge, technology, and so on). This implies enormous shifts not only within the specific domain of the digital economy but within the global economy as a whole, which run counter to the current trend toward austerity, reduction of the cost and rights of labor, and extreme competitiveness. Who is the subject that should carry on such struggle to reverse the tendency toward further impoverishment and exploitation? Where is the passage from the class in itself to the class for itself?

The ambiguity of the current condition is implied in the fact that the means through which such passage can be accomplished are given (with the possible exception of Anonymous) within the context of those social media technologies that today are fully privatized and embedded in the capitalist economy at large. It is within these media that we are witnessing the formation of social and political movements that question not so much the specific domain of social media use but the overall economic structure that supports them. The Arab Spring and the Assemble and Occupy movements are two obvious examples of this trend, but so are the innumerable initiatives and struggles that over the past decade have brought together the net, the Squares, and the Streets. It is not clear at the moment whether such struggles will manage to accumulate enough social energy not only to reverse the current trend but also to generate their own structures and political rationalities, which are truly alternative to the no-alternative diktat. The liberation of free labor, however, cannot demand anything less.

Notes

This essay has been made possible by research carried out with the support of the Virtual Society? program of the Economic and Social Research Council (grant number L132251050). I shared this grant with Sally Wyatt and Graham Thomas, Department of Innovation Studies, University of East London. The chapter has been previously published as "Free Labor: Producing Culture for the Digital Economy," in *Social Text* 18, no. 2 (2000): 33–58. Reprinted by permission of Duke University Press.

1 See Andrew Ross's ethnography of New York City digital design company Razorfish, *No Collar: The Humane Workplace and Its Hidden Costs* (New York: Basic Books, 2002).
2 See http://www.netslaves.com. And also Bill Lessard and Steve Baldwin's playful classification of the dot-com labor hierarchies in *Netslaves: True Tales of Working the Web* (New York: McGraw-Hill, 2000).
3 Lisa Margonelli, "Inside AOL's 'Cyber-Sweatshop,'" *Wired,* October 1999, 138.
4 See Paolo Virno and Michael Hardt, *Radical Thought in Italy: A Potential Politics* (Minneapolis: University of Minnesota Press, 1996); and Toni Negri, *The Politics of Subversion: A Manifesto for the Twenty-first Century* (Cambridge: Polity Press, 1989) and *Marx beyond Marx: Lessons on the "Grundrisse"* (New York: Autonomedia, 1991).
5 Negri, *The Politics of Subversion.*
6 Donna Haraway, *Simians, Cyborgs, and Women: The Reinvention of Nature* (London: Routledge, 1991), 159.
7 Paul Gilroy, *The Black Atlantic: Modernity and Double Consciousness* (London: Verso, 1993), 40.
8 Manuel Castells, *The Rise of the Network Society* (Cambridge, MA: Blackwell, 1996), 395.
9 Antonio Negri, *Guide. Cinque lezioni su Impero e dintorni* (Milan: Raffaello Cortina, 2003), 209 (my translation).
10 In discussing these developments, I will also draw on debates circulating across Internet sites such as, for example, nettime, telepolis, rhizome, and c-theory. Online debates are one of the manifestations of the surplus value engendered by the digital economy, a hyperproduction that can only be partly reabsorbed by capital.
11 Ross, *No Collar,* 9.
12 See Richard Barbrook, "The Digital Economy," nettime, June 17, 1997, http://www.nettime.org; Richard Barbrook, "The High-Tech Gift Economy," in *Readme! Filtered by Nettime: ASCII Culture and the Revenge of Knowledge,* eds. Josephine Bosma et al. (Brooklyn, NY: Autonomedia, 1999), 132–8. Also see Anonymous, "The Digital Artisan Manifesto," nettime, May 15, 1997; and Andrew Ross's argument in *No Collar* that the

digital artisan was an expression of a short-lived phase in the Internet labor market corresponding to a temporary shortage of skills that initially prevented a more industrial division of labor.

13 Barbrook, "The High-Tech Gift Economy," 135.

14 Ibid., 137.

15 Don Tapscott, *The Digital Economy* (New York: McGraw-Hill, 1996), xiii.

16 Ibid., 35 (emphasis added).

17 Ibid., 48.

18 For a discussion of the independent music industry and its relation to corporate culture, see David Hesmondalgh, "Indie: The Aesthetics and Institutional Politics of a Popular Music Genre," *Cultural Studies* 13 (January 1999): 34–61. Angela McRobbie has also studied a similar phenomenon in the fashion and design industry in *British Fashion Design: Rag Trade or Image Industry?* (London: Routledge, 1998).

19 See the challenging section on work in the high-tech industry in Bosma et al., *Readme!*

20 Martin Kenney, "Value-Creation in the Late Twentieth Century: The Rise of the Knowledge Worker," in *Cutting Edge: Technology, Information Capitalism and Social Revolution,* eds. Jim Davis, Thomas Hirsch, and Michael Stack (London: Verso, 1997), 93; also see in the same anthology Tessa Morris-Suzuki, "Capitalism in the Computer Age," 57–71.

21 See Darko Suvin, "On Gibson and Cyberpunk SF," in *Storming the Reality Studio,* ed. Larry McCaffery (London: Durham University Press, 1991), 349–65; and Stanley Aronowitz and William DiFazio, *The Jobless Future: SciTech and the Dogma of Work* (Minneapolis: University of Minnesota Press, 1994). According to Andrew Clement, information technologies were introduced as extensions of Taylorist techniques of scientific management to middle-level, rather than clerical, employees. Such technologies responded to a managerial need for efficient ways to manage intellectual labor. Clement, however, seems to connect this scientific management to the workstation, while he is ready to admit that personal computers introduce an element of autonomy much disliked by management. See Andrew Clement, "Office Automation and the Technical Control of Information Workers," in *The Political Economy of Information,* eds. Vincent Mosco and Janet Wasko (Madison: University of Wisconsin Press, 1988).

22 Barbrook, "The High-Tech Gift Economy."

23 See Kevin Robins, "Cyberspace or the World We Live In," in *Fractal Media: New Media in Social Context,* ed. Jon Dovey (London: Lawrence and Wishart, 1996).

24 See Frank Webster, *Theories of the Information Society* (London: Routledge, 1995).

25 Maurizio Lazzarato, "Immaterial Labor," in *Marxism beyond Marxism,* eds. Saree Makdisi, Cesare Casarino, and Rebecca E. Karl for the Polygraph Collective (London: Routledge, 1996), 133.

26 The Criminal Justice Act (CJA) was popularly perceived as an antirave legislation, and most of the campaign against it was organized around the "right to party." However, the most devastating effects of the CJA have struck the neotribal, nomadic camps, basically decimated or forced to move to Ireland in the process. See Andrea Natella and Serena Tinari, eds., *Rave Off* (Rome: Castelvecchi, 1996).

27 Lazzarato, "Immaterial Labor," 136.

28 In the two volumes of *Capitalism and Schizophrenia,* Gilles Deleuze and Félix Guattari described the process by which capital unsettles and resettles bodies and cultures as a movement of "decoding" ruled by "axiomatization." Decoding is the process through which older cultural limits are displaced and removed, as with older, local cultures during modernization; the flows of culture and capital unleashed by the decoding are then channeled into a process of axiomatization, an abstract moment of conversion into money

and profit. The decoding forces of global capitalism have then opened up the possibilities of immaterial labor. See Gilles Deleuze and Félix Guattari, *Anti-Oedipus: Capitalism and Schizophrenia* (London: Athlone, 1984); and *A Thousand Plateaus: Capitalism and Schizophrenia* (London: Athlone, 1988).

29 See Franco Berardi (Bifo), *La nefasta utopia di potere operaio* (Rome: Castelvecchi/DeriveApprodi, 1998), 43.

30 See Kevin Kelly, *Out of Control* (Reading, MA: Addison-Wesley, 1994).

31 Eugene Provenzo, foreword to Pierre Levy, *Collective Intelligence: Mankind's Emerging World in Cyberspace* (New York: Plenum, 1995), viii.

32 Levy, *Collective Intelligence,* 13.

33 Ibid., 1.

34 See Little Red Henski, "Insider Report from UUNET," in Bosma et al., *Readme!* 189–91.

35 Paolo Virno, "Notes on the General Intellect," in Makdisi, Casarino, and Karl, *Marxism beyond Marxism,* 266.

36 Karl Marx, *Grundrisse* (London: Penguin, 1973), 693.

37 Virno, "Notes on the General Intellect," 266.

38 Ibid., 270.

39 Ibid., 271.

40 See Maurizio Lazzarato, "New Forms of Production," in Bosma et al., *Readme!* 159–66; and Tessa Morris-Suzuki, "Robots and Capitalism," in *Cutting Edge: Technology, Information Capitalism and Social Revolution,* 13–27. n.p.: Verso, 1998.

41 See Toni Negri, "Back to the Future," in Bosma et al., *Readme!* 181–6; and Haraway, *Simians, Cyborgs, and Women.*

42 Andrew Ross, *Real Love: In Pursuit of Cultural Justice* (London: Routledge, 1998).

43 See Barbrook, "The High-Tech Gift Economy."

44 The work of Jean-François Lyotard in *The Postmodern Condition* is mainly concerned with *knowledge* rather than intellectual labor but still provides a useful conceptualization of the reorganization of labor within the productive structures of late capitalism. See Jean-François Lyotard, *The Postmodern Condition: A Report on Knowledge,* trans. Geoff Bennington and Brian Massumi (Minneapolis: University of Minnesota Press, 1989).

45 See Arthur Kroker and Michael A. Weinstein, *Data Trash: The Theory of the Virtual Class* (New York: St. Martin's Press, 1994).

46 See Howard Rheingold, *The Virtual Community: Homesteading on the Electronic Frontier* (New York: Harper Perennial, 1994).

47 See Howard Rheingold, "My Experience with Electric Minds," in Bosma et al., *Readme!* 147–50; also David Hudson, *Rewired: A Brief (and Opinionated) Net History* (Indianapolis: Macmillan Technical Publishing, 1997). The expansion of the net is based on different types of producers adopting different strategies of income generation: some might use more traditional types of financial support (grants, divisions of the public sector, in-house Internet divisions within traditional media companies, businesses' web pages, which are paid as with traditional forms of advertising); some might generate interest in one's page and then sell the user's profile or advertising space (freelance web production); and some might use innovative strategies of valorization, such as various types of e-commerce.

48 See Margonelli, "Inside AOL's 'Cyber-Sweatshop.'"

49 Andrew Leonard, "Open Season," *Wired,* May 1999, 140. Open source harks back to the specific competencies embodied by Internet users in its pre-1994 days. When most net users were computer experts, the software structure of the medium was developed by way of a continuous interaction of different technical skills. This tradition

still survives in institutions like the Internet Engineering Task Force (IETF), which is responsible for a number of important decisions about the technical infrastructure of the net. Although the IETF is subordinated to a number of professional committees, it has important responsibilities and is open to anybody who wants to join. The freeware movement has a long tradition, but it has also recently been divided by the polemics between the free software or "copyleft" movement and the open-source movement, which is more of a pragmatic attempt to make freeware a business proposition. See debates online at http://www.gnu.org and http://www.salonmag.com.

50 Leonard, "Open Season."

51 Ibid., 142.

52 It is an established pattern of the computer industry, in fact, that you might have to give away your product if you want to reap the benefits later on. As John Perry Barlow has remarked, "Familiarity is an important asset in the world of information. It may often be the case that the best thing you can do to raise demand for your product is to give it away." See John Perry Barlow, "Selling Wine without Bottles: The Economy of Mind on the Global Net," in *High Noon on the Electronic Frontier: Conceptual Issues in Cyberspace,* ed. Peter Ludlow (Cambridge, MA: MIT Press, 1996).

53 The technical and social structure of the net has been developed to encourage open cooperation among its participants. As an everyday activity, users are building the system together. Engaged in interactive creativity, they send e-mail, take part in electronic mailing lists, contribute to newsgroups, participate in online conferences, and produce websites. Lacking copyright protection, information can be freely adapted to suit the users' needs. Within the high-tech gift economy, people successfully work together through "an open social process involving evaluation, comparison and collaboration" (Barbrook, "The High-Tech Gift Economy," 135–6).

54 John Horvarth, "Freeware Capitalism," nettime, February 5, 1998.

55 Ibid.

56 Netscape started like a lot of other computer companies: its founder, Marc Andreessen, was part of the original research group that developed the structure of the World Wide Web at the CERN laboratory, in Geneva. As with many successful computer entrepreneurs, he developed the browser as an offshoot of the original, state-funded research and soon started his own company. Netscape was also the first company to exceed the economic processes of the computer industry, inasmuch as it was the first successful company to set up shop on the net itself. As such, Netscape exemplifies some of the problems that even the computer industry meets on the net and constitutes a good starting point to assess some of the common claims about the digital economy.

57 Ross, *Real Love.*

58 Chip Bayers, "Push Comes to Show," *Wired,* February 1999, 113.

59 Ibid., 156.

60 Ibid.

3

THE POLITICAL ECONOMY OF COSMOPOLIS

Sean Cubitt

On Political Economy

The political economy of cosmopolis, of a global polity that is not that of neoliberal globalization, has to be imagined, because this is the one way to stop it being planned. Michel Foucault (2007) made the case that the free market depends entirely on an unfree regulatory regime of property, contracts, money, law. So we should begin by reintroducing the political to the economic. The classical political philosophers—Aristotle, Hobbes, Rousseau—suggest that politics is a natural state for the political animal. Rancière (1999), in contrast, suggests that it is not natural at all. The state of nature might favor such natural attributes as strength, gender, and age as criteria, but politics began when these "natural" hierarchies were challenged by those who had been left out of the account. Politics is, he argues, the struggle over inclusion in the arena of the political. In ancient times, the artisans and in modern times, the landless, slaves, prisoners, and women were governed without the possibility of governing. Today exclusion of immigrants and refugees, governed by coercive actions in which they have no say (Abizadeh 2008), defines the political. As Arendt (1978) argued, the exclusion would prove definitive of the postwar politics of human rights. As Rancière has it, referencing Agamben,

> either the rights of man are the rights of the citizen, that is to say the rights of those who have rights, which is a tautology; or the rights of the citizen are the rights of man. But as bare humanity has no rights, then they are the rights of those who have no rights, which is an absurdity. (Rancière 2006: 61)

More concretely, the poor may have the right to own property but have no property to own—that is, they have a right without possessing it. Rancière disagrees, however, with the analysis that says that democracy is therefore unattainable. Instead, he sees it as the grounds of politics.

This is what the democratic process implies: the action of subjects who, by working the interval between identities, reconfigure the distributions of the public and the private, the universal and the particular. Democracy can never be identified with the simple domination of the universal (Rancière 2006: 61–2).

Politics is a question of subjects and objects: the subjects of politics, who govern, and the objects, who are governed. When an object of politics demands to be a subject, democracy arises in that demand and how it is met. The putatively universal subject of democracy is never universal, because government always means government *of:* of people, tendencies, in fine of objects deemed incapable of governing themselves. The gap between citizen and human—between those who have rights and those who do not—produces demand: for recognition, participation, and the changes to the existing polity that implies.

Rancière's interest is political, but an analogous economic exclusion appears in the analysis of labor theorist Hernando de Soto (2000). De Soto agrees with Foucault that the accumulation of wealth is not the engine of capitalism. Instead, it is the infrastructure of property rights, contracts, deeds, titles, and, crucially for our discussions, intellectual property regimes, which, together, drive the system of capital. This infrastructure excludes forms of wealth—of labor and property—which cannot be monetized. The wealth of the poor specifically is excluded: the labor of women and children, domestic labor, subsistence farming, and indigenous and common ownership systems. The difference between monetizable and what de Soto calls "dead capital" is that the capital that can be monetized is alienable; it is transferrable, mobile, liquid, and so also transformable. De Soto argues that were we to count in this dead labor, the world's poor would actually own the majority of the world's wealth.

De Soto proposes a market solution to effect this goal. For many reasons that cannot detain us here (but see Clastres 1987 and Barclay 2005), this is not only an unlikely but an undesirable result. One reason why such market solutions are likely to succeed, however, is that the tendency of the rate of profit to fall constantly drives capital into the marketization of new areas of life, each of which inevitably succumbs to the same tendency, with the results we witness today in the privatization of the public good and of the global ecology. A second reason that a market solution is unlikely is the question of whether capital in its post-Fordist, neoliberal, global phase is sustainably mobile, fluid, and transformative enough to accommodate the irruption of new modes of wealth and translate them into monetizable currents—into currency. Until the dot-com crash of 2001, the web was one of the longest-lived Temporary Autonomous Zones our generation ever knew. Capital failed to understand. Although early experimenters such as Amazon and eBay preceded and survived the crash, it was not until the years after 2001 that business models based in the web, rather than imported from magazine publishing and the broadcast industry, began to dominate the new medium. This would seem to demonstrate capital's ability to colonize any new public good.

In Marx's "Fragment on Machines" in *Grundrisse* (1973: 690ff.), the "social" or "general intellect" is manifest in two processes. In one, manual skills developed over generations are ossified into machinery and turned to purposes of exploitation. In the second, capital systematizes workers' self-organization. But, as Virno argues in *A Grammar of the Multitude* (2004), this innovative power to make new systems is no longer a side benefit of employing workers; it is written into our contracts. With the commercialized social web, capital has finally managed to turn subversion into profit. The battle for the Internet is not yet over, but in critical strategic and tactical fields such as codecs, HTML5 and Ipv6, capital is winning. Is this evidence of the universalization of neoliberal democracy, or are there grounds for a new politics?

If there are grounds, network communications will provide them. Neither weightless nor immaterial, networks accumulate debt to the most important of all the nonmonetized domains: the global environment. The server industry alone already has a greater carbon footprint than the airline business (Boccaletti, Löffler, and Oppenheim 2006). Smart server design and innovations in the generation and delivery of energy are partial solutions, but the fact remains: there is an environmental cost—in the extraction of materials, manufacture, distribution and retailing, use, and recycling—to computer-mediated communications. The exclusion that defines democracy, and that provides information capital with its core resource, is not exclusively human. Actor-network theory notes the exclusion of the natural world from political process (Latour 2004); we cannot imagine giving a vote to the environment, or to machines. But then our ancestors couldn't imagine giving the vote to artisans or slaves, women, blacks, servants, landless peasants, youths, and colonized or indigenous peoples, and today we cannot imagine giving votes to migrants. The challenge, of course, is that we cannot, nor could we ever, simply assimilate these others into an unchanged system. The system must change, radically, as it opens its political life to the now incessant demands of the ecosphere.

Environmentalism is presented largely as a matter of behavioral change—of new criteria in consumption, fundamentally as ethics rather than politics. As in the normative practices of the professions, environmentalism is presented as code of conduct. These ostensibly ethical strictures do not provide communal grounds for action—the root meaning of the word *ethics*—but rules for smooth functioning. They are self-replicating systems that, far from demanding commitment to the Good, the good life, or the infinite demand of the other, ensure that no decision need ever be taken. This is the point of Derrida's challenge:

> If I know, for example, what the causes and effects of what I am doing are, what the program is for what I am doing, then there is no decision; it is a question, at the moment of judgment, of applying a particular causality. . . . If I know what is to be done . . . then there is no moment of decision, simply the application of a body of knowledge, or at the very least a rule or a norm. For there to be a decision, the decision must be heterogeneous to knowledge as such. (Derrida 2001: 231–2)

The only true action is thus one that breaks the rules. But since the rules have emerged from consensus, breaking them is unethical. The only choice is between compliance and evil—and we know from Arendt that, at least in certain circumstances, compliance may itself be evil. This is the point at which we find ethics opposed to action, ethics as the excluded other of politics defined as the realm of action. From this standpoint, we have to acknowledge the shocking inference drawn by Esposito: "Not only is there no contradiction in principle between evil and politics, but evil, as such, is from a certain point of view always political" (Esposito 1993: 183).

The evolution of new strategies, then, depends on an escape from ethics as code of conduct. The uniqueness of every situation requires consideration if it is to provide the grounds for action. Considering where we are (and what we are to do as a consequence of how we find ourselves situated) is quite different from either the application of rules or modeling possible future scenarios in which, in the long run, we are all dead. Consideration of the actual situation should therefore seek out what is unique in it: what is unforeseen, unaccounted for in the rulebook. It is on the basis of these unforeseen elements in the situation that it becomes possible to act, to change the world as given into the world as potential. The terrain of managed possibilities debarring us from action (de Carolis 1996) reveals its contradictions. The givenness of a contingent and probabilistic world becomes future-oriented capacity for bringing about genuinely new situations.

The Crowd

The entity that best expresses this new, postindividual condition is the crowd. Inherently contingent in its complexity, it is probabilistic not in the sense of statistical management, but of virtuality; the crowd is an organ of demand that is never complete, universal, or integral—that is, it fails to exist as a unified and coherent whole (In other words, the indeterminacy is our best hope and hence a call to arms), pitching itself instead into action, which converts the actually existing into the raw material of futurity. But the new crowd is also target of capital's latest colonization, crowdsourcing. Social networking commercializes the gift of labor, not as individual activity but as aberrations from the average, which can be read as tendencies and thus both governed and exploited as such. Hence, the virtual nature of the crowd, its potential or power to act, is removed by a process of forecasting how much deviance is tolerable—and profitable—in a population. This may indeed be the actuality of the process Rossiter and Zehle in this volume refer to as "a politics beyond the actionable." Disciplinary identity no longer produced the requisite unforeseen behaviors that capital requires in its endless expansion. The capitalization of friendship by Facebook is a new trajectory, paralleled by the extension of prosumer status to the vast populations of the global South in schemes such as O3b (http://www.o3bnetworks.com), an alliance of search and telecom giants to build a satellite network capable of inducting the Other 3 Billion of the developing world into Internet culture. Geographical extension, sociological intension, and cultural diversity embrace difference as an engine of growth.

The challenge, then, is to confront network activity not with negation but intensification. What is essential is not the actual, certainly not the enforced identities of consumer capital and the management of the self, but precisely nonidentity: the nonidentical nature of the world to which Western thought perpetually ascribes identity. Beyond the shattering of the individual self, what remains to be thought is the nonidenticality of the crowd, or the masses, or populations. The implication of the shattered self is that the crowd is no longer conceivable in terms of a relation between individual and collective. For Laclau, any social or political group emerges neither because the group exists "naturally" (as in some descriptions of nationalism), nor as an aggregation of individuals, but as the concatenation of a more primal human condition:

> The unity of the group is, in my view, the result of an articulation of demands. This articulation, however, does not correspond to a stable and positive configuration which could be grasped as a unified whole: on the contrary, since it is in the nature of all demands to present claims to a certain established order, it is in a peculiar relation with that order, being both inside and outside it. As this order cannot fully absorb the demand, it cannot constitute itself as a coherent totality. (Laclau 2005: ix)

But in the database economy, demand is always the object of management. Demand management demeans demand as engine of socialization. Even where it is most lauded as the new mode of extraction of surplus value from populations, in crowdsourcing, the crowd is treated as an emergent property of probabilities whose behaviors, however, are held to be foreseeable. In this actuarial foreknowledge, it is crucial to discern the object of biopolitical management, an object that is singular. The population managed in biopolitics is a single entity. This is the sovereign people of constitutional representative democracy, the sovereign consumer of the market economy. There is only one market in the global economy. But that entity is incomplete and contradictory: neither whole nor universal, it fails in its quest for totality.

We live, politically, in a world governed by the distinction between the rights of the citizen and the rights of man. As Anthony Downey (2009: 109) expresses it, "What if the refugee, the political prisoner, the disappeared, the victim of torture, the dispossessed are not only constitutive of modernity but its emblematic subjects?" Like Agamben (1995), who provides his premise, Downey misses a key issue—that the refugee, along with those other others, is not a subject, because she is not within the population. Assimilating the stateless and the excluded will remove the last great barrier to cosmopolis, the last political refusal of a system which today encourages the free flow of money and goods and only restricts the free flow of people.

This is the first stage in building cosmopolis. It takes us beyond the Westphalian nation-state as the unit of Kant's "cosmopolitan intent." It is, after all, almost conceivable that nations open their borders to migrants, conceivable enough to be the motor of fear and protest, activism and fascist backlash, in Europe and elsewhere. What is truly inconceivable is to extend beyond the migrant into more unimaginable zones where government extends without representation or voice.

This is the mode of "any difference which makes a difference *in some later event*" (Bateson 1973: 351; emphasis in original), of the utopia without content, which Adorno and Bloch agreed in their last interview (Bloch 1988) was the grounds for political hope. Cosmopolis is the mode of politics after humanism, after we are forced to accept our cyborg assemblages—which enable population as concept and political fact, but do so only on the grounds that technologies, notably telecommunications, are excluded from the humans-only polity, which is all we have ever imagined—and after we accept the articulation of human with planetary futures. It is not a question of sustainability, because what is to be sustained in such discourse is always the exclusively human population. In any posthuman politics, the question of the good is no longer de facto defined by humans and is therefore no longer definable in the liberal regulatory and legalistic framework of rights. Contemporary humanist biopolitics has abandoned debate over how we should live; the only value is efficient management of the market. Wealth alone provides the good life, in actuality a miasma of commodities and status, of half-understood energies and half-satisfied desires. Cosmopolis makes it possible to imagine that other goods, truer understandings, and deeper satisfactions may well turn out to be both achievable beyond the unitary political economy of biopolitical capitalism.

To turn the compulsory choice of consumerism into actual freedom, we must move from the schizo individual to the particulate crowd of the demand. But we need also to recognize the interdependence of crowds, as opposed to the imagined autonomy of individuals. Twenty-first-century crowds exist in interdependence with technical and physical phyla beyond the humanist polity. Recognizing the failure of the system to encompass them in its illusory universality, the mediated crowd is the first political agency in human history with the capacity to cede autonomy to those unthinkable others: machines, animals, environments, geology, oceans, and atmosphere. The polis is not exclusively made of its population. It is rocks and earth, water and air, plants and animals, buildings, services, communications. "The creature that lives in cities" is as good a description of influenza as it is of humanity. It is pointless to speak of the rights of viruses. Cosmopolis is the goal of politics, and is unimaginable because it is truly future, truly other than the world we inhabit. It is so deeply alien because it is not exclusively human, and its polity is therefore not a matter of rights or citizenship or even of species-belonging of the kind that has structured our political philosophies as much as our actual politics. The function of human beings, Flusser (2000) held, was to produce randomness. But we are little capable of that in a self-regulating cybernetic regime dedicated to homeostasis. Our greatest hope is the unexpected, and we have vast reservoirs of that in the shape of the ancestral dead labor enshrined in our machines, and the great unknown of the natural world. As the dead capital of de Soto's poor, so Marx's dead labor of technology, and so, too, the unmonetized wealth of the living environment. What happens when we account this wealth in its own terms, not according to the correlationist economics that converts the universe into an environment *for* the human species?

Correcting de Carolis, we must understand the environment as alien, or historically alienated, to the extent that it is now no longer even the raw material of manufacture but a hostile Gaia gathering its strength to cast off its cancerously overgrown human population. It's a good time to strike an alliance, when the alternatives are all too thinkable. The alternative that holds out greatest hope for the self-replicating system of capital is the path of perpetual innovation. Technical inventions will provide sustainability; perpetual innovation will fuel perpetual growth. But innovation must come from an increasingly homogenized population, and from a technical infrastructure whose engineering solutions and organizational shape are more and more isomorphic with capital itself, that is the very forms which it is charged with renovating that are increasingly normalized around de facto standards. As a political economy premised on permanent growth, capital faces the finite limits of the unmonetized environment (accounting as carbon credits is a farce, credible only to neoliberal fundamentalists; there can be no market in the unmarketable). We cannot place our faith in a universal, popular platform of innovation through user-generated content, because the infrastructure that would permit it is itself finite. That it is also plagued by the very private property regime that enables capital—forcing each user to store his or her own intellectual property, each corporation to create silos of password-protected data, doubling, quadrupling, googleplexing the energy requirements and material infrastructure of the cloud—makes it even less likely that it will provide anything other than the short-term patch for which capital is beginning to be notorious.

Those who have rights they do not possess; those who consume least but are the most castigated; those who own enough to save for retirement but have no control over their money; those who suffer because we have divorced the making of wealth from the making of use-values; those who vainly seek accountability from those who are responsible for disaster; all of us lose when emergency overtakes pragmatism. Political economy is about value, and about the changing nature of value (Graham 2006). In late lectures, Adorno argued that any sacrifice of happiness to some other, putatively higher, always later goal is an imposition. Deferral is "a kind of economy of thrift," but "the compensation promised by civilization and our education in return for our acts of renunciation is not forthcoming" (Adorno 2000: 138). The sacrifice of happiness to rationality or to deferred gratification is a truly tragic sacrifice. Happiness is not to be passed over. But nor is it to be undersold, passing it off with nostrums and trinkets. Capital fails continuously to address famine and poverty, and thrives on pandemic and war. It has failed globally and consistently, and yet it poses itself as global necessity.

Contemporary political activism begins as it has before: in the dialectic of these contradictions, which intellectual fashion, shaped by what we have taught ourselves to recite as a litany of defeat, has placed in the dustbin of residual concepts.

The greatest of these contradictions is the human exception: that whatever constitutes the good is good exclusively for humans. The founding moment was the triumph of monotheism over animism, the dark secret of the Enlightenment's attack on superstition—ostensibly against the Roman Church but in actuality against belief systems that privileged the persons, multiple and protean, of nature rather than the single, unified and unifying Godhead. The long construction of God (Debray 2004) is a history of the brutal suppression of animism at home and in the colonies. That indigenous peoples have maintained and developed this animism should humble and inspire us.

Animism is not the religion of an atavistic Hobbesian war of each against all. Against the illusion of universality, which is the common claim of democracy, it contests the meticulous exclusion of the politics of the nonhuman. In thinking that unthinkable, we open the space for a different politics, and a different economics, that we cannot reach through shopping and voting. Under the regime of universal human rights, the much-desired goal of U.S. armed imposition of human rights is that all identities be subsumed under the single identity of humanity. What is at stake in the opening of politics to the nonhuman is the end of such a spurious and self-contradictory identity.

We possess a model for posthuman politics. As Sassen (2006) establishes, the market is no longer invisible. It is actively realized in network communications. This immense technological system is now an undeniable agent in political life. At the same time, as Knorr Cetina and Bruegger argue, the characteristic feature of markets is

> their essential incompleteness of being, which is transposed into a continuous knowledge project for participants. From a theoretical point of view, the defining characteristic of the market as an object is its lack of *'object-ivity'* *and completeness of being, its non-identity with itself.* Markets are always in the process of being materially redefined, they continually acquire new properties and change the ones they have. (Knorr Cetina and Bruegger 2002: 168)

This nonidentity is what we stand to gain in sacrificing identity as humans in a posthuman politics, which includes not only technologies, as the market already does, but the natural world as well. A central difference between market traders and us Greens is that they care far more about the liquid object of their engagement than we do. The reason why is interesting in its own right: nonidentity is, from Habermas to Deleuze, a characteristic of subjects. The market is not just an agency; for these traders it is a living, breathing subject. In many respects, we could say that it is The Subject of the contemporary globalizing political economy. The question is, then, how to move from the actor-network theory that ascribes *agency* to both physical and technological actors to a new political theory that recognizes their *subjectivity*.

Rancière's concept of the political as constituted by its exclusion points to such a phenomenon of incompleteness, of nonidentity of the putative universal, is what draws market traders to the market's lack in being. Culturalists, sociologists, and political philosophers cling to the concept of identity—gendered, regional, cultural, ethnic, sexual, but always already biological. This bounded unity is the *felix culpa* of political philosophy—the radical evil that makes possible a new world. We have three potential subjects of political economy: the market, the individual, and the crowd. All three are foundationally nonidentical. We recognize the cyborg nature of all three but have yet to recognize the dependent imbrication of the rest of the nonhuman world—a relation that is the utopian content of Harman's anticorrelationist stance (see Clough's contribution to this volume), which, however, defuses his insistence that objects precede and exceed their relationships. The political (as opposed perhaps to the ontological) is affective and mediated *because* it is relational in the first instance, and objective only as a product of that initial ontological standing. To stand as object of political economy is to be excluded and, by that token, governed and exploited. That is why, in the first instance, the challenge for Internet political economy is to reveal and release the natural and technical (ancestral) participants excluded from both wealth and citizenship. Only in such radical steps will the possibility of a human future be made possible, and a goal beyond the tyranny of instrumental reason and cash. We might begin with the only tribe who have a passion equal to Knorr Cetina's traders: the hackers celebrated by Parikka (2007) and Mackenzie (2006). We have yet to discover the passion that will make the green world integral to the problem of a new political economy of the Internet.

A fundamental question, in this framework, is whether the play we witness in social networks constitutes a demand for a political subjectivity or, indeed, extends the argument by analogy to the economic sphere, for an economic subjectivity. The peer-to-peer movement clearly articulates a new economics, and increasingly a new politics, in ways Facebook and other social networking sites absolutely do not. A traditional condition of subjectivity is awareness of the relations one has entered into. Such awareness may not be a property of immersion into social networks. Awareness is characterized by demand: by a demand for something beyond what is on offer. The demand for inclusion is only a foreshadowing. The demand is for a realignment of that Good, for the purpose of which the political exists in the first instance. This demand is not voicable, I suspect, on Facebook, but it is integral to peer-to-peer networks and to the SLOC (small, local, open, connected) model proposed by Ezio Manzini (2009). Such models, to the extent that they are practiced already, are gateways, not roads; the whole point about the future is that it is unknown. An administered future is no future at all. A political future is not constituted by emerging markets but by the unforeseeable demands of the excluded for a new polity, which must be achieved in the context of struggle with the old that renews, radically, its presuppositions, including its ethical basis. Since we cannot help but think ahead, we plan, but plan for what is genuinely unknown and unforeseeable. So a future that is imaginable but not administered out of existence. Imagine: a world of communication between a polity including the demands of the governed and excluded phyla. . . .

References

Abizadeh, Arash (2008), "Democratic Theory and Border Coercion: No Right to Unilaterally Control Your Own Borders," *Political Theory* 35, no. 1: 37–65.

Adorno, Theodor W. (2000), *Problems of Moral Philosophy,* trans. Edmund Jephcott. Cambridge: Polity Press.

Agamben, Giorgio (1995), *We Refugees,* trans. Michael Rocke, *Symposium* 49, no. 2 (Summer): 114-19, http://www.egs.edu/faculty/agamben/agamben-we-refugees.html.

Arendt, Hannah (1978), *"We Refugees." The Jew as Pariah: Jewish Identity and Politics in the Modern Age,* ed. Ron H. Feldman. New York: Grove Press.

Barclay, Barry (2005), *Mana Tuturu: Maori Treasures and Intellectual Property Rights.* Auckland: Auckland University Press.

Bateson, Gregory (1973), *Steps to an Ecology of Mind: Collected Essays in Anthropology, Psychiatry, Evolution and Epistemology.* London: Paladin.

Bloch, Ernst (1988), *The Utopian Function of Art and Literature: Selected Essays,* trans. Jack Zipes and Frank Mecklenburg. Cambridge, MA: MIT Press.

Boccaletti, Giulio, Markus Löffler, and Jeremy M. Oppenheim (2008), "How IT Can Cut Carbon Emissions," *McKinsey Quarterly,* October, http://www.mckinseyquarterly.com/How_IT_can_cut_carbon_emissions_2221.

Clastres, Pierre (1987), *Society against the State: Essays in Political Anthropology,* trans. Robert Hurley. New York: Zone Books.

Debray, Régis (2004), *God: An Itinerary,* trans. Jeffrey Mehlmann. London: Verso.

de Carolis, Massimo (1996), "Towards a Phenomenology of Opportunism," in Paolo Virno and Michael Hardt, eds., *Radical Thought in Italy: A Potential Politics,* 37–52. Minneapolis: University of Minnesota Press.

Derrida, Jacques (2001), *Negotiations: Interventions and Interviews, 1971–2001,* ed., trans., and with an introduction by Elizabeth G. Rottenberg. Stanford, CA: Stanford University Press.

de Soto, Hernando (2000), *The Mystery of Capital: Why Capitalism Triumphs in the West and Fails Everywhere Else.* New York: Basic Books.

Downey, Anthony (2009), "Zones of Indistinction: Giorgio Agamben's 'Bare Life' and the Politics of Aesthetics," *Third Text* 23, no. 2 (March): 109–25.

Esposito, Roberto (1993), *Nove pensieri sulla politica.* Bologna: Il Mulino.

Flusser, Vilém (2000), *Towards a Philosophy of Photography,* trans. Anthony Matthews, intro Hubertus Von Amelunxen. London: Reaktion Books.

Foucault, Michel (2007), *Security, Population, Territory: Lectures at the Collège de France 1977–1978,* ed. Michel Senellart, trans. Graham Burchell. Basingstoke: Palgrave Macmillan.

Graham, Phil (2006), *Hypercapitalism: Language, New Media, and Social Perceptions of Value.* New York: Peter Lang.

Knorr Cetina, Karin, and Urs Bruegger (2002), "'Traders' Engagement with Markets: A Postsocial Relationship," *Theory Culture and Society* 19, no. 5/6: 161–85.

Laclau, Ernesto (2005), *On Populist Reason.* London: Verso.

Latour, Bruno (2004), *Politics of Nature: How to Bring the Sciences Into Democracy*, trans. Catherine Porter. Cambridge MA: Harvard University Press.

Mackenzie, Adrian (2006), *Cutting Code: Software and Sociality*. New York: Peter Lang.

Manzini, Ezio (2009), "Small, Local, Open and Connected," *Rethink: Contemporary Art and Climate Change*, http://www.rethinkclimate.org/debat/rethink-technology/?show=bvc.

Marx, Karl (1973a), *Grundrisse*, trans. Martin Nicolaus. London: Penguin/New Left Books.

Parikka, Jussi (2007), *Digital Contagions: A Media Archaeology of Computer Viruses*. New York: Peter Lang.

Rancière, Jacques (1999), *Disagreement: Politics and Philosophy*, trans. Julie Rose. Minneapolis: University of Minnesota Press.

Rancière, Jacques (2006), *Hatred of Democracy*, trans. Steve Corcoran. London: Verso.

Sassen, Sakia (2006), *Territory, Authority, Rights: From Medieval to Global Assemblages*. Princeton, NJ: Princeton University Press.

Virno, Paolo (2004), *A Grammar of the Multitude: For an Analysis of Contemporary Forms of Life*, trans. Isabella Bertoletti, James Cascaito, and Andrea Casson. Los Angeles: Semiotext(e).

4

CONSIDERATIONS ON A HACKER MANIFESTO

McKenzie Wark

Here in the overdeveloped world, the bourgeoisie is dead. It neither rules nor governs. Power is in the hands of what I called the vectoralist class. Where the old ruling class controlled the means of production, the new ruling class has limited interest in the material conditions of production, in mines and blast furnaces and assembly lines. Its power rests not on the ownership of such things but in control of the logistics by which they are managed.

Vectoral power has two aspects: intensive and extensive. The intensive vector is the power of calculation. It is the power to model and simulate, but not only that. It is the power to monitor and calculate. And it is also the power to play with information, to turn it into poetry and narrative. The extensive vector is the power to move information from one place to another. It is the power to move and combine anything and everything as a resource. Again, this power has not just a rational meaning but also a poetic one.

Vectoral power can thus dispense with much of the machinery of the old capitalist ruling class. It is a matter of indifference who actually owns a furnace or an assembly line. The vectoral class contracts out such functions. The rise of the manufacturing industry in China and of the service industry in India is not the sign, then, that these underdeveloped states are joining the capitalist developed world. Rather, they now confront an overdeveloped world ruled by vectoral power.

The vectoral class is united only in desiring a world free from the compromises with labor that its capitalist predecessor was obliged to make. For all its tragedies, the twentieth century was the century of socialism—but its victories were mostly confined to the West. In the West, labor fought capital to a draw. Capital was obliged to concede to a substantial socialization of the surplus. We got free education, health care, the vote, and the emancipation of women. The tenets of the *Communist Manifesto* were indeed realized—in the West. This is the compromise that is now unraveling.

The vectoral class has few fixed assets. It tries to avoid actually owning factories. It avoids paying wages directly. It has less and less interest in the viability of national spaces of production and consumption. Fordism is dead.[1] What the vectoral class desires is a relationship with the world in which the world makes its body totally available in exchange for no commitments at all. Which is perhaps why the cultural form that best explains vectoral power is pornography.

And yet the vectoral class is not coherent in its strategies and interests. It has at least two factions. The vectoralist class as a whole we could describe as a military entertainment complex. What distinguishes its two factions is that while one pursues entertainment as a military strategy, the other pursues military strategy as entertainment. Between them is what William Gibson, in his novel *Spook Country,* calls the cold civil war.[2]

What we see playing out on the surface of U.S. politics in the early twenty-first century is the surface effect of this cold civil war. One faction is interested only in the strategics of resources. It thinks it acquired in Iraq the last untapped source of oil and natural gas and tried to build the logistical infrastructure to secure it. Far from being a failure, its Iraq adventure has proven a complete success. It never had any interest in Iraq as a democracy. In many ways, the more unstable it is, the better. The bases being built are to secure the oil, not the people.

The other faction within the vectoralist class is increasingly worried about the costs of this strategy, however. Its interest is not in the strategics of nature but in the logistics of second nature. Its business is the business of coordinating all aspects of life under the power of the brand, the patent, and the copyright. If capitalist power reduced being to having, then vectoralist power reduces having to appearing.[3] The actual qualities of things become secondary to the logistics and poetics that decorate the commodity.

This faction of the vectoralist class confronts quite different issues. The dematerialization of the commodity threatens to undermine the very principle of the scarcity of value. As soon as digital technology perfected the separation of information as content from material form, the way was open for a massive socialization of cultural material. To some extent, this took the vectoral class by surprise. It did not quite occur to them that private property is not the natural form of culture.

We are witnessing a massive, nameless, faceless social movement, which takes the raw material of commodified culture and turns it back into common property. And the good news is that this movement has essentially won. After centuries of privatization, culture is ours again. This victory is partial and limited, of course, just as the victor of socialism in the West was limited. It only applies to culture and not to many of the other aspects of vectoral power. But, still, it is worth celebrating.

Politics now for the vectoralist class is the politics of attempting to recommodify some aspect of the value of culture, to make it scarce and rare again. Consider the politics of Apple's iPod, which attempted to make a fetish object of the device.

Or Facebook, where the proposition is that we should all entertain each other and put up with advertising merely for this privilege. Far from being a step forward, such media are a decadent form of the "society of the spectacle." Not only are we to passively consume these images, we have to make them ourselves.

The model here is to reduce the paid labor force in the production of images as close as possible to zero and pay them only in the currency of recognition. We have to pay for the privilege of producing our own spectacle. The power of the vectoral class retreats from the direct ownership of the cultural product but consolidates around the control of the vector. We get all the culture; they get all the revenue.

Parts of the vectoral class are heading in quite the opposite direction—to completely closed, proprietary worlds. Online gaming is usually like this. In a game like the popular World of Warcraft, you pay for the privilege of laboring to acquire objects and status that are only artificially scarce.[4] And you never get to own them. They remain private property. You rent back the product of your own labor. World of Warcraft is the nullity of the commodity economy perfected. World of Warcraft is the fantasy version of the power of the vectoral class perfected. You pay to rent everything, and they can deport you at any time.

Caught between the social movement that tries to liberate information and that faction of the vectoral class that seeks to control it is the hacker class. Anyone who labors for someone else producing so-called intellectual property is a hacker. It's an ambivalent class. On the one hand, we depend on the vectoral class, who own the means of realizing the value of what we produce. On the other hand, we hardly profit from private property in information. If anything, it is a fetter on our own productivity.

I first proposed the idea of the hacker class in 2000, and in the intervening years have repeatedly been told that even if it exists, it can never become conscious of itself as a class. But frankly, I think the recent politics of information bears out the thesis. The hacker class does not march down the boulevard behind red banners on May Day. But it is fully capable of organizing around net neutrality, creative commons, open publishing in science, challenging stupid and harmful patents, and so on. The contemporary equivalent of the trade union consciousness of the old labor movement has well and truly arrived. It even has its vanguard, although an anonymous one.

Andrew Ross dismisses the projects of the hacker class as those of a "thwarted technocratic elite whose libertarian worldview butts up against the established proprietary interests."[5] There is some truth to that. However, if one were to look with too cold an eye at the practices of organized labor in the United States, one might come up with an equally cynical take. There's always a gap between what a class is in practice and what it could make of itself.

It's a question of pushing the often local or issue-based approach to hacker class consciousness into an entire worldview, or rather, worldviews. The challenge is to think the whole social totality from our point of view—to imagine worlds in which our own interests and the interests of the people are aligned. The way to do this, I think, is to push beyond the compromise formations of things like creative commons. What would it mean not to liberalize intellectual property but to conceive of the world without it altogether? What would it mean to really think and practice the politics of information as something that is not scarce and has no owners?

It's important, I think, to cultivate a studied indifference to the cooption of our movement by compromise formations, which offer limited liberties but leave the ownership and control of the vector in the hands of the vectoralist class. No good tactic goes unrecouperated, not least those of the most extreme of avant-gardes, the situationists. According to Christine Harold, "Perhaps this is because, like all good brands, situationism is easily appropriated towards new ends." Yet sometimes what looks like bankrupt tactics prove themselves again later, and what look like serious, professional, and mature developments of a movement can end up collapsing under their own weight. There is still a role for an avant-garde that has left the stale forms of art and politics behind and that confronts the emerging forms of power of our time with the possibility that they, too, will pass.

It was a sign of the times, of the strength of the free culture movement, that when the musicians Radiohead were released from their contract with EMI in 2007 they offered their new album *In Rainbows* via the Internet for fans to purchase at the price of their own choosing. You could even choose to pay zero pounds and zero pence, and still have it. There's a certain understanding of the gift implied in this. The gift always creates obligations in the receiver. If I sell you something, I am obliged to you. I must provide the goods and services to which we agreed. If I give you something, you are obliged to me—or at least are under a weak and very general obligation to return the gift, somewhere, to someone. Radiohead understood this. The gift of the new album created publicity, goodwill, future concert ticket sales, and even the gift of money. Many fans really want to pay for their music, but to pay as a gift because they want to honor an obligation, not because they are being forced to pay or risk legal sanctions for alleged theft or piracy.

But the limit to making a gift of culture to everyone is that doing so adds value to the vector through which it is distributed, and that is not free. The more forward-thinking strategy of the vectoral class is to retreat to this stronghold but to insist on it. This is why I suggest that free culture be considered a tactic rather than an end in itself. I think the hacker practice is to keep asking questions about property rather than just settle on one model.

An example might be what I call copygift.[6] Besides copyright there is copyleft, but both copyright and copyleft take the property form for granted. Copyleft is the dialectical negation of intellectual property. It turns it against itself. But perhaps there are other, nondialectical strategies, not for opposing intellectual property but for escaping it. What if, rather than giving one's culture to everyone in the abstract but no one in particular, one made it always a particular gift to particular people?

This would be more like the model of a chain letter, for example. Long before the Occupy Wall Street movement, occupation literature circulated, and in the curious form of PDF files. They were designed to be transmitted, if not hand to hand, then e-mail to e-mail, to not be too readily searchable and retrievable by just anybody.

Of course, vectoral power is already here. It is called viral marketing. The game is to imagine other uses to which such a strategy can be put—and to go beyond, to invent new kinds of relations. Who knows what a relation can be? We haven't seen anything yet.

Lastly, I want to caution against three of the common modes of self-understanding that we have accepted a little too willingly without thinking it through. The first is the romance of the pirate.[7] We are not pirates; we are hackers. And the distinction is this: The pirate is someone who takes another's property. Pirates take what does not belong to them. There is a romantic side to the pirate, but it is the romance of transgression. A transgression that, of course, mostly confirms the very notion of property in the act of coveting the property that belongs to another.

Call it what you like. If not hacking, then something else. But not piracy. The pirate takes another's property. The hacker makes something new out of property that belongs to everyone in the first place. Information wants to be free but is everywhere in chains. The figure of the pirate draws attention to the chains. The figure of the hacker insists that information is in its very being something that is free, that always escapes the property form. It is where we are and remain social beings. It is where, far from being on the run or in retreat, the game is only just begun.

Not that the persona of the pirate is without its uses. In 2011, the Pirate Party won seats in Berlin's municipal elections on a platform that combined support for a guaranteed minimum income with the legalization of drug use and sophisticated positions on information rights.[8] However, the future of progressive politics in the overdeveloped world may lie in a range of experiments in combining the interests of labor and the interests of the hacker class broadly defined—that is, if politics can be said to exist outside of the use of the vector for marketing purposes.

Second, I want to caution against the rhetoric of gamification. This could most broadly be conceived of as getting people to do things without paying them by offering them symbolic rewards in exchange. These rewards appeal by being rare and by being stratified. You can distinguish yourself by winning this symbolic token, which is ranked in relation to a whole hierarchy of such tokens.

Superficially, this seems like the logic of the gift economy. You do something for nothing because you want to do it, not as labor grudgingly offered in exchange for wages or other incentives but for fun, as "playbor." The difference is that the gift is not to another, and not via another to the commons in general, and the reward is not recognition by others making the same gifts. Rather, what is offered is a bit of cognitive energy that performs a task some vectoral business requires, and the reward is only a formal and abstract kind of token and ranking. It is not the gift economy; it is a simulation of it. It isn't play that creates its own games; it is a game that extracts labor in the form of play.

Gamification broadly conceived is the strategy of the vectoral class at its most sophisticated. It no longer cares all that much about mere images or stories or tunes as intellectual property. But that does not mean it has given up on property! Its interest, rather, is in two things. First, in its proprietary algorithms for managing networks. Second, in the data that can be extracted from those networks and that remains resolutely proprietary. In short, the vectoral class has brought the fabled general intellect into material existence and is doing its best to make it private property. The struggle moves onto a whole new terrain.

Finally, the concept of the social factory. This has always seemed to me to relate to the special case quality of Italy in the seventies. Italy was the last major European country to shift its economy away from industrial labor processes. The struggles of that time were less a foretaste of what was to come for the rest of the overdeveloped world as a throwback to what had already passed.

Indeed, it can be hard to find people in the overdeveloped world who have any idea of what factory labor was like. In these parts of the world, the factory is no longer the dominant form of the experience of labor, and hasn't been for a while. Rather than social factory, it might make sense to talk of the monetized boudoir. What were formerly qualities of private, affective, and intimate life are now the kinds of labor that can be commodified. One needs to present well, even to make coffee or sell shoes, not to mention negotiate the social maze of the office or take meetings that will result in temp contracts.

But one thing the Italian experience really did identify that permeates the overdeveloped world, particularly for young people, is precarity. Working conditions become temporary, with few or no benefits. Only a tiny handful of employees are to be considered permanent. Everyone else is just hired hands, or rather hands, eyes, brains, and so on.

In such conditions, the question arises as to whether making labor more secure and rewarded or extending the social compact is the better strategy. It's a question with two dimensions. Which is more tactically feasible, but also which is more desirable in the first place? Do we want to focus on labor, and securing life through labor? Or do we want to secure the conditions of life itself?

It is hard not to be pessimistic about both options. And it is also hard to argue against any and every opportunity that people might find to secure life against commodification wherever they can find it. But taking a step back, perhaps there's something to be said for the struggle to secure the conditions of life directly.

It is still something of a wake-up call for educated people in the overdeveloped world: what we do has finally been proletarianized. Logics of what Stiegler calls grammatization, or what I call abstraction, extend now to formerly white-collar and professional tasks. Meanwhile, information has escaped its embeddedness in any given materiality and can now be easily transferred from one material expression to another. The whole basis of an economy that sold information strapped to particular things has simply vanished, despite the efforts of the old culture industry to artificially restore it.

Given those two conditions, restoring the prestige of intellectual endeavor seems as vain a project as restoring the privileges of the old craft guilds. All that is solid melts into air. After the era of cheap things comes the era of cheap information.

That seems to me to shift attention to securing the conditions of life directly rather than indirectly as a reward for labor. Any particular labor for any particular firm or industry is always vulnerable, not least to competition now from the developing world. So why not struggle instead for securing life? We will consent to labor if we have to, or if we feel like it, but demand the right to live, to love, to create, to play, to struggle—to make the best of everyday life. We demand a living wage for all. We demand free education for all. We demand free heath care for all. We demand universal access to the infrastructure of life in all its forms. The rest we will make for ourselves.

Notes

1 See the classic presentation by Michel Aglietta, *A Theory of Capitalist Regulation* (London: Verso, 2001).

2 William Gibson, *Spook Country* (New York: Putnam, 2007).

3 To paraphrase Guy Debord, *Society of the Spectacle* (New York: Zone Books, 1994), p. 17.

4 Julian Dibbell, *Play Money* (New York: Basic Books, 2006).

5 Andrew Ross, *Nice Work If You Can Get It* (New York: New York University Press, 2010), 175.

6 See McKenzie Wark, "Copyright, Copyleft, Copygift," *Open* no. 12 (2007), skor.nl. Also available at http://meanland.com.au/articles/post/copyright-copyleft-copygift.

7 Peter Linebaugh and Marcus Rediker, *The Many Headed Hydra* (Boston: Beacon Press, 2001).

8 "The New Rebels," *Spiegel Online International,* September 19, 2011, http://www.spiegel.de/international/germany/the-new-rebels-germany-s-pirate-party-celebrates-historic-victory-a-787044.html.

PART II

Interrogating Modes of Digital Labor

5

RETURN OF THE CROWDS

Mechanical Turk and Neoliberal States of Exception

Ayhan Aytes

One of the most ubiquitous examples of crowdsourcing application is a human authentication tool called *captcha* (von Ahn et al. 2003; see Figure 5.1). It could be described as a reverse Turing test, in that humans convince the machine that they are indeed humans and not a software robot crawling the web and filling out random forms for spam dissemination.

Most of the time, the task required for a captcha authentication consists of reading a garbled text that is provided as an image file and then typing it into a text box. Re-captcha, a particular type of captcha, uses two sets of texts—one for the assessment purpose and the other for transcribing difficult-to-read words that were captured during optical character recognition scans. As a result, re-captcha functions not only as a human authentication tool but also as a cognitive labor platform.[1] The crucial aspect of this process is that no single individual who completes a captcha will ever be able to know the overall meaning of the text that was transcribed because of its fragmentation into single words. In most crowdsourcing platforms, fragmentation of tasks disenfranchises cognitive workers by disconnecting them from the final intellectual work. In addition, most crowdsourcing systems maintain a transient, task-based, and limited-time relationship between the worker and the requester and do not support a direct communication between the parties, further erasing the connection between the cognitive labor and the resultant work. A similar type of disconnect characterizes Amazon.com's digital labor market, Mechanical Turk.

Amazon Web Services established in November 2005 its digital labor market where workers from across the world and around the clock browse, choose, and complete human intelligence tasks (HITs) that are designed by corporate or individual contractors. The kind of labor required for each HIT varies: finding information and images about products and services, translating text from or to English,

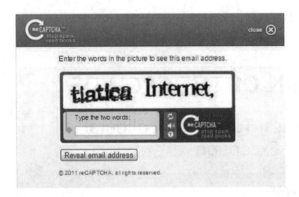

FIGURE 5.1 A typical re-captcha task.

transcribing audio, tagging images with descriptive text, or answering surveys on various topics. The products of this labor might serve many purposes ranging from spam generation to training machine learning algorithms that would eventually assume some of these human roles in the future. The payment amount per HIT ranges from one cent to several U.S. dollars, depending on the required time or difficulty of the task.

Amazon.com's initial motivation to build Amazon Mechanical Turk (AMT) emerged after the failure of its artificial intelligence programs in the task of finding duplicate product pages on its retail website (Pontin 2007). After a series of futile and expensive attempts, the project engineers turned to humans to work behind computers within a streamlined web-based system. Later, AMT made this cognitive labor platform available to private contractors in return for a commission for each completed HIT. AMT's digital workshop emulates artificial intelligence systems by replacing computing with human brainpower. Driven by what AMT calls "artificial artificial intelligence," this sociotechnical system represents a crucial formation on a global scale as it facilitates the supply of cognitive labor needs of mainly Western information and communication technologies industries from a global workforce.[2] AMT explains the value of its labor market for the software industry as follows:

> With Amazon Mechanical Turk, it may seem to your customers that your application is somehow using advanced artificial intelligence to accomplish tasks, but in reality it is the "Artificial Artificial Intelligence" of the Mechanical Turk workforce that is helping you effectively achieve your business objectives.[3]

According to Panos Iperiotis, approximately half of the AMT workers—or Turkers, as some of them prefer to call themselves—are from the United States, and the other half are from 66 different countries. Most of the non-U.S. Turkers are from India, representing 33% of the AMT workforce (Iperiotis, 2010). Ross et al. have demonstrated that the demographics of AMT are becoming increasingly international, highlighted by an expanding group of young, male, Indian workers who make less than US$10,000 per year. About a third of Indian workers reported that they partly rely on AMT "to make basic ends meet" (Ross et al., 2010).

Amazon.com branded its micropayment-based crowdsourcing platform as the Mechanical Turk, borrowing one of the names of the 18th-century Automaton Chess Player as shorthand for the relationship that the system establishes between the cognitive labor force and the seemingly automated complex tasks. In both cases, the performance of the workers who animate the artifice is obscured by the spectacle of the machine.

The idea of the chess-playing machine, which was realized by IBM's Deep Blue computer in 1997 has been a key conceptual apparatus for imagining the automatization of the operations of the human mind since the Enlightenment era. This metaphor was also central for the idealization of cybernetic discourse as a universal system during the first half of the 20th century, embodied by the postwar symbol processors, which later became the architectural basis of the contemporary computer (Bowker 1993; Shannon 1950). In this chapter, I will study a neoliberal reincarnation of the chess-playing automaton, Amazon's Mechanical Turk, in the light of its early-modern legacy of configuring the relationship between the division of cognitive labor and the automatic systems of computing and control. Particularly, in both cases, in varying degrees and methods, the labor performance of intellectual workers is an integral element of the disciplinary structure of the corresponding socioeconomic apparatus.

In the current configuration, this cognitive labor apparatus is situated within the neoliberal system of exception facilitated by the digital networks, taking advantage of legislative gray zones in the international labor regulations in order to maximize profits for multinational corporations (Ong 2006). Crowd-sourcing is one of the most significant elements of this configuration that expands the reach of the neoliberal economy through cognitive capitalism,[4] in which immaterial labor plays a key, structural role.[5] Not surprisingly, this configuration also embodies some of the conflicts whose seeds are placed during the early modern conceptualizations of the mechanization of industrial labor through division of cognitive labor. One of the most significant examples of this conceptualization was the chess-playing automaton that performed the insurmountable conflicts of the disciplining of the human mind for industrial production.

Docile Automata

Wolfgang von Kempelen's Chess Player Automaton was constructed and presented in 1770 at the court of the Empress Maria Theresa of Austria and gave the

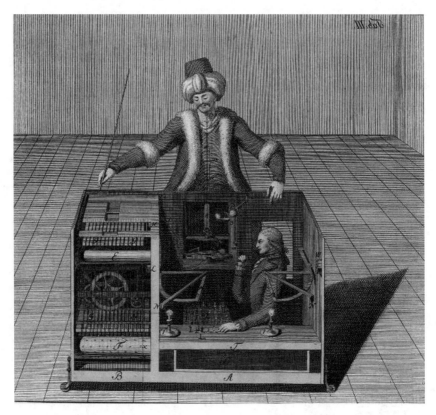

FIGURE 5.2 Engraving of *The Turk* from Joseph Friedrich Freiherr von Racknitz's 1789 pamphlet *Über den Schachspieler des Herrn von Kempelen und dessen Nachbildung.*

impression that the pipe-smoking Turk mannequin, controlled by a sophisticated mechanism under the cabinet, could play serious chess against human opponents (see Figure 5.2). However, the seemingly mechanical mind of the Turk was actually manipulated by Kempelen's chess master assistant, who was hidden beneath the pseudo-mechanism. The Automaton Chess Player was exhibited for 84 years in Europe and the Americas and attracted many notable challengers and spectators, such as Napoleon Bonaparte, Charles Babbage, and Benjamin Franklin (Carroll 1975; Windisch 1784).

In his book, *Discipline and Punish,* Michel Foucault considers the 18th-century automata as models for human body and social order (Foucault 1977). Consequently, the mechanistic conception of human body needs to be read in two registers: the *anatomico-metaphysical* register as constituted mainly through Cartesian mind/body duality, and the *technico-political* register that was constituted by empirical methods of the state for disciplining the operations of the body through the army, the school, and the hospital. In the context of these two registers, the

18th-century humanoid automata functions as a model, on the one hand, for submission and use and, on the other, for empirical analysis.

Foucault has often been criticized for ignoring the racial others in his historiography.[6] Notably, his concept of docility displaces Orientalist traces by solely focusing on the European subject in a selective genealogy. This absence becomes more critical in the analysis of an automaton that carries significations of Oriental "other," such as Kempelen's chess-playing automaton. However, I believe that the trick of the chess-playing automaton involves more than just exchanging the enacted body of the European chess player with the represented body of the Turk, animated through its mechanical artifice. It also includes initial assumptions that were set up in the audience by the automaton's chess performance that were crucial in influencing the public debates on the mechanized reason that provided the larger context for these performances. These initial assumptions are closely tied to Orientalist undercurrents that were exploited by Enlightenment discourse in order to configure the docile subject on the image of the Turk.[7]

The Orientalist assumptions that were active in Enlightenment automata were also effective in the cultural performance of Kempelen's automaton. I will focus on the two main aspects of the affordance of the image of the Turk as a significant part of the main interface of the chess-playing automaton.[8] The first critical aspect of the Turk's performance is its liminal quality. This liminality created a buffer zone against the risk associated with the idea of the man-machine that most Enlightenment humanoid automata performed. That potential risk was often associated with instigations of libertinism, atheism, and insurrection in public due to the heretical understanding of a body without a soul (Vartanian 1960). Relegating this precarious role to an Oriental figure had, in fact, a long tradition with origins in medieval romance literature (Truitt 2004). The Oriental automata, through its association with liminal spaces and experiences in these literary accounts, conveyed surveillance, discipline, and enforcement of limits of morality.

The second aspect of the Turk's performance is a particular form of docility that conveys the idea of the disciplined productive body, which played a salient role in the formation of the enlightened culture (Schaffer 1999). The association of the Oriental with docility has its roots in medieval theology, where the Muslim subjects were considered as strict followers of religious code. Linking this association with the discourse of Oriental automata, Christian theology configured a particular discourse of Muslim as automaton (Biddick 2011). Furthermore, docility prefigures the hidden chess player's performance of the intellectual labor on behalf of the Oriental automaton. This dual performance of docility highlights the question of the intellectual labor in the context of the epistemic renovation in 18th-century Europe (Foucault 1977). These two aspects of the Turk's performance—docility and liminality—are crucial for grasping its function as a model of power for the idealization of a social order in the context of the large-scale processes of mechanization of labor in Europe in the 18th century.

The chess-playing automaton performed its role as a model of power in multiple layers, the first of which was the demonstration of knowledge as a tool of power. The hidden chess player was the open secret of Kempelen's (and later Maelzel's) shows (Carroll 1975). Kempelen admitted that his automaton was just a "happy deception" (Cook 1995). As Schaffer notes, one of the roles of the Enlightenment automata was "to allow the selective entry by th[e] power to the inner workings of art and nature" (Schaffer 1999: 135). In other words, this open secret was also a conceited wink of the guardians of knowledge and power, reminding the general public about their privilege and status.

The element of mystery in Kempelen's performance can be considered within the system of representation of the natural philosophy, which perceived the whole of nature as a divine theater. The effects of this system of representation could be exploited to create a particular moral impression on its audience (Schaffer 1983). Scottish philosopher Thomas Reid expounds this moral effect as follows: "Upon the theatre of nature we see innumerable effects, which requires an agent endowed with active power; but the agent is behind the scene."[9] Kempelen's automaton benefited from the assumptions within this theater as a significant representation of the technomythical idea of the mechanized mind, and was not just a machine but also provided the language that made it possible to explicate that myth (Beaune 1989). As in every technical medium, it carried the inscriptions of discursive traditions and formulations that defined its cultural system of significations. The Automaton Chess Player performed these inscribed notions that were formulated as technical puzzles, which have remained relevant throughout the history of the mechanization of the mind. The puzzle of the mechanical chess player, or the mechanized symbol processing, has been tackled by many notable scholars and practitioners, including Gottfried Leibniz, Edgar Allan Poe, Charles Babbage, Norbert Wiener, and Alan Turing.

In Europe in the second half of the 18th century, automata performed as a secure experimental apparatus for exploring impenetrable ontological liminalities in a more systemic way and most of the time simulated life in order to redefine it (Riskin 2003). Fueled by the mechanistic philosophy, humanoid automata transformed not only the cultural attitude toward living creatures but also machines, as they performed the idea that mechanisms were also living beings. The mutual relationship between the animation of machinery and the mechanization of life was explored through the experimental apparatus of humanoid and animal automata and was popularized through the debates instigated by their public exhibition in Europe.

Wolfgang von Kempelen's Chess Player Automaton formulated the question of the mechanized life with a unique emphasis: Can the mind exist without the body? To this question, it gave two answers simultaneously: yes and not yet. The actual answer was not yet, as the automaton was indeed controlled by a human operator. However, the deceptive yes response was still valuable as a philosophical game[10] for grappling with the ideas that were later made technically possible and implemented systematically, such as self-regulating mechanisms.

In contrast to other automata of the 18th century, the Turk's apparatus did not act as mere clockwork; instead, it gave the impression of a self-regulating system that could counter external actions within the symbolic logic of chess.[11] As historian of technology Otto Mayr (1970) suggests, in contrast to the idea of clockwork universe, which was the political universe of autocratic feudalism, the mechanical, political, and economic ideas of self-regulating systems influenced the Enlightenment ideas of liberal subjects and democracy. This association is partly constructed as a result of the rationalization of the socioeconomic life through industrialization, where subjects self-regulate according to their rational economic interests. Philosophical arguments for such conflict-free social systems had already been provided by various scholars, the most famous of whom was Gottfried Leibniz.

The preceding century had seen Leibniz's proposal of a universal symbolic language or algebra of thought. Since the expansion of the commerce in Leibniz's time, there had been a search for a universal language that would allow European traders to establish a sustainable communication with the people in the new colonies. Leibniz's universal language could be manipulated by a logical calculation framework, *calculus ratiocinator* (ca. 1680), which was a precursor model of modern computing (Wiener 1948). Leibniz suggested that the mind is a spiritual automaton that operates involuntarily based on a predetermined set of laws. "The operation of spiritual automata, that is of souls, is not mechanical, but it contains in the highest degree all that is beautiful in mechanism" (Leibniz 2005: 365). However, the automaton/self-moving soul does not eliminate agency for Leibniz, because symbols and the symbolic systems of language play a constitutive role for reasoning. Based on this principle, Leibniz proposed calculus ratiocinator as an ultimate solution for all conflicts between the people of the world. This perspective finds its expression in Leibniz's Machiavellian motto *calculemus* (let us calculate!): "if controversies were to arise there would be no more need of disputation between two philosophers than between two accountants. For it would suffice to take their pencils in their hands, and say to each other: *Calculemus.*"[12]

Chess is a perfect example for computable symbolic systems; consequently, when the Turk spoke the language of the symbolic via chess, it entered "the world of the machine" (Lacan 1991: 47). But that machine denoted a particular type of subjectivity because of the nature of the actors and their limited set of behaviors that are strictly defined within a set of rules in the game of chess. As Deleuze and Guattari state:

> Chess is a game of State, or of the court: the emperor of China played it. Chess pieces are coded; they have an internal nature and intrinsic properties from which their movements, situations, and confrontations derive. They have qualities; a knight remains a knight, a pawn a pawn, a bishop a bishop.

> Each is like a subject of the statement endowed with a relative power, and these relative powers combine in a subject of enunciation, that is, the chess player or the game's form of interiority.... Within their milieu of interiority, chess pieces entertain biunivocal relations with one another, and with the adversary's pieces: their functioning is structural.... Chess is indeed a war, but an institutionalized, regulated, coded war. (Deleuze and Guattari 2004: 352)

Consequently, an automatized chessboard represents the ideal Enlightenment universe, where the subjects and their possible actions are coded according to the regulations informed by the power structure of the society. Each subject is endowed with a relative power, and they cannot go beyond the roles for which they qualify. Particularly, when these intrinsic properties are abstracted into geometric functions and when combined with the functions of other subjects, they have the potential to exhibit numerous but finite possibilities for a final outcome. This is another reason for mechanized chess being a model for imagining a society whose coded subjects articulate a plurality of results. Thus, the chess-playing Turk embodied an integration of the self-regulating liberal subject with the mechanical docility of the Oriental, performed within the coded socioeconomic universe of the game of chess.

In the mid-19th century, during the Turk's tour in the Americas, Edgar Alan Poe took this seemingly conflicting performance for his argument of why an automaton chess player would be impossible. In an editorial published in the Richmond-based *Southern Literary Messenger*, he surmised that "[n]o one move in chess necessarily follows upon any one other. From no particular disposition of the men at one period of a game can we predicate their disposition at a different period" (Poe 2009: 1). This perceived paradox was mainly due to the assumption Poe had for the possible operational principle of the automaton, which was mainly based on the linear mechanism paradigm, where the interaction between the mechanism and the environment is not a relevant factor during its operation. Poe explicitly based his argument on a comparison of the performance of the chess-playing automaton with Charles Babbage's calculating machine and concluded that:

> There is then no analogy whatever between the operations of the Chess-Player, and those of the calculating machine of Mr. Babbage, and if we choose to call the former a *pure machine* we must be prepared to admit that it is, beyond all comparison, the most wonderful of the inventions of mankind. (Poe, 1910: 84)

Poe's resistance to the idea of mechanized thinking may also be related to a particular kind of predicament that concerned his intellectual labor. The very possibility of chess automaton as a "pure machine" must have posed an uncanny prospect for Poe as an intellectual worker. The designer of the actual calculating machine, Babbage, had already implicated the particular kind of skill and labor that Poe uses for his intellectual work as part of the mechanization and division of the cognitive labor system. Charles Babbage specifically used newspapers as an example

> of a manufactory in which the division of labor, both mentally and bodily, is admirably illustrated, and in which also the effect of the domestic economy is well exemplified. It is scarcely imagined, by the thousands who read that paper in various quarters of the globe, what a scene of organized activity the factory presents during the whole night, or what a quantity of talent and mechanical skill put in action for their amusement and information (Babbage 1963: 216).

Following Adam Smith's analysis in *The Wealth of Nations*, Babbage thought that the process of division of mental labor would serve for the eventual goal of transferring the functions of the human cognitive labor to the operations of a machine. Thus, for Poe, chess-playing automaton, with its allusions to such a "manufactory of information" processing, must have posed an uncanny puzzle also for its implications about the exchange value of his previously irreplaceable intellectual labor. In one of his later speculative narratives, Poe depicted von Kempelen as an alchemist who transforms lead into gold, which results in an enormous reduction of the value of gold and an inflation in the price of lead in international markets.[13] This narrative could be read as an allusion to the expected decline in the exchange value of the intellectual labor as an unavoidable outcome of the mechanization of reason through a division of cognitive labor.

The imminent threat for the privileged labor position of the enlightened subject as a result of the division of cognitive labor was already under way in the 19th century. Industrial capitalism's premise was that any of the roles in the socioeconomic chessboard could be played by anyone when these functions are regulated into smaller units through industrial organization.

This social program as an instance of the expansion of the Cartesian mechanistic universe is mainly guided by the flow of human thinking into computational organizations and apparatuses, including the state. In this volume, Jonathan Beller's essay emphasizes this point through a close reading of Villem Flusser's works. Particularly, the scientific discourse of the Enlightenment led the trend toward the encoding of human thought into numerical representations. My historical analysis considers the Chess Playing Automaton as one of the behavioral prototypes of this trend inhabiting the associated tensions of the emergent apparatuses that later realize these initially imaginary encodings into commodified social and cultural programs such as cameras or computers. In fact, Flusser finds similarities between photographers' attempts to find possibilities within the program of the camera and the chess players' pursuit of finding new possibilities in the program of chess (Flusser 2000: 27–30). In both instances, humans and apparatuses merge into a unity, which explains how human functionaries of apparatuses both control them and are controlled by them. These apparatuses, as a codified set of social relations, are integrated into other socioeconomic apparatuses ranging from industrial production regimes to disciplinary apparatuses of the state. By emphasizing this particular definition of apparatus, Jonathan Beller guides us through a potential and common risk of ignoring the socioeconomic ground of their emergence.

There is an immense similarity between Flusser's use of apparatus and that of Michel Foucault's, which denotes strategic constellations of tangible and intangible tools, institutions, and discourses that are inscribed into politics of knowledge and power. *Apparatus/Dispositif*, according to Foucault, is "a set of strategies of the relations of supporting, and supported by certain types of knowledge."[14] Foucault uses the term *apparatus* in order to move beyond discourses to include material, behavioral, and institutional elements for describing formations of structures of knowledge. The term frequently appears in relation to his studies on governmentality from the mid-1970s.

Foucault uses the prison as an example of an apparatus by emphasizing its optic attributes that are configured based on Bentham's Panopticon architecture. The prison in this view is simultaneously a technical medium designed for seeing without being seen and consequently a tool for subjectification by internalization of surveillance. As Agamben succinctly describes, the apparatus "is first of all a machine that produces subjectifications, and only as such it is also a machine of governance" (Agamben 2009: 20). As a result, the term *apparatus* provides a very useful vantage point for studying mechanization of mind with an integrated focus on its technical, industrial mediations such as the division of cognitive labor as a disciplinary formation and its constitutive socioeconomic conditions.

Consequently, the analysis of the evolution of the industrial cognitive labor apparatus from its imaginary Enlightenment conceptual prototype to large-scale computable social systems in postindustrial capitalism needs to take into account the neoliberal grounds of its emergence.

The transfer of the functionary role of the cognitive labor apparatus from the privileged labor of the Enlightened subject to unqualified crowds of the neoliberal cognitive capitalism is primarily enabled by the digital networks of the 21st century. This transfer further extends the effect of the foreclosure of the semiosis for the cognitive worker by microdivision of cognitive tasks and its distribution across cultural, temporal, and geographical zones.

Return of the Crowds

Crowdsourcing is a hybrid concept that merges the neoliberal outsourcing paradigm with the crowds on the digital networks. In the June 2006 issue of *Wired* magazine, Jeff Howe evangelized the concept to its technologically savvy neoliberal audience as follows:

Technological advances in everything from product design software to digital video cameras are breaking down the cost barriers that once separated amateurs from professionals. Hobbyists, part-timers, and dabblers suddenly have a market for their efforts, as smart companies in industries as disparate as pharmaceuticals and television discover ways to tap the latent talent of the crowd. The labor isn't always free, but it costs a lot less than paying traditional employees. It's not outsourcing; it's crowdsourcing. (Howe 2006:1)

Crowdsourcing as an alternative to traditional employment methods also signifies an unexpected return of the concept of the crowds to the agenda of the global North. But at this time, its discursive signification is limited within the communities of the global South. As William Mazzarella expounds:

Crowds, supposedly, belong to the past of the neoliberal democracies of the global North. By the same token, they also mark the present of non- or insufficiently liberal polities in the global South... crowds are the dark matter that pull the liberal subject from its past, whereas multitudes occupy the emergent horizon of a postliberal politics. (Mazzarella 2010: 697)

Mazzarella finds the distinction between crowds and multitudes as parallel to the distinction between Foucault's "society of discipline" and Gilles Deleuze's postindustrial "control society." While crowds correspond to industrial discipline, multitudes can only be considered in the context of the postindustrial control society, where command by control is "fractal and aims to integrate conflicts not by imposing a coherent social apparatus but by controlling differences" (Mazzarella 2010: 700). Command by control also characterizes the mode of production in the postindustrial service economy with full integration of computers and digital networks.

At this point, it is useful to look at the concept of immaterial labor and some of the assumptions it conveys, because it is the most prominent activity that gives its characteristics to the multitude. Because of its reliance on the commodification of communication, which inherently forms social relationships, immaterial labor denotes the process through which "social" becomes "economic." According to Maurizio Lazzarato, as an extension of the commodification of social relationships, the subjectivity becomes the "raw material" of immaterial labor (Lazzarato 1996). This is partly because the "production today is directly the production of a social relation" (Mazzarella 2010: 700). Here, the key assumption that needs to be challenged is that the economic expression of the social relationships happens in the same sociocultural environment. However, crowdsourcing unsettles this relationship because of its effect of deterritorialization.

Consequently, we need to consider the production of subjectivity in the context of the global system of cognitive labor practices. Despite its similarity to the industrial commodity consumption/production cycles, the information production cycles are different in terms of their effects on subjectivity, since their immediate domain of effect is in the information and communication industry that forms the cultural fabric of the society by simultaneously constructing active consumer/communicator subjects. As a result, "[t]he production of subjectivity ceases to be only an instrument of social control (for the reproduction of mercantile relationships) and becomes directly productive" (Lazzarato 1996: 1). But how would this process still be valid when the communicator is no longer a consumer as a result of both the fragmentation of intellectual work and the global income gaps between the producers and the consumers of information commodities, or between the multitude and the crowd?

A similar set of assumptions characterizes Hardt and Negri's concept of multitude. They expand the characteristics of postindustrial production onto the multitude and claim that "[w]hat the multitude produces is not just goods or services; the multitude also and most importantly produces cooperation, communication, forms of life, and social relationships" (Hardt and Negri 2005: 339). Further, Hardt and Negri ascribe an autonomous character to the subjectivities that are produced through cognitive labor mainly due to its assumed collective nature. "Such new forms of labor... present new possibilities for economic self-management, since the mechanisms of cooperation necessary for production are contained in the labor itself" (Hardt and Negri 2004: 336). This characteristic of the immaterial labor is presented in distinct contrast to the industrial notion of the labor power, which is considered "variable capital" in Marxist terms of political economy, since it can be activated and formed as a productive force only by capital.

However, I believe the crowdsourcing apparatus, with its unique configuration, challenges all of these assumptions and essentially negates the essentialist distinction between the industrial and postindustrial configuration of labor. In digital labor markets maintained by crowdsourcing protocols, crowds are subjected to a form of division of labor that is reminiscent of industrial production. But this division of labor differs from the industrial division of labor in terms of its effects in its relation to the global neoliberal socioeconomic formations that constitute a distinct condition for the workers of the global South. These conditions could be described as the gray zones of international laws that are designed by neoliberal policies to take advantage of stark regional differences in labor costs, which Aihwa Ong conceptualizes as "system of exception."

Crowdsourcing as a Neoliberal Exception Apparatus

Aihwa Ong describes neoliberalism as a global system of exception, borrowing a term from German political theorist Carl Schmitt. The state of exception, in the Schmittian sense, defines a political liminality that is established outside of the juridical order, created by the sovereign rule. Ong, similar to Schmitt's description, emphasizes inclusive as well as exclusive aspects of neoliberal political formations, because these exceptions primarily work for making decisions outside of a consistent legislative framework. She formulates the neoliberal exception in relation to "the interplay among technologies of governing and of disciplining, of inclusion and exclusion, of giving value or denying value to human conduct" (Ong 2006: 5). A significant example of these technologies of exclusion is *labor arbitrage*.

According to Ong, labor arbitrage is one of the strategies that informs the conditions of governing and disciplining by way of deterritorializing labor. Labor arbitrage breaks apart the traditional relationship between the national labor legislations and the worker as citizen. Ong describes labor arbitrage as "the latest technique to exploit time-space coordinates in order to accumulate profits, putting into play a new kind of flexibility" (Ong 2006: 174). Cognitive labor is particularly susceptible to labor arbitrage technologies because computerized division of labor enables the fragmentation of tasks into smaller and standardizable units, allowing their completion by an assembly of workers across the globe (Ong 2006: 161). I believe crowdsourcing is an apparatus of a neoliberal system of exception that signifies a novel instance of labor arbitrage, where online cognitive labor markets are established as aggregation platforms that simultaneously act as a techno-immigration system.

The exploitative aspects of cognitive labor arbitrage are clearly exemplified by Amazon.com's Mechanical Turk crowdsourcing system. The Turker community seems to have varied responses to the claims of exploitation. Some U.S.-based Turkers oppose such claims and state that their interest in Mechanical Turk is solely motivated by the novelty of the experience. This fact could be explained by the seemingly negligible amount of income that can be earned through AMT for a U.S.-based worker.[15]

On the other hand, workers from countries such as India or China appear to be mostly interested in Mechanical Turk as a primary income source, though some of them find that AMT undervalues their labor. For example, Rajesh Mago, a computer freelancer from New Delhi, criticizes Mechanical Turk in his blog as follows:

> They call the assignments posted by their requester as HITs (Human Intelligence Tasks). So, is the human intelligence worth cents only? LOL! I know no one is forcing anyone to do these assignments but yet it doesn't justify the usage word "intelligence"—a mockery of human brain.[16]

Mago states that he completed more than 10,000 HITs working for a few hours a day for Mechanical Turk through 2008. He earned $572.62. His HIT approval rate was 98.2%; in other words, the requesters he worked for rejected approximately 2% of his completed tasks, for which he was not compensated at all. According to Mago, requesters do not give any credible reason for their rejection. Moreover, even the payments for accepted works are most of the time delayed, a matter that appears to affect many other Indian Turkers. Rajesh Mago does not work for Mechanical Turk anymore, and, in retrospect, he concludes that:

> Mechanical Turking was kind of addictive as I always challenged myself to test and experiment and work for low-paying HITs thinking that I will

be able to make decent money. But, Mechanical Turk requesters are pretty smart; they had done more R&D than me and were sure that they would get the work done at the lowest rates or for free![17]

Mago's case highlights the unregulated nature of the emerging global cognitive labor market and evokes the *Gastarbeiter* (guest worker) program of the economic wonder years of postwar Germany in terms of the long-term historical interest of Western industries in labor arbitrage. The German *Gastarbeiter* program has been a prominent model for establishing an *immigration without rights* legislative system and it has recently inspired U.S. lawmakers during the fiery political debate on the immigrant worker program (H-1B visa) for the U.S. information technology industry (Jacoby 2009). The German *Gastarbeiter* program initially allowed only male workers from Yugoslavia, Greece, Spain, and Turkey on a temporary immigration status. These men were required to work up to 80 hours a week, supplying the labor needs of the booming postwar German industry at a much lower minimum wage than domestic workers and were exploited in a state of exception outside of the normal legislations, rights, and union protections.

The current neoliberal system of exception advances this early form of labor arbitrage by the help of digital networks. In addition, the peculiar temporality of the digital network with its "timeless time" creates another effect—the *time arbitrage*—which further accentuates the consequences of labor arbitrage. According to Shehzad Nadeem:

> Time arbitrage can be defined as the exploitation of time discrepancies between geographical labor markets to make a profit. This operates on two scales. At the geographical scale, many companies exploit time zone differences to achieve a 24-hour business cycle. At the labor process scale, time arbitrage can mean the extension of work hours or the acceleration of the labor process. (Nadeem 2009: 21)

One may consider the acceleration of digital labor processes as an extension of the general acceleration of the pace of life on digital networks. According to Manuel Castells, digital networks replace the clock time of the industrial age with what he calls "timeless time," which is

> defined by the use of new information/communication technologies in a relentless effort to annihilate time, to compress years in seconds, seconds in split seconds. Furthermore, the most fundamental aim is to eliminate sequencing of time, including past, present and future in the same hypertext. (Castells 2004: 12)

In addition, Castells characterizes network time as "the time of the dominant functions and powerful social actors in the network society" (Castells 2009: xlii).

In the context of these sociocultural premises of the network society, it is possible to consider time arbitrage as an actualization of the allochronic temporality of the Western anthropological discourse as it casts the "other" within an *always-on* machinic zone of temporality. According to Mazzarella, the periodization of crowds to the global South is partly established by its allochronic quality, a term borrowed from Johannes Fabian for the description of a particular discourse built in Western anthropology and intellectual tradition in order to cast the "other" outside of Western historical time. According to Fabian (2002), allochronic discourse is a vehicle for domination and for maintaining global inequalities. In this case, the crowds of the global South are materially configured within the machinic always-on time of the networks through their immaterial labor in order to fuel the linear material progress that characterizes Western temporality. In other words, the Western allochronic discourse has been reified in the form of temporal arbitrage as an apparatus of a neoliberal system of exception.

I argue that the geographical and temporal detachments of the cognitive worker from the immediate cultural products of her labor, which eventually inform social relations on the other side of the globe, creates another state of exception that I call a cultural state of exception. As a result of this detachment, the cultural and the informational content of the produced commodity is consumed outside of the social context of the cognitive worker and thus does not directly alter her sociocultural conditions as a consumer/communicator. It is crucial to remind ourselves that this particular aspect of the cognitive labor apparatus was enabled by the process of disembodiment of information, which was a creation of postwar cybernetics. Corporeal decontextualization of information brought by cybernetics has had significant ideological presumptions—for example, an Anglo-American preference for digital information over context-dependent analog information (Marvin 1987). Carolyn Marvin has suggested that this preference mainly means an "ideological call for born-again unity in a clean and rigidly uniform world, a world more like ours than anyone else's" (Marvin 1987: 61). Precisely because of such ideological implications, the network *Gastarbeiter* have become much more attractive to the neoliberal agenda within the context of the post-9/11 fear rhetoric.

Concluding Remarks

If the digital network is the assembly line of cognitive labor, then the Mechanical Turk is its model apparatus. As the network shifts the object of control from the bodies to the collective mind, the Mechanical Turk achieves this objective by foreclosing the mode of collective cultural production to cognitive workers and confining them within the legislative, temporal, and cultural states of exception.

AMT divides cognitive tasks into discrete pieces so that the completion of tasks is not dependent on the cooperation of the workers themselves but is organized from outside by information and communication technologies industries. By the elimination of the cooperation aspect of the cognitive work, the labor power becomes a variable capital as it creates value only after the activation and organization of the capital.

As a result of the fragmentation of cognitive tasks, crowdsourced workers not only produce the desired information for the task algorithm, but they are, in turn, produced by the algorithm, disciplined by its process flows into a particular cognitive mode and problem solving that eventually determines the efficiency of their labor and thus their livelihood. This effect becomes more significant when we consider the fact that the processes that require the fulfilling of tasks by means of the Mechanical Turk system are mostly the culture-producing algorithms that constantly feed the production/consumption cycle of the network economy. This is the source of the innermost paradox of the system: a gradual reduction of the differences that define the economic value of its information as a product by approximating the unpredictable global variety of tastes, expressions, metaphors, and conceptual affinities into a singular ontology of the multitude.

Notes

1 In order to describe the particular type of immaterial labor that characterizes the industrial production of symbolic-analytical services, I prefer to use the term *cognitive labor*. This distinction is helpful to avoid the perceived emphasis on the immateriality of the immaterial labor under consideration, although various authors have carefully pointed out that the term does not denote solely immaterial processes in terms of production or consumption. However, I believe that immaterial labor still has the traces of some of the conventional assumptions about the processes of mind as separate from the body. Cognitive labor marks an epistemological and discursive culmination point in postindustrialism that is apparent in the academic, military, and socioeconomic prominence of the parallel systematization of the concept. As Mateo Pasquinelli describes, "Cognitive labour produces machines of all kinds, not only software: electronic machines, narrative machines, advertising machines, mediatic machines, acting machines, psychic machines, social machines, libidinous machines. In the XIXth century the definition of machine referred to a device transforming energy. In the XXth century Turing's machine—the foundation of all computing—starts interpreting information in the form of sequences of 0 and 1" (Pasquinelli 2004). Another critical advantage of using the concept of cognitive labor for a critical analysis is that by means of its embodied and distributed characteristics, it is possible to talk about the historical relationship between the particular sociotechnical systems and constitutive subjectivities.

2 Non-U.S. workers do not need to pay tax to the U.S. government for their income. Incomes of the U.S.-based workers are taxed if the total annual amount earned from a requester exceeds the tax reporting threshold defined by the Internal Revenue Service.

3 "Amazon.com Help: Mechanical Turk," http://www.amazon.com/gp/help/customer/display.html?nodeId=16465291.

4 In its various uses by Nick Dyer-Witheford, Paolo Virno, and Yann Moulier Boulang, the term *cognitive capitalism* refers to the accumulation of capital primarily characterized by post-Fordist modes of production and consumption of information in the network society.

5 According to Zizek, "Today, immaterial labor is 'hegemonic' in the precise sense in which Marx proclaimed that, in the 19th century capitalism, large industrial production is hegemonic, as the specific color giving its tone to the totality—not quantitatively, but playing the key, emblematic structural role." See Slavoj Zizek, *Objet a as Inherent Limit to Capitalism: On Michael Hardt and Antonio Negri,* Fall 2005, http://www.lacan.com/zizmultitude.htm.

6 Ann Stoler, in her work *Race and the Education of Desire,* has highlighted the oversight of racial Others in Foucault's historiography, particularly in Foucault's "The History of Sexuality," by focusing on the colonial facts in Dutch archival records (Stoler 1995).

7 In Europe until the 19th century, the term *Turk* was used interchangeably with Muslim, referring to the subjects of the Ottoman Empire, while the Ottomans never considered themselves as Turks. Ottoman elites used the term to disparage the nomadic tribes in Anatolia.

8 Cognitive scientist Donald Norman uses the term *affordance* to describe the perceived quality of an object in relation to its utility (Norman 1990).

9 W. R. Hamilton, ed., *Works of Thomas Reid* (Edinburgh, 1846); quote appears in Schaffer (1983).

10 Windisch emphasizes the boldness of the idea that the automaton conveys as one of its intended effects. "He represented it for merely what it is; a machine, which is not without merit as to its mechanism, but the effects of which appear so wonderful, only from the boldness of the idea, and the fortunate choice of means which he employs to carry on the illusion" (Windisch 1874: Letter V).

11 Kempelen was aware of the importance of self-regulating mechanisms and patented a steam turbine that was very similar to James Watt's famous invention. The governor mechanism of Watt's steam turbine is considered to be the archetype of self-regulating systems.

12 Gottfried Leibniz, *Dissertio de Arte Combinatoria* (1666); quoted in Ronald Chrisley and Sander Begeer, *Artificial Intelligence: Critical Concepts* (London: Taylor & Francis, 2000), 14.

13 Poe published "Von Kempelen and His Discovery" in 1849.

14 Foucault explains this term in his interview published in Michel Foucault, *Power/Knowledge: Selected Interviews and Other Writings, 1972–1977,* ed. C. Gordon ([City: Publisher]), 194–8. Deleuze (1992) prefers the term *social apparatus* in his translation of dispositive.

15 However, this assumption may not always reflect the entire reality. Mechanical Turk has recently gained some attention in the U.S. media, particularly after the 2008 economic crisis, through the aired stories by people who work for AMT. Although the kind of income that could be produced in Mechanical Turk may not entirely compensate for an income lost from a traditional full-time job for a worker based in the United States, many Turkers still see it as convenient and flexible work that could pay $8 to $15 per day.

16 Rajesh Mago, "Review of Mturk after Working with Them as Worker | PC Tips and Tricks," http://www.pctipstricks.com/my-review-of-amazon-mturk-after-working-part-time-as-worker-for-few-months/.

17 Ibid.

References

Agamben, Giorgio. 2009. *"What Is an Apparatus?" and Other Essays.* Stanford, CA: Stanford University Press.

Babbage, Charles. 1963. *On the Economy of Machinery and Manufactures*. 4th ed. Reprints of Economic Classics. New York: A. M. Kelley.

Beaune, Jean-Claude. 1989. The Classical Age of Automata: An Impressionistic Survey from the Sixteenth to the Nineteenth Century, in *Fragments for a History of the Human Body*, ed. Michel Feher, 430–80. New York: Zone.

Biddick, Kathleen. 2012. Dead Neighbors Archive: Jews, Muslims, and the Enemy's Two Bodies. In *Political Theology and Early Modernity*, eds. Julia Reihard Lupton and Graham Hammill. Chicago: University of Chicago Press.

Bowker, Geof. 1993. How to Be Universal: Some Cybernetic Strategies, 1943–70. *Social Studies of Science* 23, no. 1 (February): 107–27. doi:10.1177/030631293023001004.

Carroll, Charles Michael. 1975. *The Great Chess Automaton*. Dover Publications.

Castells, M. 2002. An Introduction to the Information Age. In *The Information Society Reader*, ed. Frank Webster, Raimo Blom, Erkki Karvonen, Harri Melin, Kaarle Nordenstreng, and Ensio Puoskari, 138–49. New York: Routledge.

Castells, Manuel. 2009. *The Rise of the Network Society: The Information Age: Economy, Society, and Culture*. Vol. 1, 2nd ed. Oxford: Wiley-Blackwell.

Chrisley, Ronald, and Sander Begeer. 2000. *Artificial Intelligence: Critical Concepts*. London: Taylor & Francis.

Cook, James W. 1995. From the Age of Reason to the Age of Barnum: The Great Automaton Chess-Player and the Emergence of Victorian Cultural Illusionism. *Winterthur Portfolio* 30, no. 4: 231–57.

Deleuze, Gilles. 1992. What Is a Dispositif?. In *Michel Foucault, Philosopher? Essays Translated from the French and German*, ed. Timothy Armstrong, 159–67. New York: Routledge.

Deleuze, Gilles, and Félix Guattari. 2004. *A Thousand Plateaus: Capitalism and Schizophrenia*. Trans. Brian Massumi. London: Continuum International Publishing.

Fabian, Johannes. 2002. *Time and the Other: How Anthropology Makes Its Object*. New York: Columbia University Press.

Flusser, Vilém. 2000. *Towards a Philosophy of Photography*. London: Reaktion.

Foucault, Michel. 1977. *Discipline and Punish: The Birth of the Prison*. London: Allen Lane.

Hardt, Michael, and Antonio Negri. 2005. *Multitude: War and Democracy in the Age of Empire*. New York: Penguin.

Howe, Jeff. 2006. The Rise of Crowdsourcing. *Wired* 14.06 (June). http://www.wired.com/wired/archive/14.06/crowds.html.

Ipeirotis, Panagiotis G. 2010. Demographics of Mechanical Turk. *SSRN eLibrary* (March). http://papers.ssrn.com/sol3/papers.cfm?abstract_id=1585030.

Jacoby, Tamar. 2006. "Guest Workers" Won't Work. *Washington Post*, March 26. http://www.washingtonpost.com/wp-dyn/content/article/2006/03/24/AR2006032401719.html.

Lacan, Jacques. 1991. *The Ego in Freud's Theory and in the Technique of Psychoanalysis, 1954–1955*. Book 2. New York: W. W. Norton.

Lazzarato, Maurizio. 1996. *Immaterial Labor*. Trans. Paul Colilli and Ed Emery. http://www.generation-online.org/c/fcimmateriallabour3.htm.

Leibniz, Gottfried Wilhelm. 2005. *Theodicy Essays on the Goodness of God, the Freedom of Man and the Origin of Evil*. Trans. E. M. Huggard. http://www.gutenberg.org/ebooks/17147.

Marvin, C. 1987. Information and History. *The Ideology of the Information Age*, ed. Jennifer Slack and Fred Fejes, 49–62. Norwood, NJ: Ablex Pub.

Mayr, Otto. 1970. *The Origins of Feedback Control*. Cambridge, MA: MIT Press.

Mazzarella, W. 2010. The Myth of the Multitude, or, Who's Afraid of the Crowd? *Critical Inquiry* 36, no. 4: 697–727.

Nadeem, Shehzad. 2009. The Uses and Abuses of Time: Globalization and Time Arbitrage in India's Outsourcing Industries. *Global Networks* 9, no. 1 (January): 20–40.

Norman, Donald. 1990. *The Design of Everyday Things.* New York: Doubleday Business.

Ong, Aihwa. 2006. *Neoliberalism as Exception: Mutations in Citizenship and Sovereignty.* Durham, NC: Duke University Press.

Pasquinelli, Matteo. 2004. *Radical Machines against the Techno-empire: From Utopia to Network.* Trans. Arianna Bove. http://multitudes.samizdat.net/Radical-machines-against-the.

Poe, Edgar Allan. 1910. *Works.* Leslie-Judge Company, New York.

Pontin, Jason. 2007. Artificial Intelligence, with Help from the Humans. *New York Times,* March 25. http://www.nytimes.com/2007/03/25/business/yourmoney/25Stream.html.

Riskin, Jessica. 2003. Eighteenth-Century Wetware. *Representations,* no. 83 (July): 97–125.

Ross, J., L. Irani, M. Silberman, A. Zaldivar, and B. Tomlinson. 2010. Who Are the Crowdworkers? Shifting Demographics in Mechanical Turk. In *Proceedings of the 28th International Conference Extended Abstracts on Human Factors in Computing Systems,* 2863–72. New York: ACM.

Schaffer, S. 1983. Natural Philosophy and Public Spectacle in the Eighteenth Century. *History of Science: An Annual Review of Literature, Research and Teaching* 21, no. 51, pt. 1 (March): 1–43.

Schaffer, S. 1994. Babbage's Intelligence: Calculating Engines and the Factory System. *Critical Inquiry* 21, no. 1 (October): 203–27.

Schaffer, S. 1996. Babbage's Dancer and the Impresarios of Mechanism. *Cultural Babbage: Technology, Time and Invention,* ed. Francis Spufford and Jennifer S. Uglow, 335–52. Boston: Faber and Faber.

Schaffer, S. 1999. Enlightened Automata. In *The Sciences in Enlightened Europe,* ed. William Clark, Simon Schaffer, and Jan Golinski, 126–65. Chicago: University of Chicago Press.

Shannon, C. E. 1950. Programming a Computer to Play Chess. *Philosophy Magazine* 41: 256–75.

Smith, Adam. 1976. *An Inquiry into the Nature and Causes of the Wealth of Nations.* Oxford: Clarendon Press.

Stoler, Ann Laura. 1995. *Race and the Education of Desire: Foucault's History of Sexuality and the Colonial Order of Things.* Durham, NC: Duke University Press.

Truitt, E. R. 2004. "Trei poëte, sages dotors, qui mout sorent di nigromance": Knowledge and Automata in Twelfth-Century French Literature. *Configurations: A Journal of Literature, Science, and Technology* 12, no. 2: 167–93.

Vartanian, Aram. 1960. *La Mettrie's L'homme Machine: A Study in the Origins of an Idea.* Princeton, NJ: Princeton University Press.

von Ahn, Luis, Manuel Blum, Nicholas Hopper, and John Langford. 2003. CAPTCHA: Using Hard AI Problems for Security. In *Proceedings of Eurocrypt,* 2656, 294–311. Warsaw, Poland, May 4–8. Published by Springer.

Wiener, Norbert. 1948. *Cybernetics: Or, Control and Communications in the Animal and the Machine.* Actualités scientifiques et industrielles 1053. Paris: Hermann.

Windisch, Karl Gottlieb. 1784. *Inanimate Reason; Or a Circumstantial Account of That Astonishing Piece of Mechanism, M. de Kempelen's Chess-Player; Now Exhibiting at No. 8, Savile-Row, Burlington-Gardens; Illustrated with Three Copper-plates, Exhibiting This Celebrated Automaton, in Different Points of View: Translated from the Original Letters of M. Charles Gottlieb de Windisch.* Printed for S. Bladon, no. 13, Pater-Noster-Row.

6

FANDOM AS FREE LABOR

Abigail De Kosnik

Fanatics or Workers?

Historically, fan activity has been derided as frivolous, irrelevant, and even patho-logical. In his book *Textual Poachers,* Henry Jenkins traces the uses of the word *fan* from its origins in the Latin word *fanaticus,* which bore connotations of (Jenkins cites the *Oxford Latin Dictionary* and *Oxford English Dictionary*) "orgiastic rites and enthusiastic frenzy," "excessive and mistaken enthusiasm," and "possession by a deity or demon." The associations between fandom and insanity persisted into the late 20th century, Jenkins argued:

> [T]he fan still constitutes a scandalous category in contemporary culture, one alternately the target of ridicule and anxiety, of dread and desire. Whether viewed as a religious fanatic, a psychopathic killer, a neurotic fantasist, or a lust-crazed groupie, the fan remains a "fanatic" or false worshipper, whose interests are fundamentally alien to the realm of "normal" cultural experience and whose mentality is dangerously out of touch with reality.[1]

In the two decades since *Textual Poachers* was published, the increasing process-ing power of personal computers, the decreasing costs of digital authoring tools, and the ease of publishing on the Internet have facilitated a boom in fan activity. Today, fan websites, blogs, and message boards are common, and fan groups have organized on every social media site; in these online communities, fans post their works: commentary and close readings, stories and poems, songs and videos, reen-actments and animations and mash-ups, wallpapers and screen shots and icons. Fan productions permeate the Internet. This flow of audio, visual, and textual material from fans into the realm of public consumption has not greatly altered some cul-tural critics' negative assessment of fandom. Rather, the abundance of fan content online has led some to disparage fans as prolific amateurs who make nothing of importance or value. Andrew Keen writes in *The Cult of the Amateur,* referring to T. H. Huxley's theory that matching up an infinite number of monkeys with an infinite number of typewriters will eventually yield a masterpiece:

Today's technology hooks all those monkeys up with all those typewriters. Except in our Web 2.0 world, the typewriters aren't quite typewriters, but rather networked personal computers, and the monkeys aren't quite monkeys, but rather Internet users. And instead of creating masterpieces, these millions and millions of exuberant monkeys—many with no more talent in the creative arts than our primate cousins—are creating an endless digital forest of mediocrity.[2]

But fans' profuse contributions to the Internet can be regarded otherwise: as *labor*. Online fan productions constitute unauthorized marketing for a wide variety of commodities—almost every kind of product has attracted a fandom of some kind. This chapter will argue that fan activity, instead of being dismissed as insignificant and a waste of time at best and pathological at worst, should be valued as a new form of publicity and advertising, authored by volunteers, that corporations badly need in an era of market fragmentation. In other words, fan production is a category of work.

To date, the vast majority of fans' work has been unpaid. Like many creative activities that produce content for the Internet, fandom is a form of what Tiziana Terranova calls free labor. Terranova writes:

> We call this excessive activity that makes the Internet a thriving and hyper-active medium "free labour"—a feature of the cultural economy at large, and an important, yet unacknowledged, source of value in advanced capitalist societies....Far from being an "unreal", empty space, the Internet is animated by cultural and technical labour through and through, a continuous production of value which is completely immanent in the flows of the network society at large.[3]

At the start of the second decade of the 21st century, as the question of pay for creative online labor is becoming critical for a wide variety of industries, including journalism and higher education, and as creative workers' organizations such as the Writers Guild of America and the Freelancers Union loudly campaign for more recognition of online production as deserving of payment, we are at a ripe moment for establishing the fact that fandom is a form of free labor and for calling upon fans, scholars, and the corporations that benefit from fan activity to seriously consider the question of whether fans should be compensated for their work.

Hebdige: Subcultural Style

This chapter's primary objective is to make clear that fan activity constitutes a kind of work. To that end, we will review key works in cultural studies, particularly scholarship on subcultures and fan communities, which argue that fandom is a form of active production, not passive reception.

In his landmark book *Subculture*, Dick Hebdige points out how queer subcultures and youth subcultures (teddy boys, punk rockers, biker gangs) transform ordinary objects into signifiers of style—style that marks the difference, the distinction, of the subculture's members from (what constitutes in the subculture's view) normative, homogeneous, dominant society. Hebdige writes:

> [O]bjects are made to mean and mean again as "style" in subculture.... [T]his process begins with a crime against the natural order—the cultivation of a quiff, the acquisition of a scooter or a record or a certain type of suit. But it ends in the construction of a style, in a gesture of defiance or contempt, in a smile or a sneer. It signals a Refusal.[4]

Affinity groups, Hebdige says, collectively act upon everyday commodities, such as scooters or records or suits, and infuse those objects with a certain sensibility that is reflective of the group's values and interests; the commodities come to "mean and mean again" as the affinity groups reconfigure and redefine their meanings. A safety pin in the hand of a housewife is not the same as a safety pin in the cheek of a punk rocker. "[T]he most mundane objects—a safety pin, a pointed shoe, a motor cycle—...take on a symbolic dimension.... [T]hese objects become signs of forbidden identity, sources of value."[5] Without affinity groups' specialized uses and recontextualizations of these "most mundane objects," which are commodities readily available in the marketplace, the objects would never acquire their symbolic dimension and would not be "sources of value; that is, they would not possess multiple values, they would not be valuable to different groups in different ways—they would not be *special* objects.[6]

Hebdige's work is thus an early articulation of the type of labor that this chapter calls fan labor. Fans act upon commodities and imbue them with worth via their performances, which consist of displays of certain expressions and specific actions, which can all be summed up in the concept of attitude. Fans start to regard certain physical objects, manners of dress and hairstyles, and behaviors as integral components of the attitude that marks their difference from other groups and from what they consider to be the mainstream. In Hebdige's study, the work performed by subcultures on commodities, the work of meaning-making, the work of recontextualizing commodities as crucial components of their performances of attitude and style, is undertaken in self-interest, for subcultures wish more than anything to be visibly distinctive and apart from the rest of society. An affinity group invests time, effort, and imagination in everyday objects in order to make those objects serve their needs, which include helping to consolidate and represent the group's collective identity, which often stands in clear opposition to societal norms.

An irony that does not surface in subcultural and fan studies until decades after Hebdige's work is that affinity groups, by endowing ordinary things with special meanings, actually increase those things' market value; in other words, subcultures work on objects in order to make them markers of their nonconformist attitudes and values, but their work confers on objects new value and appeal, and so is effectively a type of advertising. The work of even the most rebellious subcultures therefore conforms to one of the most significant social norms of all, the norm of capitalist labor: all who live under capital's regime must labor to promote, sell, and consume commodities.

Thornton: Taste Cultures

While Hebdige draws attention to affinity groups' reworking of things into artifacts of style, Sarah Thornton, in her study of the 1990s British techno music dance club and rave scene called *Club Cultures,* highlights the ways that subcultures use everyday objects to create new modes of social engagement. In the present day, as it becomes increasingly common for people to join online communities via social media sites, the observation that subcultures create entertaining forms of group participation may seem obvious. But Thornton lays out a set of concepts and terms that prove as useful today for understanding how subcultures create modes of online interactivity as they were fifteen years ago for comprehending the face-to-face techno club and rave scene.

Thornton categorizes club culture as a type of "taste culture." Taste cultures, Thornton writes, "congregate on the basis of their shared taste . . . , their consumption of common media and, most importantly, their preference for people with similar tastes to themselves." Taking part in a particular taste culture "socializ[es] participants into a knowledge of (and frequently a belief in) the likes and dislikes, meanings and values of the culture." These cultures are not often permanent institutions of affiliation; rather, they are "*ad hoc* communities with fluid boundaries which may come together and dissolve over a single summer or endure for a few years." Also, taste cultures are "riddled with cultural hierarchies," such as, in the example of club cultures, the privileging of what is considered authentic over what is deemed phoney, the hip over the mainstream, and the underground over the media.[7]

What Thornton describes here are the social innovations of fandoms. Thornton's taste cultures can also be called fan cultures, and these types of groups coalesce around certain objects, which can be "common media" such as music, films, television programs, and comic books but can also be other types of commodities. Around these commodities, fans build societies with particular hierarchies, values, and belief systems. A great deal of the work of fans consists of the construction of the rules and codes of participating in fan cultures; fans moderate the interactions of other fans, establish the terms of the fans' discussions and play (e.g., make clear what is authentic versus phoney), and initiate and teach newcomers to the fandom. Status games—the struggle for newbies to become "big name fans" or moderators in a community, or the struggle for a faction of fans who wish to modify the group's value system to gain recognition—are common in fandoms and provide a great deal of the emotional interest and entertainment for community members. Thornton's was one of the first studies to shed light on the importance of the social dimension of fandom. She reveals that a great deal of effort and time goes into the constitution of and participation in fan communities (although that participation may be fleeting), and she emphasizes that without activities such as the learning and policing of rules, the gaining and losing of status, the adhering to or breaking from shared belief systems, ordinary commodities would not hold much interest for many people. In other words, the community-building labor of fans endows objects with much of their appeal. Without fan labor, there would be little or no social aspect to consuming; buyers of things would not associate those things with the pleasures of joining and taking part in societies comprising people with similar tastes and values.

Jenkins: Fascination/Frustration

Hebdige and Thornton's early theorizations of fan labor are complemented by Jenkins's and Matt Hills's analyses of fan labor's contradictions and complexities. Jenkins notes that fans choose to work on objects (he studies primarily fans of television productions) because they experience a multiplicity of affect when engaging with the objects:

> The fans' response typically involves not simply fascination or adoration but also frustration and antagonism, and it is the combination of the two responses, which motivates their active engagement with the media. Because popular narratives often fail to satisfy, fans must struggle with them, to try to articulate to themselves and others unrealized possibilities within the original works. Because the texts continue to fascinate, fans cannot dismiss them from their attention but rather must try to find ways to salvage them for their interests.[8]

Jenkins illuminates that the internal emotional conflict that fans feel toward the objects of their interest—both fascination *and* frustration, affection *and* loathing—drives fans to work on those commodities. Media fans, Jenkins observes, write fan fiction and fan commentary, and make art and music and videos, as a way to create *their* version of a text, the text as they would like it to be, the text that serves their needs best. From Jenkins, we learn that fan labor is often the work of *customization,* the making of mass-produced things into things that serve individuals' particular and peculiar desires and wishes.

We also learn that fandom is not devotion, or rather, that it is not *only* devotion but also antagonism, and that fans feel they must labor—that is, dedicate time, attention, creativity, intellect, and energy to commodities—to make those things be what they want them to be. Fans work on objects in order to master them. Jenkins writes, "Far from syncopathic, fans actively assert their mastery over the mass-produced texts which provide the raw materials for their own cultural productions and the basis for their social interactions."[9] So, far from the notion of the fan as slavishly enthralled by commodities, we here find the concept of the fan as an individual who asserts her or his mastery over commodities by forcibly altering those objects to better serve them. The fan regards commodities as "raw materials for their own cultural productions"—echoing Hebdige's writing on subcultures' making over of ordinary things into icons of style and props of public performance—and as "the basis for their social interactions"—just as Thornton claims (four years after Jenkins) that taste cultures constitute communities that engage individuals with status games and unique value systems.

Jenkins allows us to see that the fan's position is that no object of fandom is complete or perfect or whole in itself. Fans are eager to praise what is right about an object, point out what is wrong, and propose solutions and new directions for the development of that object because they think that fandom is what completes and perfects the object. *The object is about the fan.* It is not the fan who is devoted to the object so much as the object that serves the needs of the fan—and, initially, does not do a very good job of that; the fan must invest work into the object to customize the object to better suit the fan's wishes.

Jenkins also enables us to grasp that, from the fan's perspective, there is a clear separation between his or her labor on a commodity and the labor of the official producers of that commodity. If fans must smooth out the rough edges of an object, if they must explore and actualize the unrealized possibilities of an object, then it is the official producers who are to blame for giving the object its undesirable attributes and suppressing its more interesting potentials. The fact that fans feel compelled to labor on things means that the labor that went into bringing that thing to the marketplace was shoddy or insufficient or, at best, left much to be desired. This distance between the fan laborer and the official producer is one reason that fans have not often regarded themselves *as* laborers. The fans' efforts to customize mass commodities are for themselves and their fellow fans only, not for the marketplace and not for average consumers (i.e., nonfans). One might hypothesize that fans think of their activities as driven by an interest in unleashing the best and highest promise of their favored objects rather than being motivated by financial gain, as official producers are; many fans therefore think of their motives as purer than those of official producers and see themselves as above questions of market value, advertising, and sales. The frustration and antagonism that fans frequently feel toward official producers have largely prevented fans from regarding themselves as part of the same capitalist system within which official producers operate.

Hills: Fans and Exchange-Value

However, as Hills argues in *Fan Cultures,* fans are, in fact, essential components of the capitalist system within which official producers operate. Hills addresses the prevalent concept of the "resistive" fan, stating that "an expressed hostility within cult fandoms towards commercialisation and commodification... [has] led to the theorization of cult TV fandom (and other related media fandoms) as somehow anti-consumerist."[10] But there is an inherent contradiction in fandom, Hills writes:

> While simultaneously "resisting" norms of capitalist society and its rapid turnover of novel commodities, fans are also implicated in these very economic and cultural processes. Fans are, in one sense, "ideal consumers" since their consumption habits can be very highly predicted by the culture industry, and are likely to remain stable. But fans also express anti-commercial beliefs (or "ideologies", we might say, since these beliefs are not entirely in alignment with the cultural situation in which fans find themselves).[11]

Hills thus views the fan experience as having (at least) two competing aspects: the "anti-commercial ideology" side and the "commodity-completist" side.

Hills's proposal of these two halves of fandom allows him to articulate, more clearly than the subculture and fan studies scholars who preceded him, how fan labor adds value to commodities and why fans disavow or simply refuse to acknowledge that their value-adding activities constitute labor. Looking at the way that fans who have collected old, no-longer-manufactured items are able to sell them for sometimes quite high prices on eBay, Hills says,

> Many commodities offered for sale on eBay should, according to the conventional logic of use and exchange-value, be almost worthless. However, due to many of them having been intensely subjectively valued by fans, such commodities take on a redefined "exchange-value".... [F]an-based "use-values" interact with systems which belong to the economy "proper", meaning that the existence of a marketplace for media-related collectibles is underpinned by the lived experiences of fandom.[12]

What gives these commodities value beyond their initial sales price is what fans add to them—the new uses to which fans put old things and the emotional landscapes that fans construct around them. Hills states that "fan 'appropriations' of texts or 'resistances' to consumption can always be reclaimed as new instances of exchange-value,"[13] and, conversely, we can say that *without* fan appropriations, many commodities would have much lower exchange-value, a much shorter shelf life of value, and a much smaller base of potential consumers. Without fans working on them, many items would be, in Hills's words, "almost worthless" a short while after coming to market.

But fans and fan studies scholars have historically been reluctant to regard fans' value-adding actions as labor since "fan identities are typically viewed against consumer identities."[14] Particularly relevant to this essay is Hills's observation, citing a study by Taylor and Willis,[15] that fans criticize members of their own communities who *do* regard their activities as work worthy of compensation: "[F]ans whose practices are 'clearly linked with' dominant capitalist society (e.g. they may be trying to sell videos recorded off-air) are likely to be censured within the fan culture concerned."[16] As I have written about elsewhere, using the example of the case of a *Star Wars* fan fiction author who briefly listed her fan novel on Amazon,[17] fan communities frequently severely criticize members who attempt to sell their fan works. Because fans generally conceive of their activities as "resistive" to consumerism, they refuse to consider that their works might constitute either promotional materials or ancillary products that increase the value of the objects of fandom and therefore might be deserving of compensation, either from official producers or from other consumers.

Linking Hebdige's and Thornton's theories to Jenkins's and Hills's, then, we can discern that fans do not think of objects of fandom as commodities even though that is what they are, even though they spend a lot of money (in some cases, a great deal of money) acquiring those objects, and even though fandom is what gives those objects market value far greater than their initial sales price. Fans, therefore, do not regard their own activities as work that adds or creates exchange-value (rather, they think of their efforts as adding personal use value) and do not seek compensation for their activities.

In the digital era, however, as fans circulate their works publicly to wider audiences than was possible with analog distribution technologies, it is evident that the energy and time that fans devote to making objects "mean and mean again" (as Hebdige would say) is labor, and the vast majority of this labor is performed for free. The issue of how the Internet consists primarily of free and voluntary creative labor has been worked through by scholars such as Tiziana Terranova and Andrew Ross.

Terranova's concept of the continuous need for *updating* required by the digital economy maps well onto our discussion of fan labor. Terranova writes in *Network Culture* that the digital economy "challenged the postmodern assumption that labour disappears while the commodity takes on and dissolves all meaning. In particular, the Internet foregrounds the extraction of value out of continuous, updateable work and is extremely labour-intensive."[18] She points to the work of web designers and maintainers to constantly update a website to ensure it is a "good" site, and the work of programmers to repeatedly update software to keep an application relevant and in use:

> It is the labour of the designers and programmers that shows through a successful website and it is the spectacle of that labour changing its product that keeps the users coming back. The commodity, then, is only as good as the labour that goes into it.[19]

Similar to Terranova's examples is the work that fans put into existing products to update them, to contribute new material in the form of commentary, stories, videos, and music that refreshes the products and feeds (and creates) consumer demand for them.

Terranova also addresses the contradiction inherent in affinity groups about which Hills writes—that is, the contradiction between communities' feeling that what they do is *not* work and does not warrant compensation versus the communities' creation of a great deal of real economic value. Terranova observes that "the sustainability of the Internet as a medium depends on massive amounts of labor (which is not equivalent to employment [. . .]), only some of which was hyper-compensated by the capricious logic of venture capitalism (during the late 1990s dot-com boom). Of the incredible amount of labor which sustains the Internet as a whole (from mailing list traffic to websites to infrastructural questions), we can guess that a substantial amount of it is still free labor."

Free labor, however, is not necessarily exploited labor. Within the early virtual communities, we are told, labor was really free: the labor of building a community was not compensated by great financial rewards (it was therefore free, unpaid), but it was also willingly conceded in exchange for the pleasures of communication and exchange (it was therefore free, pleasurable, not imposed).[20]

The fact that members of self-organizing communities such as the first AOL chat groups did not mind giving away their labor mirrors the way that fans freely donate their time, energy, and creativity to making fan productions that they then share online; both groups do it for the "pleasures of communication and exchange," and both groups feel their Internet labor is "not-imposed." Terranova refers to the Internet "gift economy"[21] as one framework that affinity groups use to characterize their modes of exchange without pay, but the fact that groups do not regard what they voluntarily do as work does not make it less value-producing. "[I]n 1996, at the peak of the volunteer moment [in AOL chat room moderation], over 30,000 'community leaders' were helping AOL to generate at least $7 million a month,"[22] Terranova states. Today, the fan moderators, writers, and artists who post and comment on YouTube, Facebook, Twitter, and other social media sites number in the millions, and their activities contribute to far more massive corporate revenues than the $7 million monthly garnered by AOL in the late 1990s.

Ross, in his lecture "On the Digital Labor Question," builds on Terranova and Hills, emphasizing that the United States is transitioning to an "Internet-based economy based on the widespread use of non-paid or amateur user labor." For Ross, this transition raises numerous questions about fairness of wages and working conditions that both corporate employers and creative workers are, for the most part, ignoring. Ross writes:

> In the world of new media, where unions have no foothold whatsoever, the formula of overwork, underpayment, and sacrificial labor is entirely normative. The blurring of the lines between work and leisure, the widespread use of amateur or user input on the Social Web or in open source, and the systematic expropriation of Tiziana Terranova first described as "free labor" has prompted some commentators to ask whether the experience of digital

environments should direct us to rethink entirely our basic understanding of labor and enterprise.[23]

Ross sees this expropriation of Internet users' free labor as a form of "self-exploitation among creative workers." What one of Ross's informants calls "work you just couldn't help doing," work that seems like play and recreation, is, states Ross, "value-adding work" that can be "digitally extend[ed]...into every waking moment of an employee's life"—and one need not even be an employee to perform this work. Applying Terranova's conclusions regarding 1990s-era AOL chat rooms to present-day social media sites, Ross claims that wage-free labor infuses all such sites with their financial value, which is a huge boon to the sites' founders:

> [F]or the business entrepreneur, [establishing a social networking site] is a virtually wage-free proposition. There are costs involved for bandwidth, hosting, and maintaining commercial platforms, but as far as the monetizable product goes, it is the users, or prosumers, as industry strategists call them, who create all the surplus value (which could be described as the difference between the value such free services offer to users and the value they create for business).[24]

Ross, like Terranova, acknowledges that the "pleasures of communication and exchange" and the fact that fan labor is "not imposed" prevent fans from seeking compensation for their value-adding activities. For many fans, the donation of labor is willingly given in exchange for the opportunity to enjoy and play in a relatively open, unrestricted Internet. Ross clarifies this point of view in his writing:

> [T]he role the social web is currently playing in new modes of capital accumulation is simply the price one pays for preserving a free medium of exchange whose scope of activity is large enough to outpace any government or corporate surveillance. It's another kind of trade-off, in other words, and the balance, for the time being, is still in favor of the commons. From this point of view, all of the interactive free labor that goes into user-generated value can be seen as a kind of tithe or tribute we pay to the Internet as a whole so that the expropriators stay away from the parts of it we really cherish.[25]

The fact that wealth is unevenly distributed between social media companies (and, we can add, all companies that benefit from social media sites) and the fans who produce content and value for those entities is willingly accepted by fans who regard their volunteering labor as a prerequisite for their attainment of the benefits of Internet participation.

Fan Volunteerism

We can now postulate several reasons for fans' refusal to labor under anything other than a model of volunteerism.

As mentioned at the start of this chapter, the concept of fandom has, for a long while, borne connotations of madness, social marginalization, and abnormality, and inherent in those connotations is the assumption that fans are possessed—psychologically and emotionally enslaved—by particular objects and texts. This definition of fandom as a state of passive reception verging on, or tipping into, insanity has undoubtedly set a low bar for what fans hope to define as their rights vis-à-vis larger society. When a group is categorized as deviant or subnormal, it typically strives for no more than the right to exist and to operate without interference. Moral panics have arisen around a number of media fandoms, from comic book fans in the 1950s to rap and hip-hop fans in the 1990s, and social censure has been applied to a far greater range of fandoms, from Trekkies to soap opera viewers to video gamers; because so many fan groups have experienced rejection and criticism for their enthusiasms over the course of the last century, an integral part of fan sensibility is knowing when to conceal one's fannish interests and when to out oneself as a fan. The pseudonymity of online communication permits people to operate as fans discreetly, and this can be thought of as a form of closeting, for many people rarely discuss their Internet fan activities in their face-to-face social interactions. The Internet permits individuals to hide their fan identities, or rather, to protect their "real" identities and social spheres from any associations with fandom. A group that is largely closeted is usually far from eager to publicly organize and issue economic demands.

The notion of fandom has become a more accepted and privileged term in marketing and consumer circles—companies understand that their products need fans, followers, and friends online and in the real world—but even when considered a worthwhile use of time and money, fandom is regarded as a marginal, recreational, just-for-fun activity, not as central to a person's professional development or as a legitimate foundation for a career in the creative industries.

In addition to the fact that fandom is widely categorized as pure leisure and completely outside the "serious" realms of people's lives, such as work, fans' perception that what they do is explicitly anticommercial prevents them from considering what they do as warranting pay. Subcultures often organize in opposition to social norms, as Hebdige points out, and their members remake, rework, and find new uses for ordinary objects partly to defy those objects' advertised uses as a method of disrupting society's habitual flows. Style can be a signal of disturbance, of breaking with the behaviors and beliefs that characterize the mainstream, and infusing commodities with nonnormative meanings to define a subcultural style is one way to reject capitalism's proclivity for treating everybody as exactly the same as everybody else, reducing all to equivalent, interchangeable consumers.

Hills informs us that fans can also be "resistive" to the commodity aspect of their favorite texts and objects because they see their appropriative activities as pure of financial motives—fans are interested in specific things because they feel an emotional, intellectual, psychological, or artistic connection to them, not because fans wish to profit from them. In fact, fans often think that it is official producers' profit-seeking motives that lead them to make incorrect or less-than-optimal decisions about their products, leaving fans to salvage or modify the products to which they have become attached, spurred by love and frustration, not by money. The opposition between finances and fandom posited in a great deal of fan discourse and fan studies scholarship does not provide fertile ground for fans to consider lobbying to receive payment for the value they add to companies' products.

And Ross and Terranova claim that even when fans do think of their productivity as labor, they can justify giving away their time, energy, and creativity for free in ways that benefit corporations by regarding that donation as a necessary trade-off for the ability to participate in the Internet's largely unregulated social media sites. Their free labor buys them a free Internet.

The very idea of fans organizing officially, as a kind of labor union, is somewhat contrary to the underlying principles of fandom. For fans, although they do gather in groups around specific objects, do the work of *customizing* mass-produced things to fit their own unique desires and needs. The goal of most fan labor is to modify a commodity, which is made to suit everybody, so that it suits the fan laborer, and other fans who share the laborer's particular tastes, much better. It is unlikely that any sizeable number of fans would all come to agreement about the types of work they all wanted to perform on various corporate-made objects and texts and propose some kind of pay schedule commensurate with clearly defined categories of production. Fan labor is, by nature, idiosyncratic, and each fan production arises from, and is shaped by, the peculiar interests of the fan producer.

Also, because it is unclear how much revenue is generated for companies by the brand extensions, publicity, and marketing materials created by fans, it would be difficult for fans to seek payment on a commission or revenue-sharing model. Fan-made videos, websites, commentary, posters and other artworks, stories, songs, and reviews merge with the stream of official advertising and promotion that surrounds any given product—fan labor can ramp up the buzz and reputation of the product, and it can reinforce the pull or allure that the product exerts on would-be consumers, but it would be impossible to tell what percentage of sales of the product had resulted from fans' efforts versus those of the paid corporate marketers.

Fan Compensation

However, as much as the digital economy relies on unpaid, user-generated labor, the Internet has also been the site of some innovations in compensation that might serve fans well in the future. Garnering revenue from advertising has proved feasible for bloggers and video makers who attract significant audiences; fan producers could similarly benefit from Google AdSense or the YouTube Partner Program if companies would allow them to use copyrighted images, text, video, and sound, as most fan productions make use of proprietary media (companies could give permission tacitly, by not suing fans or serving them with cease-and-desist letters for copyright infringement).

Another form of compensation that has benefited a few fans, and could benefit many more, is the elevation of fan laborers from amateurs to paid professionals. Some companies have included fan works with their official products or have used them as advertisements for the products, which have boosted those fans' careers in the creative industries; other companies have hired talented artists, writers, and moderators whose works they first encountered on fan sites. Fan labor could eventually be regarded as the first rung on the reputation ladder for aspiring creative professionals, with the highest rung on the ladder being full-time employment.

The realization of any possibility for fans to earn payment for their labor would depend on both fans and corporations acknowledging that fandom is a form of labor that adds value to mass-produced commodities and is worthy of compensation. The history of discourse about fandom, especially within fan communities, makes such an acknowledgement unlikely. But if companies could begin to regard fan groups as the potential developers of their greatest promotional campaigns, and if fans could start to see that their productions have, not just personal use value, but market exchange-value, then fans could conceivably be one of the first social groups to formulate workable solutions to the important questions of Internet labor and pay. In this scenario, fans would help to shape how creative labor is fairly compensated in the digital economy rather than being the economy's marginalized victims.

Notes

1 Henry Jenkins, *Textual Poachers: Television Fans and Participatory Culture* (New York: Routledge, 1992), 12.
2 Andrew Keen, *The Cult of the Amateur: How Today's Internet Is Killing Our Culture* (New York: Doubleday/Currency, 2007), 2–3.
3 Tiziana Terranova, *Network Culture: Politics for the Information Age* (New York: Pluto Press, 2004), 73–4.
4 Dick Hebdige, *Subculture: The Meaning of Style* (1979; reprint, London: Routledge, 2006), 3.
5 Hebdige, *Subculture,* 2–3.
6 I do not mean to privilege the subculture of youth gangs over the subculture of housewives, or any other group, in this discussion. Although Hebdige is concerned with subcultures that identify themselves as rebellious against mainstream society, one can regard safety pins as endowed with special meaning by homemakers just as much as by punks, although the meaning of the safety pin may be very different in each affinity group. The French saying, "*tiré à quatre épingles,*" or "pulled by four pins" (immaculately

dressed), demonstrates how the ordinary pin (though not necessarily the safety pin, in this case) has been given special meaning in fashion culture.

7 Sarah Thornton, *Club Cultures: Music, Media and Subcultural Capital* (Middletown, CT: Wesleyan University Press, 1996), 3–4.

8 Jenkins, *Textual Poachers,* 23.

9 Jenkins, *Textual Poachers,* 23–4.

10 Matt Hills, *Fan Cultures* (New York: Routledge, 2002), 28.

11 Hills, *Fan Cultures,* 29.

12 Hills, *Fan Cultures,* 35.

13 Ibid.

14 Hills, *Fan Cultures,* 28.

15 Lisa Taylor and Andrew Willis, *Media Studies: Texts, Institutions and Audiences* (Oxford: Blackwell, 1999).

16 Hills, *Fan Cultures,* 29.

17 See my article "Should Fan Fiction Be Free?" *Cinema Journal* 48, no. 4 (Summer 2009).

18 Terranova, *Network Culture,* 90.

19 Ibid.

20 Terranova, *Network Culture,* 90–1.

21 Terranova, *Network Culture,* 93.

22 Terranova, *Network Culture,* 92.

23 Andrew Ross, "On the Digital Labor Question," paper presented at the Internet as Playground and Factory pre-conference at The New School, September 29, 2009. Available at https://lists.thing.net/pipermail/idc/2009-November/004039.html.

24 Ibid.

25 Ibid.

References

Hebdige, Dick. *Subculture: The Meaning of Style.* 1979. Reprint, London: Routledge, 2006.

Hills, Matt. *Fan Cultures.* New York: Routledge, 2002.

Jenkins, Henry. *Textual Poachers: Television Fans and Participatory Culture.* New York: Routledge, 1992.

Keen, Andrew. *The Cult of the Amateur: How Today's Internet Is Killing Our Culture.* New York: Doubleday/Currency, 2007.

Ross, Andrew. "On the Digital Labor Question," paper presented at the Internet as Playground and Factory pre-conference at The New School, September 29, 2009. Available at https://lists.thing.net/pipermail/idc/2009-November/004039.html.

Taylor, Lisa, and Andrew Willis. *Media Studies: Texts, Institutions and Audiences.* Oxford: Blackwell, 1999.

Terranova, Tiziana. *Network Culture: Politics for the Information Age.* New York: Pluto Press, 2004.

Thornton, Sarah. *Club Cultures: Music, Media and Subcultural Capital.* Middletown, CT: Wesleyan University Press, 1996.

7

THE DIGITAL, LABOR, AND MEASURE BEYOND BIOPOLITICS

Patricia Ticineto Clough

This chapter turns to recent technoscientific developments in order to rethink the value of affective labor in relationship to mathematical (digital) forms of measure. I focus especially on the work of Luciana Parisi because my aims here, like hers, are both to draw out the political, cultural, economic, and social implications of these developments and at least to sketch what transformation in thought, or in the thinking about thought (as well as the unthought) they may incite. As Parisi takes philosophical discourse both as a guide to critical analysis of technoscientific development and as the discourse to which she finally hopes to contribute, I hope to do so as well. While philosophies focused on process—those of Gilles Deleuze and Alfred North Whitehead especially—are those to which Parisi is drawn, I contrast those philosophies with speculative realist philosophies and object-oriented ontologies. I propose that this contrast shows that philosophy, even if unconsciously, is being drawn to the implications of the technoscientific development of nanotechnology and the issue of measure it raises in its effort to make productive the micro affects of matter. Or, to put it otherwise, philosophy presently is registering the reconfiguration of economy, affective labor, and biopolitical governance.

Nanotechnology and Measuring Matter's Affects

In her recent analysis of nanotechnology, Luciana Parisi has reported that the specific novelty of nanotechnologies is that nanomachines can "rearrange the very position of every atom" (2012: 48, n. 2). This means that "each atom can be placed in a selected position to become an active or structural component of a living system that is being redesigned." In particular, this new capacity of controlling the position of atoms suggests that "the high speed oscillation and fuzziness of molecules, which was central to the discoveries of quantum physics, is no longer an absolute indeterminacy defined by atomic superposition between particles and waves." Rather, the fuzziness provides a chaotic instability that could be turned into a "weird dynamic productivity" (Parisi 2012: 49, n. 2). At the nanoscale, Parisi continues, "particles can become probability waves which leap across impenetrable barriers, occupy two places at the same time and anticipate future states" (Parisi 2012: 33).

From the science of nanotechnology to the nanodesign of artificial atoms for what has been trademarked "programmable matter," the aim, as Parisi sees it, is "to neutralize the distinction between the physical composition of materials—atoms, photons, protons, electrons—and their properties, such as color, shape, smoothness, brightness, and so on," such that "material can change their substance instantaneously like the design and debugging of software" (Parisi 2012: 38). Parisi sums up by proposing that,

> by entering the realm of pure potentials—of color, shape, roughness, electricity, vectoriality, etc., programmable matter promises an architecture of instantaneous realization of potentialities.... At work here no longer is control intended as the calculation of the future by means of prediction, or the calculation of the unknown through pre-set probabilities. The disappearance of bio-physical contingencies instead is directly proportional to the nano-programming of uncertainties as the inclusion of fuzzy states in the design of thought and extension. (Parisi 2012: 39)[1]

I have quoted at length from one of Parisi's essays to situate my discussion of measure, as she situates her discussions of calculation and computation, in relationship to technoscientific development (Parisi 2009a, 2009b, 2009c). Nanotechnological development also is meant to frame my return to an earlier moment of engagement with labor, affect, and measure in a 2007 publication that I co-authored with Greg Goldberg, Rachel Schiff, Aaron Weeks, and Craig Willse titled "Notes Toward a Theory of Affect-Itself." We drew on George Caffentzis's disagreement with Hardt and Negri's claim that the value of immaterial or affective labor is immeasurable. Arguing instead that capitalism "imposes an extremely quantified form of life on its constituents," Caffentzis warned against claims of immeasurability, proposing that capitalists have sought and still do seek a way to measure what at first seems immeasurable. Caffentzis not only argued that exploitation still was measureable in terms of laborers' production of surplus value, but he also proposed that those who would resist capitalism must have quantitative capacity to match the quantitative capacity at the service of capitalism.[2]

While taken with Caffentzis's interest in measure and capitalism's quantitative capacity, we felt that the question of the measurability or immeasurability of affective labor had to be posed differently than in terms of laborers' productive time, since affective labor as Paolo Virno (2004), among others, would have it, goes even beyond the labor of communicative and cognitive capacities in a knowledge society or information society, beyond what Marx called the labor of a general intelligence to the laboring of affect in a biopolitical society where affect refers to a preindividual, nonconscious, noncognitive, asubjective bodily capacity to affect or be affected. Here, affect is a vector of unqualified intensity opening to future actualization, a pure potential. Defined in this way, affective labor raised questions for my coauthors and me about the embodiment of pure potential or vectors of intensity in contrast to the organic body of the laborer. We asked what kind of body is the affective body or what is an embodiment of vectors of intensity. We doubted that it could be the body modeled on the human organism or the human laborer. If measure is central to affective labor as much as any other labor, we asked how should the measuring of affect be thought.[3]

Bodies, Affect, and Media Technology

The preceding definition of affect is drawn from the philosophical tradition employed by Brian Massumi, the philosophies of Deleuze and Whitehead, and before them Spinoza and Bergson. Although Massumi (2002) develops his conceptualization of affect for the most part in relationship to the human subject—or, more specifically, the autonomic nervous system of the human organism—his very conceptualization of affect as preindividual potential, resonant with Deleuzean virtuality, would seem to let affect slip from the human organism. Indeed, Massumi at times does point to the various scales of matter at which affect is potential or indeterminism. It would seem, then, that affect points to the reconfiguration of bodies and matter/energy; affect may be experienced by and be the experience of bodies other than human bodies or bodies conceived as organisms.

In "Notes Toward a Theory of Affect-Itself," my coauthors and I focused on the technical frame of affect, starting with the technologies with which Massumi measured affect as a fraction of time before conscious experience, a technological enhancement or measuring device theoretically overlooked by Massumi but seemingly necessary to his examples of preconscious affect as a measurable fraction of time before consciousness, a measurement that necessarily moves affect toward consciousness, virtuality toward actualization, although without depleting virtuality or affective potential. That is to say, ontologically, affect is potential and, as such, cannot be realized, only actualized; actualization can only be a matter of invention out of virtuality, which itself ontologically remains virtual. It seemed to my coauthors and me that it might be possible to imagine the body of affect as a technological assemblage or a technology of measurement, where measure measures without depleting or fully capturing, a computationally open technology of measure.

In "Heat-Death: Emergence and Control in Genetic Engineering and Artificial Life," Parisi and Tiziana Terranova (2000) provided a way to begin to address our queries. Offering a genealogy of the (re)configurations of bodies, technologies, and labor, "Heat-Death" makes it possible to think of the body-as-organism as only one figure, a historically specific one, of what the body is or what it can do. Focusing on autopoiesis, characteristic of the body-as-organism, Parisi and Terranova argue that it was in the 19th century that the body-as-autopoietic-organism becomes the figure of what the body is and what it can do. They go on to propose that this figure of the body is befitting the disciplinary society of late-19th-century industrial capitalism, "where the fluids which were circulating outside and between bodies, are folded onto themselves in order to be channeled within the solid walls of the organism/self/subject" (Parisi and Terranova 2000: 4). The body-as-organism is organized for "reproduction within a thermodynamic cycle of accumulation and expenditure; and trained to work" (Parisi and Terranova 2000: 5). Here, Parisi and Terranova are suggesting that a body is a historically specific mode of organization of material forces, invested by capital into being as well as elaborated through various discourses of biology, physics, neuroscience, medicine, and so on that reconfigure work, bodies, production, and reproduction.

If the turn to affect is registering a reconfiguration of the body, labor, and technology, as my coauthors and I went on to argue, then we also wanted to propose that it is due, in no small part, to digital technologies and to the technosciences of information that now propose that information is the general theory of matter/energy and that thermodynamics is only a special case.[4] Here, affect at every scale of matter points to the self-organization inherent to matter or matter's capacity to be informational or informing. It points as well to the digital technology that supports a mathematics that is able to attach to and modulate the informational substrate of bodily matter and matter generally, such that technosciences—for example, biomedia and new media—introduce what Keith Ansell-Pearson (1999) has called the "post-biological threshold" into "life-itself." That is to say, these technologies are changing what the body can do or its affective capacity, with the postbiological as a threshold or a limit. However, in what follows I suggest that in her treatment of nanotechnology, Parisi raises a question as to the status of this limit in thinking of bodies, affect, technology, and labor—a question that also points to recent philosophical debate over ontology.

In the years since the 2007 publication of "Notes Towards a Theory of Affect-Itself," the thought of affect as a technological assemblage has been refined through interdisciplinary discussions about affect, media, technology, governance, and economy. This has occurred as media studies discourse has been shifting its focus from technologies and uses of mass communications to affect or capabilities of perception and sensation, and not only human perception and sensation. In fact, media are being defined in terms of a subtraction of human perception as the presumed center of being and feeling. Steve Goodman, writing on sound technologies and leaning toward the process philosophies of Deleuze and Whitehead, argues: "If we subtract human perception, everything moves.... At the molecular or quantum level, everything is in motion, is vibrating" (Goodman 2009: 83). For subjectivity and objectivity, all that is required is that an entity be felt by another entity. "All entities," Goodman continues, "are potential media that can feel or whose vibrations can be felt by other entities" (Goodman 2009: 83). Here media are understood in terms of nonanthropocentric affect, where "affects are transitions, gateways, and passages between dimensions," as Jussi Parikka has put it (Parikka 2010: xxvi).

In these terms, media is more broadly described as "contractions of forces of the world into specific resonating milieus" (Parikka 2010: xiv), such that mediation is contingent and immanent. Mediation (if it even should be called that) is less about connecting two or more entities, although by the above definition of entities, they are media and they do connect other entities. Still, for theorists such as Goodman and Parikka, it might be better to describe mediation as modulation, intensifying or deintensifying rhythmicities and forces that are of but also below, above, and other than human perception. Here media are extended to various platforms organic, nonorganic, chemical, and neurochemical. As Parikka concludes: "we do not so much *have* media as we *are* media and *of* media; media...cast a plane over the chaos" (Parikka 2010: xxvii).

This definition of media borrows from contemporary thinking about assemblage as a mode of affective (de)intensification—that is, an affordance to sensations, percepts, and concepts and the modulation of their intensities at every scale of matter. As such, an analysis of effects engages them not as the end result of a predefined condition, but immediately as a cause or a condition of possibility of affect and further effects. This is the working of what Massumi has called a "quasi-causality"—that is, the (eternal) return of indeterminacy in every actualization or individualization.[5] These actualizations and individualizations might well be thought of as bodies of affect, the bodies that this discussion of media provokes. If all entities are affective media, then they may share the definition of bodies that Elizabeth Grosz offers: "discontinuous, nontotalizable series of processes, organs, flows, energies, corporeal substances and incorporeal events, speeds and durations" (Grosz 1994: 164), and, as such, they are open to the affordance of a media assemblage and its modulation of intensities. Given this take on media as affective embodiments and bodies as affective media, questions arise as to how an entity or object should be thought, or how relation might be thought when the body-as-organism is no longer the figure of life, and organic matter is no longer privileged over nonorganic matter. And, finally, what does addressing these questions have to do with measure and affective labor?

Prehension, Media Technologies, and Measure

While Parisi has relied on Deleuze, increasingly she also turns to Whitehead. It is Whitehead's philosophy that accompanies Parisi in observing the ongoing investment in technoscience and its elaboration of mathematical technologies that are transforming, as nanotechnology means to do, the biophysical strata of evolution, adaptation, and change and thereby are displacing the postbiological as horizon of thought and extension in matter. This turn to Whitehead, I would argue, is due in part to the difference between his thinking about process and Deleuze's. While Whitehead is concerned with how entities become, nonetheless, entities do become; they become and they perish (Whitehead 1978). In this way, they generate space/time, while Deleuze's conceptualizations of virtuality, pure past, and duration put everything in time, put all entities in relationship, if not to each other, to virtuality. For Whitehead, while there is becoming, it is a matter of what he describes as "concrescence," the actual becoming through a novel production of togetherness or the coming together of multiple prehensions, where prehension is the preconscious, preindividual act by which one actual occasion (entity) takes up and responds to another. Everything, not just humans, prehend in that each thing orients toward; it withdraws from or advances toward the world as it experiences its becoming. Prehension is a "decision," to use Whitehead's term, eliminating potential occasions and delimiting a specific occasion, which, after perishing, becomes the past or "datum" for another occasion or for a grouping of occasions that endures as a "society"—again to use Whitehead's term. It is precisely to prehensions that Parisi imagines nanotechnology to be directed.

After all, nanotechnology, as Parisi sees it, aims "to substitute bio-physical materialities with the nanoprogram of matter and thought" (Parisi 2012: 40). This goes beyond a joining of technology and human; it goes beyond the cyborg and genetic engineering as well. This is because nanotechnology initiates "the process of inorganic reprogramming of the organic nature of matter all together," forcing "biotic life to confront the far from equilibrium dynamics of its quantum condition" (Parisi 2012: 40). Nanotechnology means to reprogram the experience of prehension at all levels of matter, especially the prehension of what Whitehead refers to as "eternal objects," or potentialities that will belong to each entity, "ingressing" into each entity as it becomes itself. For Parisi, then, nanoprogramming is not aimed at the atom but at its prehension—especially its prehension of the potentiality of the eternal object. As Parisi puts it:

> If atoms prehend their transmutation in colour, shape, dimension, electrical power, it is because they prehend eternal objects ingressing their actuality. Yet these atomic prehensions are but appetites for more potentialities, for pure power to become new forms of space and time, new skins and new cognitive architectures. The nanoprogramming of matter therefore indirectly allows atomic appetites to become data for the coming of new actual occasions of experience. (2012: 48)

In other words, nanotechnology is aiming to program potentiality by artificially providing the datum of an experience not actually experienced at any level of matter. Making potentiality experienceable (and not just to humans) is not to control potentiality so much as to make it more productive, weirdly productive. And Parisi concludes: "We have entered the field of pure speculation where reality does not need to be lived in order to be experienced and where thought does not need to be embodied in order for it to be real." If and when this truly becomes the case, it will be at least in part through the further development of a mathematical technology or the "mathematization or computation of the living and of thought" (Parisi 2012: 48). Here mathematization works as a technology of measure, where we enter the realm of the incalculable or the computationally open.[6]

But, of course, it is not so surprising that focusing on technoscientific modulation of potentiality, or what is referred to as affect above, points to a calculation or measure that is computationally open. After all, affect or potentiality cannot be measured without modulating it, or the far from equilibrium dynamics of its quantum condition, without affecting vectors of potentiality, moving potential toward actualization. It is for this reason that affect or potentiality as stated at the start of this essay have been thought to be immeasurable. But what Parisi refers to as the computationally open or the incalculable points to a kind of mathematics, a kind of measure that might very well enable measuring affect or potential. This is because the mathematics that operates in relationship to the digital architecture she is exploring engages with the curvilinear.

In her treatment of what she calls the digital prehension of a symbiotic architecture, Parisi returns to the ancient debate about the line and the curve, to those architectures that "seem too indebted to the finitude of the line and do not fully follow the labyrinth of the curve" (Parisi 2009c: 349). She explores the development of parallel algorithms that are moving software architecture beyond the genetic algorithms to a deployment of a "parasiting architecture" for interactive art and media (Parisi 2009c: 348). This architecture allows for the "ingression of an unforeseen curvature" and directs attention to a mathematics that attests to the viral ecologies or dense folds of information between 0s and 1s (Parisi 2009c: 363). These work as speculative activators of the future or potentiality. As Parisi puts it: "parallel algorithms are nested into each others' activities, trading and distributing variations across milieu of interaction." This allows "simultaneous communication between different processors and the sharing of memory and message transmission." These communications involve many very simple algorithms, which, however, do not lead "to the evolution of one algorithm or the other but to a new algorithmic behavior" (Parisi 2009c: 357).

Here, Parisi draws on Lynn Margulis's conceptualization of endosymbiosis, concerning the origin of multicellular organisms or eukaryotes. Endosymbiosis differs from a genetics of cumulative selection of random mutations. Instead, evolution comes by way of parallel entities whose independent activity remains independently active in any new composite. Parallel processing cannot be contained in a single lineage, nor is it inheritable in a filiative fashion; it points instead to "a labyrinth in evolution" (Parisi 2009c: 358). A symbiotic architecture of parallel algorithms then can take account of and effect experiential dimensions of what has not been experienced, or transition between blocs of space-time, from one state to another, virally transgressing boundaries. For Parisi, this is an abstract machine that entails "an engineering patchwork of partialities passing from one state to another, fusing and breaking into each other, and yet belonging together at points of transitions, which are less irreducible dots than inflections, critical thresholds, curvatures of imperceptible continuities" or an "incomputable materiality" of "the insides of and spaces between atoms, the atomic and subatomic particles" held together in virtuality (Parisi 2009a: 82). Thus, the symbiotic algorithm of software programming accounts for curvature as part of its computational design; it involves "biomathematical features of extension" (Parisi 2009c: 360).

Drawing on the work of mathematician Gregory Chaitlin, Parisi argues that this is a sensual mathematics that would add to the calculus of probabilities "vague or incomplete quantities at the limit of 0s and 1s" (Parisi 2009c). These indeterminacies "transform the logic of binary states, yes and no, into the fuzzy states of *maybes* and *perhaps.*" "These indeterminacies," Parisi continues, "are not merely qualitative renderings of a digital binarism" but are to be understood in terms of new processes of quantification that recognize "the full densely packed zones of information that are the intensive surrounds of zero and one," zones defined by "an intrinsic numerical variability which remains computationally open" (Parisi 2009c: 363). Parisi also draws on Greg Lynn, whose software architecture makes use of infinitely small intervals of information as well. In such cases, the computation remains open, or "extension becomes inflection or *infection,*" where "active and passive parasitic forces mark the obliqueness of the environment that never reaches a point of equilibrium in so far as any stability is mobile directed by vectors of attraction and repulsion" (Parisi 2009c: 364).

This mathematics allows a software design that exposes curvature, going beyond probabilities as nanoprogramming of the futurity of thought and extension in matter would necessitate and as measuring affect or potentiality also would require. It is a mathematics that allows for a measure other than the measure of probability; such a measure is singular but productive, as measuring cannot but modulate and change the intensity of potential or affect. As such, the metric of measure necessarily will change with each and every measure. In this sense, the measure is an aesthetic measure or affective measure, understanding aesthetic measure to be singular, nongeneralizable, and particular to each event or each modulation of potentiality. It is a measure that allows for the experience of imperceptibles, of prehensions, and, as such, permits their modulation. This experience, however, is not a human-centered experience but is experience at every scale of matter; indeed, there is a gesturing toward a scaleless matter. Yet, for Parisi, this is not a mathematical measure that claims ultimate transparency but rather one that she describes, drawing on Whitehead, to be carrying with it "the dust of the world," "the dark affectivity of matter," the incomputable (Parisi 2009c: 266–7). Yet, with nanotechnology, it would seem that there is an effort to get even closer to this dark matter to be able to modulate its potentialities, to get closer to "affective power, whose order, structure or pattern are yet to be universalized and rather remain scattered, discontinuous, infinite instances of a multiplicity of modes of thought and extension" (Parisi 2012: 37).

I turn now to the political and cultural implications of the mathematization or computation of the thought and extension in matter, after which I will return to a discussion of the contrasts between process philosophies more prevalent in Parisi's work and the speculative realist philosophies that I will argue are also implicated in the mathematics and technoscience that has drawn her to philosophical reflection. Of course, Parisi is not only engaged with philosophical reflection; she also attends to the implications of the entanglement of technoscience, politics, and economy. Drawing on current discussion of what Gilles Deleuze has called "control society," Parisi joins others in a discussion of preemption, a mode of governing that pre-empts the future by modulating the experience of memory and time, and at every scale of matter; she also introduces what she calls "preemptive/hensive power," referring to the nanotechnological aim to "invisibly restratify the biological ground of human-bound bodies and thought" (Parisi 2012: 48).

Control society, after all, is a term meant to point to a normative, if not compulsive, attending to the self, a dispersion of power, even to preindividual impersonal domains such as affect, with the accompanying smoothening of the space of civil society institutions, capitalizing on their increasing reluctance or inability to socialize, to interpellate individuals to the ideal of the nation-state. It points as well to a global extension of media, especially digital media, and their reconfiguring of the private and pubic spheres, economy, the state, and the market. While control society coincides with the shift from disciplining the subject to what Foucault called biopolitics, which focuses more on species life, expressed in terms of the capacity for life across populations, the shift to preemptive/hensive power is an intensifying of control at every scale of matter, a cosmological politics. It is the meeting of control with the curvilinear. As Parisi puts it: "mathematics of smooth space has become operative in a postcybernetic control of aesthetic curavature or continual variation...the curving space of control itself" (Parisi 2009b: 9).[7]

This intensification of control hearkens back to the way Foucault has discussed measure in his 1970s lectures on biopolitics and neoliberalism. As Tiziana Terranova has argued:

> Foucault's lectures in particular allow us to think about the process by which the economic-institutional reality of capitalism... has not simply subsumed life in its economic processes of production, but actually has drawn on life as a means of redefining a whole new political rationality where economic and vital processes are from the beginning deeply intertwined. (Terranova 2009: 235)

The market, as Foucault sees it, drives governance to be concerned with securing circulation through a milieu, moving into life or nature to make it work well. Securing nature, or being able to optimize natural processes artificially, serves to limit the function of sovereignty in governance, as governance becomes the biopolitical action on a milieu: first the town and finally something more abstract like an oblique environment that never reaches a point of equilibrium.

The milieu refers to what Foucault describes as a series of events, a seriality that is heterogeneous, without origin or end or that is marked by the reversibility of effects and causes (Foucault 2007: 20), a seriality much like the series Deleuze (1990) writes about. The series should be understood in terms of a spatiotemporal topology that accounts for the nonlinear chaotic action at a distance of bodies one on another, of one memory on another, a quantum nonlocality. Here we see the governing of a neoliberal capitalism moving to a measure beyond probabilities of statistical populations, the latter being what Foucault saw as central to neoliberal biopolitical governance. The move is to the excess created beyond the capture of probability. It is a move to preemptive/hensive power, to the curvilinear that evokes another measure of a lively mathematics for the lively interval between 0s and 1s.

With this measure, a digital depth offers the incomputable measure, a measure of potentiality befitting the power beyond biopower aimed at the condition of emergence or of potentiality—the prehensive. It is this measure that is set to work in a financial capitalism where wealth is produced external to capital's organization of labor or external to the accumulation of capital through production. What has been called the knowledge economy or the information economy or, most recently, the affect economy points to an accumulation of wealth through the working on the prehensive, what was referred to above as affect—itself a generalized affect, an abstraction brought through past investment in the education and welfare of workers and the upgrading of technical management, which increasingly is not considered to be opposed to creativity and invention. However, through the privatization and rarefication of education, health care, control of fertility, social security, and other social welfare provisions, and as the openness of digital networks continues to hold allure for governments and giant corporations that wish to contain it, creativity and invention are being made scarce. And it is this scarcity that lends motivation for a measure other than or more than the measure of probability. It is a measure that generates enthrallment with measure, integrating words, numbers, images, and diagrams to turn measure into alluring evidence of an already present future, a preempted future not only because it modulates human time memory but also the time memory at every scale of matter, the becoming of the programmable matter of nanotechnology.

Aesthetics, Measure, and the Object

As measure becomes increasingly particular and affective, necessarily changing the metric for each next measure, there is an increase of interest in aesthetics as part of philosophy's return to ontology; it is a return to affect as a first principle for the ontological grasp of all entities. This orientation suggests an ahumanism, or a democracy of objects, that does not presume the human as center of being and feeling. Thus, an object orientation proposes that all objects have the same ontological weight to throw around—that is, each object can affect other objects and can be affected by them. This certainly displaces the human as the only agency about which there should be philosophical concern; surely this concern is shared by Deleuze and Whitehead.

However, object-oriented ontologies offer a critique of what has been described as "correlationism," or the assumption that "it is impossible to speak of a world that preexisted humans in itself but only of a world pre-existing humans *for humans*," as Graham Harman puts it (2009: 122); he also adds to a critique of correlationism a critique of what he calls "relationism." Against the view that objects are constituted through relations with other objects, Harman emphasizes that objects are not reducible to their relations. No relation exhausts an object; it endures beyond its relations. In his critique of relationism, Harman is taking a more radical object orientation than Deleuze or Whitehead.

Deleuze and Whitehead argue, albeit differently, that relations are external to objects—that is, objects are not reduced to their relationships; nonetheless objects cannot exist outside all relations, as Harman argues they must. Harman's position points back to the virtual or virtuality assumed in Parisi's writings when she is following Deleuze and to the potentiality of eternal objects when she is following Whitehead. For Harman, the assumption of virtuality or potentiality "undermines" objects, suggesting that a dynamism lies beneath or outside them, often at the scale of the preindividual. It also "overmines" objects and leads, as Harman sees it, to the accusation that there is a falseness to objects; that what matters must be sought in process, eventness, and dynamism that are part of the object but as an eternally returning excess of indetermination. While Harman recognizes Whitehead's difference from Deleuze, appreciating Whitehead's specification of objects that exist and perish, which Parisi takes up in her "incomputable materialism," Harman's object orientation nonetheless leads him to criticize Whitehead's notion of eternal objects, in that they point to a potentiality outside the object. Harman also suggests that the speculative turn of an object-oriented ontology also rethinks materialism and is critical of it. Materialism, by his account, fills in all the gaps between objects in some combination of undermining and overmining them. All this is to say that the way objects become related and the way relations become themselves objects is for Harman the work to be done by "a metaphysics worth its name."

Clearly, an ontological orientation toward objects means for Harman that there is nothing outside the object that contributes to its realness; there are no other agents that make an object real or that are not of the real object-itself. Thus, for Harman, what can be said of objects and how they can enter relationships is this: Arguing for a fourfold characterization of objects, Harman proposes that objects are of two types: real objects and sensual or intentional ones. The real object is withdrawn from relations, which, nonetheless, exist simultaneously as part of the object's sensual profile (or sensual object). Thus, the real object is distinct from the primary qualities needed for it to be what it is (in this sense, a real object is something like an essence but not one that is eternal). The real object also is distinct from the secondary qualities that appear in the specific sensual translation for another object—or what, in the human realm, we have called a subject. Sensual objects appear with secondary qualities that are immediately available for relationship. The totality of all the qualities of a sensual object, however, is submerged and distinct from the intentional or sensual object: the sensual object is always less than all of its qualities (Harman 2009: 135–48).

Thus, real objects, inaccessible, cut off by a "firewall," can enter relations only through sensual objects. In contrast, sensual objects can only touch through real objects. Harman refers to a "vicarious causality" to explain how the relationship between real objects is caused vicariously or where the sensual object is vicar of the real object. Further, the relationship thus formed forms a new object. The sensual object allows two real objects to relate, which forms the new object in which the sensual object and real object contact. For Harman, causation is alluring or affective at the point where real objects touch through sensual ones, and, as such, all objects may be alluring to all other objects, albeit some objects have a stronger allure than others.

I have emphasized Harman's posture toward objects because it turns attention toward the primary and secondary qualities of objects, given that the latter—color, taste, or heat—are understood to be qualities of a subject's perception. In contrast, primary qualities belong to the object itself, such as length, width, and depth. But in questioning correlationism and relationism, the distinctions between primary and secondary qualities are troubled. It is suggested that all qualities might be thought of as secondary, while being transformable in the relations objects have with each other, removed from the privilege of human consciousness. And yet in the withdrawal of the real object, as the sensual object allures other objects, there is a philosophical protection of the real object while its primary and secondary qualities are opened to profound transformation—let us say by a technoscience such as nanotechnology. After all, Parisi proposes that nanotechnology is turning attention to mathematical technologies that seem to be rendering curvilinearity, making extension in matter, or the prehension of eternal objects, operative and experienceable; nanotechnology means to neutralize the distinction between the physical composition of materials—atoms, photons, protons, electrons—and their properties, such as color, shape, smoothness, brightness, and so on, such that material can change their substance instantaneously.[8]

In such a situation, the tension between process philosophies and object-oriented ones might reveal a particular political, economic, and governmental configuration of labor, technology, bodies, and affect. While the process philosophies have enabled critics such as Parisi to keep an eye on technological transformation and the resulting capacity for the capture and manipulation of potential, thereby affecting life, labor, and matter, the object-oriented ontologies might be put to critical use as the investments of technoscience and capital keep seeking to capture every excess of measure; the object-oriented philosophies might give us philosophical ground when potential and virtuality no longer have a positive valence or only a positive one. When labor is considered the work of affect, the stakes of philosophical debates may well be high; the abstractness of these debates is perhaps just what can give us purchase on critiques of politics, economy, and governing in relationship to the digital.

Notes

1 In presenting what he calls "nanofacture," Peter Galison suggests that nanotechnology is changing measure from representation to an ungoing doing in which measure is a making and manipulation all at once. Through the use of devices that allow touching and manipulation of nanotubes or even viruses, the technoscientist is allowed "virtual interaction," or he or she obtains "virtual presence on the surface scaled by a factor of about one million to one.... Imagining in the nano-domain has shifted from a form of passive receptivity to an integral part of manipulation, an everyday increasingly haptic tool to be exploited in the fabrication of a world of the very small" (Galison 2007: 173). Gallison concludes: "Our philosophical ideal, formed in an early time may need to catch up to a very different form of science" (2007: 173). My efforts here are to present works that are critically responding to this reconfiguring of the ontological basis of knowing.

2 Caffentzis also has suggested that physics was critical for the labor theory of value: "physics... provides definite analyses of work and new plans for its organization. Its models may appear abstract, but they are directly related to the labor process" (Caffentzis 1992: 220). And more, Caffentzis has argued that just as thermodynamics provided a uniform approach to energy in industrial labor, with the invention of the Turing machine, computers provide a uniform approach to the computational procedures of all labor usually identified as skilled labor, but which are "implicit in all parts of the division of social labor" (Caffentzis 1997: 52).

3 In considering the labor theory of value, the importance of including labor other than the labor of humans also is taken up in Sean Cubitt's essay in this collection. There also is a connection to be made between affective labor and Ned Rossiter and Soenke Zehle's critical engagement with the culture of the code and algorithmic technologies. Yet in neither of these essays is there a rethinking of the body figured as organism and the effect of that figuring on thinking labor, affect, and its measure.

4 Information now is thought of in terms of a new law, which is: "information can neither be created nor destroyed," which speaks to the physicality of information. (See C. Seife 2006.)

5 For Massumi, quasi-causality "is sensitive-affective, or creative (adding a surplus-value to response). It expresses a global ability to sense and be affected, qualitatively, for change. It injects a measure of objective uncontrol, a margin of eventfulness, a liveliness" (Massumi 2002: 225).

6 There is much to say about calculation and what is incalculable. I would point to David Berry's *The Philosophy of Software: Code and Mediation in the Digital Age* (2011) for its thinking of these questions in philosophical terms befitting the object-oriented philosophies and the process philosophies being discussed here.

7 In response to a draft of this essay, Sean Cubitt asked me an important question and made a request for clarification. I will answer here with regard to the political implications of his question about singular measure and a changing metric with each measure. Cubitt points to repetition of units of measure in his comments to me, but what I am

after here (and I think, as I said above, it resonates with his essay in this collection) is that what we have thought of as immeasurable and therefore vibrant and supportive of a resistance to the foreclosure of chance may become measureable, asking us to think differently or think again about chance or indeterminacy or an open future. I am suggesting that nanotechnology and its mathematics is already asking us to think differently about virtuality, potentiality, and indeterminacy with regard to dynamic matter, because it is bringing a new way of measure that makes the ongoing manipulation, if not capture, of indeterminacies possible and not merely as a repetition of the same. The question of politics is a large one, and I am suggesting that measure must be central to the answer to that question. Cubitt grounds his politics in those who are excluded from the probabilities of crowds or populations. I have argued elsewhere that the politically excluded often are economically included as populations (targeted for social services and/or policing) (Clough and Willse 2011). This is another way that the affective capacities or incapacities of these populations are open to measure and the productivity of the profitable labor of the measuring of affect. This understanding of the economic inclusion of the politically excluded populations is the contribution Foucault makes in his discussion of neoliberalism and biopolitics to which Cubitt also is responding.

8 It is far from clear whether object-oriented ontologies of speculative realism constitute an unhealthy symptom of the current capitalist mode of production or they are offering a ground for a criticism and politics. I only want to emphasize that these philosophical trends ought to be linked to transformations of technoscientifc development invested by capital.

References

Ansell-Pearson, K. (1999) *Germinal Life, The Difference and Repetition of Deleuze*. New York: Routledge.

Berry, D. M. (2011) *The Philosophy of Software: Code and Mediation in the Digital Age*. New York: Palgrave Macmillan.

Caffentzis, G. (1992) "The Work Energy Crisis and the Apocalypse," in *Midnight Oil: Work, Energy, War, 1973–1992*. New York: Autonomedia.

Clough, P., Greg Goldberg, Rachel Schiff, Aaron Weeks, and Craig Willse (2007) "Notes Towards a Theory of Affect-Itself," *Ephemera* 7, no. 1: 60–77.

Clough, P., and Craig Willse (2011) "Gendered Security/National Security: Political Branding and Population Racism," in *Beyond Biopolitics: Essays in the Governance of Life and Death*, eds. Patricia Clough and Craig Willse, 46–64. Durham, NC: Duke University Press.

Deleuze, G. (1990) *The Logic of Sense*. Translated by Charles Stivale. New York: Columbia University Press.

Foucault, M. (2007) *Security, Territory, Population: Lectures at the Collège de France, 1977–78*. New York: Picador.

Gallison, P. (2007) "Nanofacture," in *Sensorium: Embodied Experience, Technology, and Contemporary Art*, ed. Caroline A. Jones, 171–3. Cambridge, MA: MIT Press.

Goodman, S. (2009) *Sonic Warfare: Sound, Affect and the Ecology of Fear*. Cambridge, MA: MIT Press.

Grosz, Elizabeth (1994) *Volatile Bodies: Towards a Corporeal Feminism*. Bloomington: Indiana University Press.

Harman, G. (2009) *Prince of Networks: Bruno Latour and Metaphysics*. Melbourne: re.press.

Massumi, B. (2002) *Parables for the Virtual*. Durham, NC: Duke University Press.

Parikka, J. (2010) *Insect Media: An Archaeology of Animals and Technology*. Minneapolis: University of Minnesota Press.

Parisi, L. (2009a) "The Adventures of a Sex," in *Deleuze and Queer Theory*, eds. Chrysanthi Nigianni and Merl Storr, 1–25. Edinburgh: Edinburgh University Press.

Parisi, L. (2009b) "The Labyrinth of the Continuum: Topological Control and Mereotopologies of Abstraction," Presented at Changing Cultures: Cultures of Change, University of Barcelona.

Parisi, L. (2009c) "Symbiotic Architecture: Prehending Digitality," *Theory Culture and Society* 26: 347–79.

Parisi, L. (2012) "Nanoarchitectures: The Arrival of Synthetic Extensions and Thoughts," in *Digital Cultures and the Politics of Emotion: Feelings, Affect and Technological Change,* ed. Adi Kuntsman, 33–51. New York: Palgrave.

Parisi, L., and Tiziana Terranova (2000) "Heat-Death: Emergence and Control in Genetic Engineering and Artificial Life," *CTheory,* May 10, http://www.ctheory.net/articles.aspx?id=127.

Seife, C. (2006) *Decoding the Universe: How the New Science of Information Is Explaining Everything in the Cosmos, from Our Brains to Black Holes.* New York: Viking Press.

Terranova, T. (2009) "Another Life: The Nature of Political Economy in Foucault's Genealogy of Biopolitics," *Theory Culture and Society* 26: 234–62.

Virno, P. (2004) *A Grammar of the Multitude.* Translated by I. Bertoletti et al. New York: Semiotext(e).

Whitehead, A. N. (1978) *Process and Reality,* New York: Free Press.

8

WHATEVER BLOGGING

Jodi Dean

1

In 2007, e-commerce types were agog at the success of American teenager Ashley Qualls. By the time she was seventeen, Qualls was making over $1 million per year from Whateverlife.com, the busy pink website she designed to market MySpace page layouts. *Market* is not quite the right word, though. Her layouts and add-on weren't for sale. They were free. Her income came from advertising. Because Whateverlife.com gets more than 60 million hits per month, exceeding the circulation of several of the most popular English-language teen magazines combined, it supplies advertisers with a valuable commodity: the eyeballs of teenage girls. Qualls, or AshBo as she calls herself, started Whateverlife.com in 2004. By 2007, she had expanded her site into a sort of community for girls, a go-to site where girls could find tutorials for making their own layouts as well as a variety of images, banners, captions, buttons, and boxes for decorating their MySpace pages. In addition to the revenue-generating ads, Whateverlife.com (with its growing staff of writers and designers) features a magazine and a link to AshBo's blog on her MySpace page.

Although Qualls's popularity is exceptional, her profile fits the dominant one for U.S. bloggers: she is under thirty and female.[1] The Pew Internet and American Life Project report on Teens and Social Media provides some context: only 8% of adult Internet users in the United States have created a blog, but 28% of online teens blog, and these are most likely to be girls. Describing her site as "a place to express yourself," Qualls repeats the reason most U.S. bloggers give for blogging: a wish to express herself creatively.[2] By 2007, she was earning enough from Whateverlife.com to drop out of high school and purchase a house.[3]

Ashley Qualls provides an image of blogging as a popular technological practice of content production, media use, and multiple platform integration inscribed into everyday life such that there is little difference between being on- or offline. Together with the statistical snapshots provided by the Pew Internet and American Life Project, this image might create the sense that we are accessing a truth about blogs and social networks: they are by and for teenage girls. Both blogs and social networks produce affective spaces where girls express them-selves, share their feelings, and reach out with a little hope that someone will be touched and reach back. Accessed through the intense emotional world of networked adolescence, blogs aren't confined to a sphere separate from other media. They are situated in a rich communicative habitat consisting of multiple platforms and applications (mobile phones, social network sites, video, music, and photo-sharing sites). Blogs seem then to be ways that any of us could report on, share, experience, and even market our social lives. With a little luck, we could even earn revenue on ads accompanying each and every heartfelt expression. Feelings can be profitable.

2

The image constituted through the combination of statistics and the experience of a single blogger is too easy, even as it highlights the juxtaposition between the singular and the many characteristic of contemporary networked media. Rather than relying on one to stand in for an impossible whole, we do better to consider the rise of personalized media as a mass phenomenon and practice. By 2008, there were from 80 million to 120 million blogs.[4] The overwhelming majority of these blogs appears and dies in a matter of months, having been seen by few, if any, read-ers. Blogs are many and innumerable, an open, changing set of unique expressions. At the same time, the standardization supplied by blog services—the basic page lay-outs, archival features, titles, banners, ads, and widgets—format blogs as ultimately interchangeable, the same, one virtually indistinguishable one from another.

The common format that makes blogs blogs is a condition for the unique productions of singular bloggers. And vice versa: without the unique offerings, indeed, the promise that each voice can be heard, each experience documented, each opinion expressed, blogging has no point.

We can approach this same entanglement from a different direction: blogs offer exposure and anonymity at the same time. As bloggers we expose ourselves, our feelings and experiences, loves and hates, desires and aversions. Yet we often write as if we've opened ourselves to nearly no one, to just a select few, to a small com-munity of those we trust, perhaps because we cannot see them. Knowing full well that we are one among millions, we may find ourselves relieved not to have so many hits, so many comments. Strangers and opponents remind us of our expo-sure, our visibility, vulnerability, and ultimate lack of control.

Blogs can be useful political tools: they let activists report on their activities, plans, and aspirations. They help them meet up and coordinate. At the same time, they deliver a lot of knowledge to activists' opponents—the university officials wanting to know which students are responsible for the sit-in, the law enforce-ment officials trying to diminish the impact of planned demonstrations to dis-courage activists from *going too far*. Privacy and consumer protection advocates remind us of the accumulation of data on consumers, data easily mined for the sake of the increasingly specific and personalized targeting of ads. Yet this information in need of protection is the open content of millions of blogs and social network profiles. Blogs make monitoring easy. *There's no need to spy! I'll tell you everything—and more!* In short, blogging relies on a fantasy of exposure without exposure correlative to the indistinguishable mass of the singularly unique. It's like the thrill of telling a secret without being burdened by anxiety over its being told—exposure without exposure.

Social networks such as MySpace and Facebook deploy a similar fantasy—one can share one's life with one's friends without repercussion. On the one hand, because one has specifically friended those in one's network, one can rest assured that one's secrets are safe. *If you can't trust your friends, whom can you trust?* On the other hand, the drive to grow one's network *(Look! I'm somebody! I've got thousands of friends—they like me; they really like me!)*, to friend people with whom one works, people from different parts of one's life, belies the illusion of control over one's personal information. Not only is one's data shared with third parties, but the surveys and games that flourish in social network environments expand third-party access: access to my friend is a way of getting access to me. A typical Facebook profile reveals a person's name, age, birthday, location, occupation, high school and/or university, relationship status, sexual orientation, political affiliation, religion, and personal appearance. Add to this the fact that most users mention events they attend, groups to which they belong, and causes they support, and the result is a high degree of exposure.[5]

Typically, we respond to these seemingly paranoid lines of thought with deflection—it isn't *me* about whom data is collected; it's *us*—an aggregate. It's *our* patterns, not *mine*. It's how many of *us* refer to a new movie or click on an ad, not whether I do. As with blogging, our participation in social networks relies on the supposition that we expose but are not exposed, that we are unique but ultimately indistinguishable.

3

Developing a notion offered by Giorgio Agamben, Dominic Pettman considers the problem of the interchangeable yet irreplaceable in terms of "whatever being." For Pettman, as for Agamben, whatever being points to new modes of community and new forms of personality anticipated by the dissolution of inscriptions of identity through citizenship, ethnicity, and other modern markers of belonging. Describing the character actor as exemplary of whatever being, Pettman glosses the concept as "an enactment of existence without qualities, or at least qualities so interchangeable and obvious that they erase all identity." In positive terms, whatever being is a tag for the "sheer generic potentiality of being."[6]

Agamben emphasizes that the "whatever" in whatever being relates not to singularity as indifference to a common property, "but only in its being *such that it is.*" He writes:

In this conception, such-and-such being is reclaimed from its having this or that property, which identifies it as belonging to this or that set, to this or that class (the reds, the French, the Muslims)—and it is reclaimed not for another class nor for the simple generic absence of any belonging, but for its being-*such,* for belonging itself. Thus being-*such,* which remains constantly hidden in the condition of belonging ("there is an *x such that* it belongs to *y*") and which is in no way a real predicate, comes to light itself: The singularity exposed as such is whatever you *want,* that is lovable.[7]

There is belonging, but not to anything in particular. Something in particular is, insofar as it belongs. Asking "to what?" Pettman and Agamben suggest, mistakenly prioritizes the set over the very condition of belonging. What matters is belonging, not that to which one belongs.

At the same time, mattering triggers an intervention into what could seem little more than another way of designating indifference. Mattering matters. It's the interjection or scission of love and desire, of *wanting.* What matters stands out from the mass or multiple because it matters. As Pettman suggests, that I love it, desire it, separates it from the endless, open, uncountable set of indistinguishable members.

There are over 100 million blogs. At least one of them is mine.

4

In U.S.-American popular vernacular, "whatever" is an affective, verbal response that deflects another's comment. It is not generally uttered in response to a question, but to a statement or observation through which another might be attempting to harness the recipient or hearer.

"You haven't cleaned your room."

"Whatever."

One of multiple video mash-ups of Liam Lynch's punk-pop "Whatever" combines images of George W. Bush and his vice president, Dick Cheney, Lynch's guitar tracks, and a Bush-impersonation voice-over. Bush yells:

> I'm George W. Bush, leader of the free world. I want to bomb Iraq. And when the world says, "no!" I say, "whatever!"
> Saddam has started to meet our demands. Yeah, whatever.

He sings the refrain, "'cause this is my United States of whatever."

The response "whatever" registers the fact of another utterance, of a communicative effort or engagement. It acknowledges communicativity through the deflection of the communicative effort. The sender's message (whether understood in terms of its content or its intent, whether conscious or unconscious) is neither accepted nor rejected. Rather, the "whatever" response distills the message into the simple fact of utterance.

"Whatever" resembles the response of Herman Melville's Bartleby, the scrivener who replies, "I would prefer not to," when given a task or instruction.[8] For some contemporary philosophers (for example, Michael Hardt and Antonio Negri), Bartleby provides a figure of refusal, opposition, or resistance; a model of escape or disentanglement from the relations of power constitutive of contemporary capitalist control societies. The argument is premised on power's dependence on resistance: the transgression of the law calls law into being. Or protestors need police brutality in order to demonstrate the validity of their protests. Bartleby, then, suggests a way out of the dialectic of law and its transgression. Sidestepping resistance, he deprives power of its hold.

Yet even as Bartleby evades the circuit of power and resistance by refusing to refuse, he continues to rely on his position as a singular subject: he says "I," referring to himself as a subject—and not just any subject, but a subject with a view, a preference. As such, he remains exposed to power. He still cares. In response to a request, Bartleby does more than acknowledge communication, the fact that a message has been delivered and received. His answer affirms the intelligibility of the request even as it challenges the normative expectations informing it. And rather than challenging the sender of the message's authority to make the request, Bartleby asserts himself as what matters—*he* would prefer not to. He is a subject with preferences, and these preferences must be attended to.

In contrast, the only affirmation in "whatever" is of communication as such. Another has communicated. This communication in no way obligates me as the recipient of the message. By responding, "whatever," I have signaled the minimum degree of awareness of communicative being: a message is sent in expectation of a response (after all, I didn't completely ignore you). "Whatever" asserts no preferences. It neither affirms nor rejects. And it doesn't expose the subject as a desiring subject to whom something matters.

There is also an affective dimension to "whatever," an insolence or attitude or provocation that arises out of its function as a nonresponsive response. By acknowledging communication without attending to the content of the message, "whatever" denies the sender the sense that her message has been received because its content remains unaddressed. The sender is challenged, her position as sender undermined. "Whatever" forestalls a communicative exchange even as it adopts communicative form. It refrains from establishing the subject position of the one who responds with "whatever," and it unsettles the position of the one who initiates the exchange. It's a glitch in orality.

If communicativity such that it is whatever communicativity tags forms of subjectivity and belonging discernible in contemporary media practices, who and what is likely to benefit? What kinds of political and economic relations are likely to flourish in these new communicative habitats?

Whatever it takes.

5

An extensive literature exists documenting the production of national identities through media and communication technologies. Susan Buck-Morss's *Dreamworld and Catastrophe* is one of the best contributions to this research. Buck-Morss explores the mass identities of utopian and project-based states such as the United States and the Soviet Union during the twentieth century. She highlights the dreams and fantasies enabled by the movies, the imaginings of collectivity that film incited. For communists and capitalists alike, twentieth-century technological projects were also identity projects. Four components of Buck-Morss's account are particularly compelling: mass media's direct addressing of society, the way mass media change the nature of crowds, the spectacular function of mass media, and the compensatory logic of mass media's organization of space.

First, many have noted the ways mass media address, well, masses. Radio brought leaders' voices directly into people's homes, integrating leaders into their intimate spaces. Broadcast television likewise occupied a domestic space as it addressed its audience as personal members of a nation, perhaps imagined like a family (respected newscaster Walter Cronkite was affectionately referred to as "Uncle Walt"). But film in particular, with its large screen and grand scale, organized and spoke to the masses as a collective. The nation as national society is produced through the media address (whether newspaper, radio, television, or film), with no existence as such prior to this address.

Second, in a nuanced reading of the role of film production in the United States and in the Soviet Union during the 1930s, Buck-Morss observes,

> Whereas the radio voice allowed mass identification with political leaders, cinema, traveling to towns and villages to meet audiences halfway, represented a moving image of the masses that allowed audiences to recognize *themselves*. Such mirroring can be important in transforming the accidental crowd (mass-in-itself) into the self-conscious, purposeful crowd (the mass-for-itself), with at least the potential of acting out its own destiny.[9]

Unlike the moving carnival whose spectators aggregate and disperse, cinema organizes, locates, and seats its spectators. Their attention is directed to a single place, to the screen. The unity of the screen produces out of the disunity of persons a singular audience that can see and recognize itself as a collective: "we" are watching this movie. For the Soviets, the films of Sergei Eisenstein played a particularly powerful role. Eisenstein captured and glorified intense scenes of revolutionary masses, images that became the memories of the October Revolution. Buck-Morss writes:

> The particular characteristics of the screen as a cognitive organ enabled audiences to see the materiality not only of the new collective protagonist, but

also of other ideal entities: the unity of the revolutionary people, the idea of international solidarity, the idea of the Soviet Union itself.[10]

Similarly, in the United States, cinema changed the nature of the crowd by providing an imaginary mass body. In the early-twentieth-century United States, ethnic groups, religions, political organizations, and racist law worked against the image and goal of a unified political identity. Film countered these forces, offering massive cinematic bodies as points of singular identification. It was a crucial vehicle for mass assimilation via the production of a common culture and collective experience.[11] And, as Buck-Morss emphasizes, the potential power of this new collectivity was enormous, whether as a force of production, consumption, or politics.

Third, Buck-Morss points out the potential for manipulation in cinema. In an argument reminiscent of Guy Debord's critique of the society of the spectacle, she notes how both Hollywood and Soviet cinema "affirmed official culture and denied certain bleak realities of social development."[12] The former presented dream versions of commodity consumption. Monumental stars, awesome production numbers (Busby Berkeley) and special effects (*King Kong*), and luxurious lifestyles captivated Depression-era audiences and attempted to channel their desire toward fantasies of consumption. The latter idealized production. Although Soviet film in the 1920s continued the avant-garde experimentation of the revolutionary period (which was itself heavily influential in the United States) even as it imported Hollywood movies, by the 1930s, socialist realism and the glorification of collective projects was culturally dominant. The chief of Soiuzkino (Soviet Cinema), Boris Shumiatskii, rejected Soviet art cinema as overvaluing formalism and aesthetics. A better model for socialist realism could be found in Hollywood, which employed a factorylike model of artistic production and a realistic style of "joyful spectacles" accessible to the masses.[13] One of the most successful Soviet films of this period was *Chapaev*, an action movie about the defeat of the White Russians in the Civil War that out–cowboy-and-Indian-ed the Hollywood movies it was modeled on.

Finally, the fourth aspect of Buck-Morss's discussion of the role of film in the production and imagining of mass national identities important for my argument is the division between public and private spheres. Here the Soviet and U.S.-American cultural imaginaries are inversions of each other: the space that for one was a fantasized site of fulfillment was for the other a site of drudgery. "The forced intimacy of the communal apartment was a particular kind of terror affecting the most banal practices of every day," Buck-Morss explains. Insofar as public life under Stalinism was itself presented as the location of purpose and fulfillment, "there was no need for retreat into a private domain."[14] Conversely, in the United States, factory work generally appeared as a particularly brutal, humiliating kind of labor. Workers were subjected to control, subjection, the daily constraints and degradations of the assembly line. Rather than a source of fulfillment, industrial work was necessary drudgery. In return, workers received compensation in the form of consumption, enjoying consumer goods in the context of the love and warmth of the nuclear family. Buck-Morss writes, "the ideology of the private home came to bear a tremendous burden, that of legitimating the entire system of industrial capitalism, and nowhere more so than in the United States."[15]

6

What fantasies, what possibilities, what kinds of subjects, do multiply intersecting and increasingly personalized media and communication technologies stimulate? Differently put, how might changes from the media constitutive of projects of national utopian imagination lead in the direction of whatever beings? The pleasures of parallels with Buck-Morss's discussion of film and national mass identities suggest that answers might be found in at least four domains.

First, if mass media addressed society directly, organizing and speaking to masses as collectives, contemporary networked communications have multiple addressees—addressees known and unknown, friends and strangers. Bloggers may write for others who they imagine share their interests, a group of the uninformed they might enlighten, or future versions of themselves. The set of friends who receive my updates on Facebook, my network, are uniquely mine. Each user's network is different, even as they overlap and intersect. Blogs and social networks do not provide broadly shared symbolic identities from which we see ourselves. Blogs don't address society writ large. They invite singular readers to consider what they have on offer. Or they just make themselves available to be found by search engines' crawlers. Unlike mass media's calling of collectives, publics, and nations into being, blogs don't unite bloggers and readers. To this extent, they are more like pencils than cinema. They remain specific in their multiplicity.

Second, whereas mass media made crowds visible to themselves as a unity, providing the crowd with an imaginary collective body, networked communication and entertainment makes particularities visible to themselves as particularities. I can tweet my current location, update my friends on my current mood, check what's trending. With multiply convergent and turbulent media, I don't have to settle on any one direction or theme. I can live in the momentary. Not only do these multiple, circulating impulses incite in me a kind of permanent indecision or postponement, a lack of commitment—*what else is out there?*—but the fragmenting, networking thrust of drive turns my particular body, my very face into a montage: a wrinkle here, a bump there, a nose too large, lips too small. Fortunately, I can update my photo at any time—and I can animate it, too! There is no us. There is no me (although I can google myself to see if I turn up). Buck-Morss argues that "Cinema creates an imagined space where a mass body exists that can exist nowhere else."[16] My point is that blogs—standing in for the networked information and entertainment media of communicative capitalism—not only do not create such a space for a mass body but dissolve any sense of it. They dis-place it, producing instead ever-accelerating circuits of images, impulses, fragments, and feelings. Blogs cannot be counted; they resist inclusion into sets or categories. Yes, cinema still exists, and sometimes it lets us feel ourselves as something like an us—and then I can tweet about it. Blog-mapping projects attempt to make multiple disparate blogs appear as a sphere, a collective, as points in a shared space. But the space they map is in the imaginary of the researcher, not in bloggers' presence to themselves as a collective.

Third, the cinematic spectacles produced by Hollywood and the Soviet Union in the 1930s generally sought to affirm official culture and deny the grimmer aspects of economic and social life. In contrast, blogs persist in a setting of total mediality: anything can be found, said, seen on the Internet. With publicity as the ideology of communicative capitalism, everything can be said; nothing need be denied. Every aspect of contemporary life is reflected upon, criticized, mocked—and then the reflections, criticisms, and mockeries are themselves reflected upon, criticized, mocked... *did we go too far?* In this setting, nothing is unworthy of comment or commentary. Every aspect of the ordinary and everyday matters to someone—*for like a second*. Blogs say that whatever happens to me matters—in and of itself. And in this reflexive environment, even the fact that my posts are boring, that the arguments in my little segment of the blogipelago have an intensity far beyond merit, that the escapades of celebrities captured by TMZ are trivial, even all these facts are known and discussed. Most of the time, the repetitive intensities of blog drama are inversions of politics, rapidly circulating differences and modulations that ensure that nothing changes. Sometimes the intensities accumulate, "punctuated by catastrophic events, which are both creative and destructive."[17] Markets boom and bust; terrorists attack; a children's book becomes a global sensation. The circuits adjust and recalibrate, capturing the new again in the snares of communicative capitalism.

Fourth, just as the official myth of fulfillment through factory labor collapsed with the end of Stalinism (people didn't have to pretend anymore that it was true; they still had to go to work), the myth of idealized domesticity crumpled in the United States, in part because of the achievements of feminism, in part because the realities of divorce, infidelity, addiction, and abuse made its fantasy impossible to sustain. Television and feminism both made the personal political, erasing the fragile and imaginary boundaries between public and private, a line that made little sense after the rise of the social. In the remnants of the myth of idealized domesticity, ideals of individual freedom and creativity are promoted. Personal satisfaction takes the place of familial duty. Differently put, family life is supposed to be *personally* rewarding (rather than a duty or expectation). When family life fails to satisfy, it is examined and diagnosed, offered remedies and supplements—the family *better* succeed, because the brutal competition of neoliberalism offers neither shelter nor respite. Communicative capitalism provides the form and vehicle for the individualized consumption, participation, and creative needs expression of subjects compelled to be personally satisfied.

Correlative to the erasure of the always-tenuous distinction between the public and private spheres is the dissolution of the boundary between work and play.

From the initial electronics boom in the 1970s through the larger shifts associated with personal computers and the Internet, informatization has promised those who work with symbols and ideas increased ease and comfort. Early versions celebrated telecommuting and the paperless office. Later versions preyed on fears of being left behind, out of the loop, not as quick as the competition. Consultants urged corporations to restructure work, to encourage creativity and team building, to make work more like play. At the same time, with ever more games and interactions moving online, onto screens, play seemed a little more like work. In the circuits of communicative capitalism, the repetitions of drive suggest work without work (in the forms of work without pay or work that is fun) and play without play (in the forms of play for which one is paid and play for which one pays with enjoyment). This, then, is the setting wherein blogs are not escapes from the drudgery of part of one's life. They are not fantastic experiments in virtual reality. Rather, blogs instead extend out from, amplify, and reflect on whatever aspect of whatever life.

7

The change marked by the end of the Cold War has been tagged the end of ideology, the end of the Keynesian welfare state, the decline of the Fordist model of production, and the beginning of globalization, the information age, the network society, communicative capitalism. In their account of the new formation, Michael Hardt and Antonio Negri accentuate the passage from disciplinary society to the society of control. Focusing on the capitalist societies of the United States, the United Kingdom, and Europe, they point out how disciplinary logics worked primarily within the institutions of civil society to produce subjects. By the end of the twentieth century, these mediating institutions—the nuclear family, the prison, the school, the union, and the local church—were in crisis. The spaces, logics, practices, and norms previously coalescing into social and economic institutions have broken down and apart. Their efficacy is now indeterminate. In other words, in some instances, the release of an institutional logic from its spatial constraints has given it all the more force; in other instances, the opposite has occurred.

Corresponding to this pervasive dissolution and indeterminacy (which itself necessarily correlates with the economic changes of informatization and the ubiquitous spread of networked communications) is an "indeterminacy of the *form* of the subjectivities produced."[18] Hardt and Negri argue that the old political subject—the citizen-subject of an autonomous political sphere, the disciplined subject of civil society, the liberal subject willing to vote in public and then return home to his private domesticity—can no longer serve as a presupposition of theory or action. Racial, ethnic, and sexual identifications are similarly less fixed, less stable, less available as determinate subject positions. In their place, we find fluid, hybrid, and mobile subjectivities who are undisciplined, who have not internalized specific norms and constraints, and who can now only be controlled.

Put in psychoanalytic terms, symbolic identity is increasingly meaningless in the society of control. What we have instead are imaginary identities sustained by excess *jouissance*—that is, by an injunction to enjoy. More specifically, symbolic identity involves the subject's identification with an ego ideal—that is, with a perspective before whom the subject sees himself and his actions. Imaginary identification refers to the image that the subject adopts of himself. Symbolic identification, we might say, establishes the setting that determines which images appear and how it is that some are more compelling or attractive to us than others. Imaginary identification refers only to my self-image.

In disciplinary society, normative expectations coalesced around determinate social roles. Presuming the gaze of the school, church, family, or state, one could imagine oneself in different positions, positions that would either comply with or transgress institutional norms. I can be a conscientious student, faithful believer, dutiful daughter, good citizen. I can also be a delinquent, backsliding, worthless traitor. Even as the images differ, the symbolic identity of the gaze remains the same. In the wake of the decline of symbolic efficiency, the dissolution of disciplinary society, this gaze loses its prior force. We aren't sure if it's operative, if others believe it: is the good student a cog, uncreative, *thinking inside the box, a goody-two-shoes?* Does the Other actually admire and applaud transgression, and, if so, is it then more transgressive not to be transgressive since that's what the Other wants? Encountering the endless possibilities of contemporary reflexivity, postdisciplinary subjects are propelled to move through a variety of imaginary identities. We imagine ourselves one way, then another, never sure of how we appear because we don't know before whom we appear.

Lacking the ability to imagine how we appear to another, how another sees us, we lose the capacity to take the position of another, to see or think from another's perspective. We can choose any identity, but we lack the grounds for choosing or the sense that an identity, once chosen, entails bonds of obligation.[19] Rather than following norms—which ones? How do *they* know? Who made *them* the expert?—we cycle through trends, whether these come from fashion, diet advice, or the hope for an anchor in a particular subculture. The society of control places limits on the mobility and fluidity of contemporary hybrid identities, but these limits are not those installed by a master signifier or symbolic law. Subjects experience these limits as either groundless intrusions, irrational barriers to enjoyment, or as hypothetical or instrumental injunctions as means for achieving enjoyment later. Caught in reflexive networks—always another move, another level—we lose the capacity for reflection. Our networks are reflexive so that we don't have to be.

We are not bloggers. We are not Facebook. The networked interactions of communicative capitalism do not provide symbolic identities, sites from which we see ourselves as loci of collective action. Rather, they provide opportunities for new ways for me to imagine myself, a variety of lifestyles that I can try and try on. This variety and mutability makes my imaginary identity extremely vulnerable—the frames of reference that give it meaning and value are forever shifting; the others who can rupture it might appear at any moment, and their successes, their achievements, their capacities to enjoy call mine into question: *I could have had more; I could have really enjoyed.* This insecurity is not only psychic; it's a reasonable response to struggles to persist in global, reflexive financial and information networks. Most of the economic benefits of neoliberal capitalism—of the new economy celebrated by digital media gurus—follow a power-law distribution. A lucky few will get nearly everything. Most will get very little, almost nothing.

Hardt and Negri describe the ungovernable, mobile, and fluid singularities arising in the aftermath of disciplinary subjectivity in terms of an anthropological exodus. Hence, they emphasize that "those who are against" Empire's exploitation and domination "must also continually attempt to construct a new body and a new life."[20] Communicative capitalism facilitates and incites these attempts, employing ever-innovative upgrades to ensure not just that the attempts continue but that they accelerate. Hardt and Negri acknowledge that the methods of anthropological exodus are the methods of Empire. But they don't accept that their response is also Empire's: do more, go further, radicalize, create something new, make tools into prostheses, migrate and mutate into information technologies. They write, "The will to be against really needs a body that is completely incapable of submitting to command."[21] An undisciplined body incapable of submission is a body of immediacy and enjoyment, driven to move from image to image, intensity to intensity. Lacking discipline, how can it resist, how can it form a will at all? Far from constructing something new, such a body forecloses the possibility and hope of self-governance.

Networked media in the society of control amplify the challenge that post-Fordism poses to collective identity. Yes, they enable people to sign petitions. Yes, they enable people to give money. Yes, they enable people to express their opinions. Yes, *Obama had like a million Facebook friends.* But these particular motions of clicking and linking do not produce symbolic identities; they are ways that I express myself—just like shopping, checking my friends' updates, or following tabloid news at TMZ.com. I may imagine others like me, a virtual local, but this local remains one of those like me, my link list or followers, those who fit my demographic profile, my user habits. I don't have to posit a collective of others, others with whom I might need to cooperate or struggle, to whom I might be obliged, others who might place demands on me. The instant connection of networked association allows me to move on as soon as I am a little uncomfortable, a little put out. Petitions, social network groups (the one on Facebook that aims to get a million people to say they oppose capitalism has 24,672 members), blogs—they are the political equivalent of just-in-time production, quick responses circulating as contributions to the flows of communicative capitalism. In her compelling analysis of flash mobs, Cayley Sorochan takes the argument even further. Countering enthusiastic appropriations of flash mobs as new instances of democratic engagement, Sorochan presents them as instances of the "fetishizing of pure participation removed from any meaningful political project." She concludes, "Hopes that flash mobs might represent a future form of political organization reflect a desire for a politics of convenience where getting together with others is easy and does not involve conflict, commitment and struggle."[22] In the circuits of communicative capitalism, convenience trumps commitment.

8

Agamben affiliates whatever being with the capitalist commodification of the human body and the technologization of its image in the spectacle.[23] The photographic images proliferating out of advertising and pornography are "neither generic nor individual, neither an image of the divinity nor an animal form." In them, the body "now became something truly *whatever.*" The "whatever" Agamben invokes here suggests a new approach to Guy Debord's society of the spectacle, one that takes back from the spectacle the positive properties of being in language and being in common that it expropriates. For Agamben, whatever being is the mode of being in the coming community. Produced in capitalist spectacle, whatever being is harbinger of a better future, one wherein the division held together in the unity of the spectacle is ultimately overcome. Because he wants to wrest transformations of human nature from their entrapment in the spectacle, Agamben suggests the "geometrical splendor" of the legs of a long line of dancing girls.

Another way to think about the idea of "neither generic nor individual" is to link it to the normalizing, aggregating aspect of disciplinary power. Modern disciplinary institutions, be they home, school, factory, or state, produced individuals as types, as occupants of social roles or positions. Recall photographs of Levittown, of soldiers in training, of graduates in their caps and gowns. The self-governing, reflective subject idealized as the outcome of the disciplines may have understood himself to be an individual, but more than that, he was an instance of a form. Autonomy appeared through individuality.

Agamben associates the planetary petty bourgeoisie with a frustration with and impropriety toward identities rooted in physical particularities or differences in language, tradition, or culture. He concedes that fascism and Nazism had already recognized in the petty bourgeoisie the "decline of the old social subject."[24] He jumps quickly over their nationalism as a false popular identity, though, as he asserts a new planetary refusal of identity.

With this jump, Agamben omits the mass as a modern collective force that is also neither generic nor individual. The mass is a displaced mediator between the planetary bourgeoisie and whatever being. In Jean Baudrillard's formulation, "The mass is without attribute, predicate, quality, or reference."[25] Agamben's whatever beings appear as singularizations of the mass. Bereft of qualities of their own, they are not the same as the mass resolved into its components: masses were masses of subjects, combinations and aggregations and accumulations of people across and against modernity's attempts to separate and order them. If the mass results from a combination of bodies that omits their specificities, whatever being skips the step of amassing to treat the indistinction, the without-qualities, not as a result of belonging to the mass but as the condition of belonging as such.

Agamben's version of co-belonging inverts the political imaginary of radicals from the 1960s and 1970s: many feared erasure, being commodified, being indistinguishable, being one of a mass. They rejected the terms of mass society and mass media, the forced collectivizing of their self-perception into the envelope of "us." Agamben accepts the mass without its collective form, thereby reformatting the momentary joy of dissolution into a whole as the singularity of belonging. Whatever beings do not shed or overcome their identities in an experience of massness. They already lack them. They can simply be as they are. The mass is the missing link—displaced mediator—the function of which is a chiasmatic inversion of properties. Baudrillard writes, "Banality, inertia, apoliticism used to be fascist; they are in the process of becoming revolutionary—without changing meaning, without ceasing to have meaning."[26] Baudrillard's warning to leftists in the 1970s hits its target today: how is it that the evacuation of politics comes to embody the political as such?

Nevertheless, for Agamben, the petty bourgeoisie displace or stand in for the mass, presenting thereby a new opportunity, an opportunity for a form of belonging unhindered by the division and specificity of "belonging to." Agamben writes:

> Because if instead of continuing to search for a proper identity in the already improper and senseless form of individuality, humans were to succeed in belonging to this impropriety as such, in making of the proper being-thus not an identity and an individual property but a singularity without identity, a common and absolutely exposed singularity—if humans could, that is, not be-thus in this or that particular biography, but be only *the* thus, their singular exteriority and their face, then they would for the first time enter into a community without presuppositions and without subjects, into a communication with the incommunicable.[27]

We have been produced as subjects unlikely to coalesce, subjects resistant to solidarity and suspicious of collectivity. Central to this production is the cultivation and feeding of a sense of unique and special individuality. Every sperm is sacred: so began the story of our unique cellular lives. Or every potential genetic combination carries with it the remarkable potentiality we locate in our individuated selves. Each voice must be heard (but they don't combine into a chorus). Each vote must be counted (but they add up to less than a movement). Each person must be visible (but then we don't see a group). Personalized participatory media is a problem not only because of its personalization of participation. More than that is its injunction that we participate ever more in personalization: make your own avatar, video, profile, blog, mobster, video, app. Participation becomes indistinguishable from personalization, the continued cultivation of one's person. Leave your mark.

What would happen if we just stopped? Agamben's evocation of singularity and belonging detached from a compulsion to cultivate an individual identity or to identify with a specific group opens up the potential for another form of belonging, one unlimited by the divisions and restrictions of being this or that. He suggests, moreover, that the beings who would so belong are not subjects in the sense that European philosophy or psychoanalysis might theorize. If some sort of identity served as a locus of ethical personality, and the search for this identity has been configured as an important ethical task (perhaps, as some philosophers would have it, the task of each human life), then whatever beings would emerge as those who are not subject to such tasks. Unburdened by the obligations of being this or that, of being bound by choices or words or expectations of meaning, whatever beings could flow into and through community without presuppositions.

Agamben asks what the politics of whatever singularity could be, what sort of politics could accompany "a being whose community is mediated not by any condition of belonging (being red, being Italian, being Communist)...but by belonging itself."[28] Because the course of his exposition of whatever being takes him through Saint Thomas Aquinas and limbo as the habitat of the souls of unbaptized children, the political question seems particularly vexing. Those in limbo lack God, but they don't suffer from this lack; they know nothing of it: "Neither blessed like the elected, nor hopeless like the damned, they are infused with a joy with no outlet."[29] With limbo long synonymous with a certain stuckness, with an in-between condition of persistence that is neither here nor there, with an inability to go forward or back, it is difficult to register a politics that we might admire or seek.

More specifically, I can locate here neither a politics I admire nor any sort of struggle at all. What could motivate whatever beings? What might move them? As Agamben conceives them, they seek nothing, they lack nothing. They co-belong without struggle or antagonism. It would seem, then, that they are not political beings at all; their being is apolitical, beyond politics. They neither attack nor resist; they are neither inside nor outside. Perhaps it makes better sense, then, to think of the politics of whatever beings in terms of their setting. They are moved and propelled; they circuit through contemporary networks.

Souls in limbo belong in neither heaven nor hell. This condition of belonging to neither is limbo. It is also Agamben's model for a politics of absolute enmity toward the state. Agamben writes that "a being radically devoid of any representable identity would be absolutely irrelevant to the State."[30] And so the state or, better, states, would continue, unbothered and unlimited by the demands of people. States could attack and imprison, exploit and ignore—the future unfolding in and through militarized predatory robot drones. Whatever beings lack nothing and therefore demand nothing (and, presumably, they all get along just fine). No wonder they are irrelevant to the state. *The state can do what it wills. Whatever.*

For Agamben, however, rather than easing the way for unchecked state power, whatever being is the "principal enemy of the State." The state, he tells us, "cannot tolerate in any way... that the singularities form a community without affirming an identity, that humans co-belong without any representable condition of belonging."[31] Leaving to the side the question of whether this intolerance is a property of the state or a more complex matter of a human subjectivity that is constitutively split, it seems clear enough that the state has, from time to time, tolerated and used the mass, a form of co-belonging without representable condition. The mass can threaten or support the state, can subvert or sustain it. In Baudrillard's conception, for example, the mass is neither a group subject nor an object. On the one hand, the mass generally fails to become a conscious revolutionary force. On the other, it refuses attempts to make it speak. Surveys and statistics may simulate it, but the mass remains ungraspable, particularly as these very surveys are implicated in the reflexive constitution of the mass they survey. The absence of the mass, Baudrillard says, "is nevertheless intolerable."[32] It drives the repetitive processes of polling and testing. So not only can and has the state tolerated forms of co-belonging that do not affirm an identity, but the absence of an identity can itself generate processes of surveillance and incitement to speech useful for producing and maintaining power.

Agamben conceives the spectacle as language or communicativity. It is a form for the expropriation of linguistic being, a form that alienates people from language. He works here from the dilemma expressed by Debord: in the society of the spectacle, "the language of real communication has been lost," and a "new common language has yet to be found."[33] Debord writes:

> Spectacular consumption preserves the old culture in congealed form, going so far as to recuperate and rediffuse even its negative manifestations; in this way, the spectacle's cultural sector gives over expression to what the spectacle is implicitly in its totality—*the communication of the incommunicable.*[34]

Agamben's response is to turn the problem into the solution and in so doing find in the spectacle "a positive possibility that can be used against it."[35] Communication of the incommunicable dissolves the gap between them. It tells us that even the incommunicable can be communicated, that it cannot be separated. Thus, the spectacle as the extreme expression of estrangement from linguistic being enables its own overcoming. The expropriation of language in the spectacle opens up a new experience of language and linguistic being: "not this or that content of language, but language *itself*, not this or that true proposition, but the very fact that one speaks."[36] Failure to communicate provides its own satisfaction, the enjoyment of language itself.

Sigmund Freud describes the circular movement of the drives as a turning back round about the self and a change from activity to passivity.[37] Expressed in terms of language, the active aim, to say something, is replaced by the passive aim, to have said. Agamben's reflexive treatment of communication, his turn from *what is said* to *that something is said,* employs this dynamic of drive. Not only is a negative condition (estrangement from linguistic being) treated as a positive opening (new experience of belonging), but its positivity is a result of reflexivity. Language turns on *itself.* Whatever beings turn their attention from the content of language, from trying to communicate something, back to themselves as speaking beings. They shift from focusing on something outside or beyond themselves to turning back round upon themselves. Subjects of drive, whatever beings are passive. The very excesses of their communicative activity are the form of passivity.

9

Contemporary networked media perform and repeat communicativity as such, the taking place of language. As applications for the expression of any idea whatsoever, of an opinion, such that it is, blogs continue the severing of expressions from their content and their authors. Ideas and opinions link together and circulate, expressions of themselves neither completely generic nor completely individual. Posts may link and gesture, but they don't represent themselves or anything else. They are expressions, such that they are. The measuring and counting, the hits and rankings remind bloggers that we are set in intensive, reflexive communication and entertainment networks. It's as if the compulsion to make the mass speak, to poll and survey it, now takes whatever being as its target. Blog stats don't track truth or meaning. They track blogging, the addition of posts, responses, and page views. Differently put, they track the fact of the spoken as they direct us away from what is said.

A better instance of language without referent, of language that refers only to the "it was said," is the word cloud, a graphic representation of the content of a text understood in terms of frequency of word use. For example, a word cloud made after the first debate between presidential candidates John McCain and Barack Obama during the 2008 election shows that McCain frequently used the words *know, spending,* and *got.* Obama used the words *think, make,* and *going.* He also used the word *got* with high frequency. We don't know what this means. But we do know that words were used and speeches were made. The irony here is that language as language itself, language reflected to itself as language—Agamben's ideal of the coming community—takes the spectacular form of the image.

In word clouds, frequency and proximity displace meaning. Which words appear with which other words? The combination of these elements determines intensity—words that appear only once either don't count (they aren't counted) or they appear very faint and tiny, type as atmosphere. Words matter, not stories and not narratives. Words index communication—they mark that they are being communicated. Word clouds shift away from a space of linguistically constituted meaning, away from a language constituted out of sentences that are uttered in contexts according to rules that can be discerned and contested.

What's lost? The ability to distinguish between contestatory and hegemonic speech. Irony. Tonality. Normativity (how can there be an ethics of the address if the words are not part of an address, if they are extracted from their position within speech acts to become artifacts and toys?). Critique. The terms prominent in a discourse can be discerned, but not what they mean, not even in relation to each other. We don't know the rules governing truth and falsity, which may suggest that there are no rules (other than those of frequency, proximity, and duration). Note that frequency can be citational or monological—that is, it can come from circulation or from self-repetition. Message force multipliers are more important than the message. Word clouds capture the shift from message to contribution characteristic of communicative capitalism.

The word image of the word cloud is prefigured in avant-garde art from the late nineteenth and early twentieth centuries. Cubists included words as images. Even more disruptive were the posters from Russian communist and Soviet revolutionary artists. On the one hand, their word art was effective because of its revolutionary impulse, its challenge to the status quo of late Russian painting. It performed the revolution, disrupting prior meanings. On the other hand, precisely because it depended on its context for its performative efficacy, it reinforced the fact of symbolic meaning. Its disruption was not only to index language but to create a new one, to bring about a new world, a new man, a new register of meaning. The point wasn't to destroy meaning. It was to change it.

Word clouds aren't revolutionary. They are elements of communicative capitalism, elements that reinforce the collapse of meaning and argument and thus hinder argument and opposition. Any words can be clouded. At Wordle you can make a new one out of speeches from Kennedy and Khrushchev, Ann Coulter or Sean "Puffy" Combs. Anyone you like.

The word-cloud image doesn't stand in for or provide a prosthetic word. It marks a feeling, an intensity. It doesn't ask that the viewer understand it. All the viewer is expected to do is register that the word has been, that it has appeared. The word-become-image is a feeling-impulse, like a badge. It's identificatory, relying on an identity between word and object. The word image is this impulse identity.

One can't argue with a word cloud. It doesn't take a position. It marks a moment. It registers aspects of the intensity of that moment: repetition entails intensity in this equation. But one doesn't know why or whether it's called for or what it's in relation to. It's just intense. The word cloud might transmit the intensity, it might incite a feeling or a response, but it doesn't invite the interrogation of that response or what induced it. It offers representation without understanding: issues are out there. A word cloud is like a Möbius strip where meta-data becomes noise: "she said a lot about politics and technology." Whatever.

Notes

1 The Pew Internet and American Life Project reported on July 19, 2006, that the majority of U.S. bloggers (54%) are under thirty; Amanda Lenhart and Susanna Fox, "Bloggers: A Portrait of the Internet's New Storytellers," http://www.pewInternet.org/pdfs/

PIP%20Bloggers%20Report%20July%2019%202006.pdf. Pew reported on December 19, 2007, that "girls dominate the teen blogosphere; 35% of all online teen girls blog, compared with 20% of online teen boys"; Amanda Lenhart et al., "Teens and Social Media," http://www.pewInternet.org/pdfs/PIP_Teens_Social_Media_Final.pdf.

2 Lenhart and Fox, "Bloggers."

3 See Chuck Salter, "Girl Power," *Fast Company*, September 1, 2007, http://www.fast company.com/magazine/118/girl-power.html?page=0%2C0. See also www.whatever-life.com.

4 "State of the Blogosphere/2008," http://technorati.com/blogging/state-of-the-blogos phere/.

5 See also James Grimmelmann, "Saving Facebook," *Iowa Law Review* 94 (2009): 137–1206, http://works.bepress.com/james_grimmelmann/20/.

6 Dominic Pettman, *Love and Other Technologies* (New York: Fordham University Press, 2006), 9.

7 Giorgio Agamben, *The Coming Community*, translated by Michael Hardt (Minneapolis: University of Minnesota Press, 1993), 1.

8 Herman Melville, "Bartleby the Scrivener," was first published in *Putnam's Monthly Magazine* in 1853.

9 Susan Buck-Morss, *Dreamworld and Catastrophe* (Cambridge, MA: MIT Press, 2000), 140.

10 Buck-Morss, 147.

11 One significant study of film as a vehicle for assimilation is Michael Rogin, *Blackface, White Noise* (Berkeley: University of California Press, 1998).

12 Buck-Morss, 161.

13 Buck-Morss, 159.

14 Buck-Morss, 201.

15 Ibid.

16 Buck-Morss, 147.

17 Mark C. Taylor, *Confidence Games: Money and Markets in a World without Redemption* (Chicago: University of Chicago Press, 2004), 294.

18 Michael Hardt and Antonio Negri, *Empire* (Cambridge, MA: Harvard University Press, 2000), 197.

19 Zygmunt Bauman, *Liquid Love* (Cambridge: Polity Press, 2003), 50–1.

20 Hardt and Negri, 214.

21 Hardt and Negri, 216.

22 Cayley Sorochan, *Flash Mobs and Urban Gaming: Networked Performances in Urban Space.* Master's thesis, Department of Art History and Communication Studies, McGill University, Montreal.

23 Agamben, 47–8.

24 Agamben, 63.

25 Jean Baudrillard, *In the Shadow of Silent Majorities*, translated by Paul Foss, John Johston, Paul Patton, and Andrew Berardini (Los Angeles: Semiotext(e), 2007), 38.

26 Baudrillard, 61.

27 Agamben, 65.

28 Agamben, 85.

29 Agamben, 6.

30 Agamben, 85.

31 Agamben, 87.

32 Baudrillard, 56.

33 Guy Debord, *The Society of the Spectacle,* translated by Donald Nicholson-Smith (New York: Zone Books, 1999), 133.

34 Debord, 136 (emphasis in original).

35 Agamben, 80.

36 Agamben, 83.

37 Sigmund Freud, "Instincts and Their Vicissitudes," in *The Standard Edition of the Complete Psychological Works of Sigmund Freud,* Vol. 14 (1914–1916): *On the History of the Psycho-Analytic Movement, Papers on Metapsychology and Other Works,* ed. James Strachey (London: Hogarth Press, 1915), 109–40; 127.

PART III

The Violence of Participation

9

ESTRANGED FREE LABOR

Mark Andrejevic

It is hardly controversial these days to observe that one of the dominant business models for the online economy relies upon consumers' willing submission to increasingly detailed and comprehensive forms of monitoring. As the mainstream rightward-leaning *USA Today* put it, "The coolest stuff on the Internet actually comes at a notable price: your privacy."[1] And this price continues to grow thanks to the development of new frontiers for data mining ranging from start-ups mining the social web in real time to a host of mobile applications that collect data from users' smartphones and laptops.

If the ability to track online behavior started out as somewhat serendipitous—the by-product of the convenience afforded by a strand of code that allowed websites to remember previous visitors, now monitoring is being designed into the system. The entire app layer of interactive services, for example, provides as many new dimensions of computer monitoring as it does innovative conveniences. If you download an application for surfing or knitting, you have simultaneously joined a new demographic group for the purposes of target marketing. The more targeted or unique the service, the more detailed and unique the information about the user it provides. Even upgrades to the computer language (hypertext markup language, or HTML) that supports the web incorporate new capacities for online monitoring and tracking. As one press account noted,

> The new Web language and its additional features present more tracking opportunities because the technology uses a process in which large amounts of data can be collected and stored on the user's hard drive while online. Because of that process, advertisers and others could, experts say, see weeks or even months of personal data.[2]

These technological developments are complemented by the growth of online and mediated culture: the fact that large swaths of the population are conducting an increasing share of their social, professional, and personal lives on interactive platforms. It would be futile to attempt to catalogue the myriad forms of information that are collected about users; suffice it to say that pretty much anything one does using a smartphone or an Internet connection can and will be tracked, sorted, stored, and aggregated. Those dimensions of one's activity that are not yet captured by interactive devices soon will be, as interfaces become more sophisticated and multidimensional—eventually capable of recognizing (and thus recording) expressions, evaluating mood, monitoring vital signs, and tracking eye movements.

The ease with which this type of monitoring has insinuated itself into the digital media landscape is breathtaking, perhaps in part because of the novelty of the technology and its applications. The seductions of the convenience and gadgetry of the smartphone far outstrip concerns about its use as a sophisticated and multidimensional monitoring and tracking device. Transposed into a somewhat less novel landscape, the shift might appear more objectionable. The fact is, however, that the current embrace of commercial digital culture amounts to an unprecedented leap in the ability of institutions both public and private to collect, sort, and store information about members of the public. The flashy wizardry of new commercial technologies serves as a form of distraction or misdirection, averting or postponing direct engagement with the fact that we are constructing a culture in which commercial surveillance has become a crucial component of our communicative infrastructure. While the actual effects of this surveillance remain to be seen, it is worth pointing out that in developing a surveillance-based commercial infrastructure, we have effectively wagered on the prospect that it will prove effective in manipulating and channeling consumer behavior.

Privacy Issues

While it is true that popular culture portrayals of an emerging surveillance economy are starting to emerge—the *USA Today* article, for example, is headlined, "Online Tracking Takes a Scary Turn"—but they tend to frame the issue in terms of personal privacy. "As digital shadowing escalates," the article observes, "so too have concerns about the erosion of traditional notions of privacy."[3] Much of the discussion of online tracking has focused on the fate of privacy and the rights that pertain to it. This is an important set of issues, but it is complicated by the way in which it frames privacy in terms of personal choice (thereby dismissing challenges to the choices made by consumers as patronizing at best and at worst an affront to their personal freedom) and overlooks the way in which their information has become the *private* property of the commercial entities that do the work of harvesting it. It also tends to invoke the counterargument that there is little need for concern since many forms of monitoring that take place in interactive contexts are anonymous in the sense that the aggregators and their clients are not particularly interested in the personal identity of those monitored and do not personally inspect the details of their profiles (as if somehow the fact that no one is reading our personal e-mails means that there should be no cause for concern that they are being electronically scanned to determined how best to manipulate us). Privacy, in short, has a tendency to frame the discussion in personal, individual terms.

Because of the potential shortcomings of privacy as a means of addressing monitoring concerns, this chapter proposes an approach to the commercial use of personal information that draws on a notion more conducive to collective action and the recognition of the role played by social relations: that of exploitation. The notion of exploitation has long been used in Marxist-inflected critiques of capitalism to destabilize the very notion of free choice that underwrites the type of exchange described by *USA Today:* the process whereby, as individual consumers, we freely give up something of our own (our privacy—in the form of personal information) in exchange for something we desire or need. The "or" in this formulation is admittedly a vexed one—it might be argued that it makes all the difference in the world whether we are talking about need or desire, about livelihood or convenience. Perhaps—although the notion of what constitutes an acceptable standard of living (beyond some baseline notion of physical survival) is, as Marx, among others, has noted, a historically and culturally conditioned one.[4] While it is possible to mark the difference that separates sustenance from starvation, it is less easy to mark that which clearly delineates the boundary between need and desire.

This is not to dismiss the distinction outright, but rather to assert its socially conditioned character as a way of considering a similar issue that arises with the notion of exploitation. It is possible, as I will argue in the following pages, to make the case that the commercial appropriation of commercial information meets an abstract definition of exploitation, but to do so risks lumping together under the same name forms of brutal workplace exploitation with something that looks a lot more benign: people shopping or networking online. It is crucial to recognize the difference between types and levels of exploitation and to prioritize critical response accordingly—just as one might distinguish between different types of material deprivation. However, mobilizing the notion of exploitation raises questions about the social relations that characterize the online economy and their role in reproducing the privatization of productive resources, social and economic inequality, and resulting forms of alienation.

Exploitation and Free Labor

Although forms of online activity that take place beyond the workplace proper do not fall within the realm of wage labor, they can nevertheless generate value. Because the capture of personal information is used to create targeted marketing campaigns, the online marketing model has created a market in feedback commodities. In some cases, this information is used directly by interactive companies to customize advertising; in others, it is bought and sold to marketers. As the *Wall Street Journal's* investigative report on data mining put it in a description of a company that profiles Internet users, "tastes can be sold wholesale (a batch of movie lovers is $1 per thousand) or customized (26-year-old Southern fans of *50*

First Dates)."[5] Even when information is not directly bought or sold, the interactive economy relies on the capture of the value generated by users whose contributions help build the economic value of social media services such as Facebook or, earlier on, Internet portals such as America Online.

The value of activity captured by interactive platforms has generated a growing literature on the exploitation of so-called free labor. In what has become a canonical discussion of the labor provided by chat room moderators in exchange for access to online services, Tiziana Terranova notes that such productive activities can, in some contexts, be described as both voluntary and subject to exploitation: "Free labor is the moment where this knowledgeable consumption of culture is translated into productive activities that are pleasurably embraced and at the same time often shamelessly exploited."[6] Similarly, Michael Hardt's discussion of the network economy notes that, "in those networks of culture and communication, collective subjectivities are produced and sociality is produced—even if those subjectivities and that sociality are directly exploitable by capital."[7] Petersen's (2008) account of the exploitation of user-generated content argues that the commercial "architecture of participation turns into an architecture of exploitation and enclosure, transforming users into commodities that can be sold on the market."[8]

For Ritzer and Jurgensen (2010), the capture of value online represents the extension of the logic of capital into new spaces and temporalities: "it appears that capitalists have found another group of people—beyond workers (producers)—to exploit and a new source of surplus value. In this case, capitalism has merely done what it has always done—found yet another way to expand."[9] For Comor, forms of interactive participation reinforce rather than revolutionize the social relations upon which exploitation relies: "as long as private property, contracts and exchange values are dominant mediators of our political economy, disparities and exploitative relationships will remain largely unchallenged—unchallenged, at least, through the auspices of presumption."[10]

The notion of exploitation, in short, has become a recurring theme in recent accounts of the productivity of networks. Most of these critiques refer to the conscious productive activity of users beyond the confines of the workplace proper—activity such as fan labor, chat room moderation, and the creation of user-generated content—that users engage in voluntarily but that also generates value for commercial entities that are able to piggyback on user activity (for more on fan labor, see Abigail De Kosnik's chapter in this volume). The tendency has been to locate this kind of creative activity in the category of immaterial labor described by Lazzarato as the "activity that produces the 'cultural content' of the commodity," noting that it "involves a series of activities that are not normally recognized as 'work'—in other words, the kinds of activities involved in defining and fixing cultural and artistic standards, fashions, tastes, consumer norms, and, more strategically, public opinion."[11]

However, it might be useful to distinguish between some of these different forms of value generation—including users' active participation in marketing to themselves, the appropriation of user-generated content, and the capture of information that can be turned back upon users. This is not to say that any of these categories are exempt from exploitation, but rather to argue that we might need to think a bit differently about how exploitation functions in these varying instances.

One of the challenges of mobilizing the notion of exploitation in online contexts is that it takes a critical concept traditionally associated with industrial labor's sweatshop conditions and transposes it into a realm of relative affluence and prosperity—that is, a realm inhabited by those with the time and access to participate in online activities. For good reason, it is harder to get worked up about the allegedly exploitative conditions of user-generated content sites than about the depredations of sweatshop labor and workforce exploitation. In the case of user-generated content, we are talking in many cases about affluent consumers engaging in what might be described as optional activities: you don't *have* to join Facebook or Twitter, it is not necessary for survival in contemporary society (yet?) to get a Gmail account or to shop online.

Thus, rejoinders to critiques of exploitation in such contexts typically invoke both the lack of coercion and the pleasures of participation. As Nancy Baym and Robert Burnett (2008) put it in their account of the promotional work done by indie music fans: "We are loath to dismiss their claims of affective pleasure and the desire they feel to spread what brings them joy as evidence of exploitation."[12] Their study invokes the claim, so familiar to accounts of the promise of interactive technology, that the fans' activities recapture the pleasures of pre–mass society: "Their social response to the pleasures of music is situated in deeply meaningful social phenomena that hearken back to much earlier phases of musical history, phases before there was an industry, when music was always performed in communities by locals for locals rather than by distant celebrities for adoring fans."[13] Such forms of enjoyment are, then, allegedly, incompatible with the notion that fans are being exploited: "To claim that these people are exploited is to ignore how much these other forms of capital matter in the well being of well rounded humans."[14]

It is not clear, however, that the Marxist-inflected critiques of exploitation invoked by such accounts are incompatible with a sense of enjoyment or pleasure. The fact of exploitation need not prevent workers from taking pleasure in their craft or in the success of a collaborative effort well done. Nor is it the case that accounts of exploitation necessarily denigrate the activities or the meanings they may have for those who participate in them rather than the social relations that underwrite expropriation and alienation. The point of a critique of exploitation is neither to disparage the pleasures of workers nor the value of the tasks being undertaken. To argue otherwise is to stumble into a kind of category confusion: an attempt to reframe structural conditions as questions of individual pleasure and desire. The critique of exploitation does not devalue individual pleasure any more than such pleasures nullify exploitative social relations. More work needs to be done to define what might be meant by exploitation in nonwage labor contexts to bolster the critique of exploitation in the digital economy and to address the way in which it is so often dismissed (for failing to acknowledge the benefits and pleasures received by those engaged in various forms of free labor).

Digital Alienation

To what extent can analytic definitions of exploitation be applied to unwaged forms of participation that generate value appropriated by those who control the platforms upon which this participation relies? Holmstrom offers a clear summary of a Marxist conception of exploitation: "The profits of capitalists, then, according to Marx's theory, are generated by surplus, unpaid and forced labor, the product of which the producers do not control."[15] Central to such an account is the notion that coercion is embedded in the relations that structure so-called free choices. That is to say, coercion does not require someone standing over the worker with a gun or some other threat of force. The further point to be made is that exploitation is not simply about profit, but also alienation. As Holmstrom puts it, "what workers really sell to the capitalists, according to Marx, is not labor, but the capacity to labor or labor power, which capitalists then use as they wish for the day."[16] Alienation subsists not just in the surrender of conscious control over productive activity, but also, consequently, in its product. Exploitation, then, is not simply about a loss of monetary value, but also a loss of control over one's productive and creative activity. To push a bit further, it is the latter sense of exploitation that drives the critique, insofar as the deprivation of economic resources, in the end, is about reproducing the forms of scarcity that compel freely given submission.

In his critique of attempts to apply the notion of exploitation to free labor, David Hesmondhalgh invokes Erik Olin Wright's formulation of the three principles that define a Marxist understanding of exploitation:

> First, exploitation occurs when the material welfare of one class is causally dependent upon the material deprivation of another. The capitalist class in modern societies could not exist without the deprivations of the working classes. Second, that causal dependence depends in turn on the exclusion of workers from key productive resources, especially property. Third, the mechanism through which both these features (causal dependence and exclusion) operate is appropriation of the labor of the exploited.[17]

Although Hesmondhalgh might disagree, I would argue that this definition highlights crucial aspects of the emerging online economy, perhaps most significantly the privatization of the infrastructure for new forms of creativity, communication, and information sharing. One of the things that is not at all new about digital media is the way in which it reproduces the logic of private ownership of productive resources. Even as it fosters new forms of creativity and participation, it does so on privately owned and controlled commercial platforms such as Facebook and YouTube.

Many sites are not commercially controlled, but they still rely on the commercial infrastructure of the Internet—one that is likely to become even more tightly administered as the technology for inspecting data that passes through private servers and routers continues to develop. Even in the world of bits and bytes, matter still matters—as does ownership and control of material resources. It's a bit of instrumental fiction to assert along with futurists such as Esther Dyson and Alvin Toffler that,

> The central event of the 20th century is the overthrow of matter. In technology, economics, and the politics of nations, wealth—in the form of physical resources—has been losing value and significance. The powers of mind are everywhere ascendant over the brute force of things.[18]

This is the digital ideology that masks the material infrastructure that supports the production and distribution of the fruits of the "powers of mind."

A critique of the exploitation of free labor, then, would highlight the very real ways in which control of new productive resources is concentrated in the hands of the few, allowing them to appropriate and profit from the activity of the many who must surrender their personal information to secure access to the productive and informational resources of the digital era.

I suspect the sticking point for Hesmondhalgh would be the first element of Wright's formula: in particular, the "material deprivation" of the many. It is certainly possible to argue that lumping together the capture of personal data with other more physically severe forms of exploitation like sweatshop labor risks sensationalizing the former and trivializing the latter. It is also possible, however, to argue that, even though the effects in terms of immiseration are vastly different, there are structural, analytic similarities and, further, that this similarity cuts across and links capitalist class relations in ways that warrant concern and intervention in the name of social justice. The privatization and commercialization of the Internet is a form of material deprivation and enclosure insofar as it separates users from the infrastructure that supports their communicative activities. It reinforces and reproduces the structure of social relations wherein a small group controls the productive resources used by the many and allows economic advantages to accrue from this control. The ownership class that includes the founders of Facebook, Google, Yahoo, and so on could not exist without capturing and controlling components of the productive infrastructure. The value that they appropriate stems in large part from their ability to capture aspects of the activity of those who access their resources, and their ability to do so is directly related to their ownership and control of these resources. Bluntly put, the ability to exploit this activity for commercial purposes for the economic benefit of the few would disappear if these resources were commonly owned and controlled.

The obvious objection is that going online to converse, shop, explore, and network is clearly not a form of wage labor, even if people are in a sense compensated with free access to useful resources in exchange for submitting to detailed forms of value-generating monitoring. This activity is not a job (at least not for most of those who go online): they are not submitting their activity to the direct dictates of a supervisor, and they are not receiving wages. Exploitation can clearly take place in the absence of wages, but does it retain any meaning in a context in which users do not sacrifice control over their productive activity? The question is potentially misleading insofar as the digital environment facilitates what might be described as a redoubling of creative or productive activity. When we create a blog or post an item on Facebook or even purchase an item or view a web page, we do so in ways that are, in many cases, unsupervised and minimally controlled. At the same time, however, we generate information about our activities over which we sacrifice control in exchange for access to the infrastructure and the services it supports. In a sense, then, we lose control over some aspects of our online productivity even when this remains free from familiar forms of oversight and control.

Just as we sacrifice a degree of control over the use of our productive activity when we enter into a workspace, so too do we sacrifice a degree of control over how our activity is used when we agree to the terms of service for a particular website or online service (or even when we browse the Internet, which collects information about our activities without notifying us). Those who control the means of online sociability have the power to set the terms of access, and these terms include the establishment of certain rights over the information provided by users—rights that tend to be outlined in cursory, often incomprehensible and qualified fashion. Separation (the private control over online resources for sociability) begets separation (the establishment of rights of use over information generated by users). The various "terms of use" and end-user license agreements posted by social networking sites establish their rights over the use, sale, and transfer of information collected online.

That is to say, forms of socializing, interacting, and transacting that once relied upon other resources, as well as new forms of sociability, are increasingly dependent upon an infrastructure provided by a third party. This is not to say that the introduction of a third party is entirely novel. Certainly the phone company, for example, served as a for-profit intermediary (although not an advertising-supported one). In the current context, rather, we can identify an increasing tendency toward the use of a commercially supported mediated infrastructure for a growing range of activities: the replacement, for example, of a cash purchase in a store by an online purchase; the tendency to text a friend or a colleague in the next dorm room or office instead of knocking on his or her door; as well as the creation of new forms of sociality that are integrally tied to developing commercial infrastructures (such as "friend-ing" someone on Facebook), and so on. When we are separated from the means of socialization, this does not mean we do not have access to them; rather, we come to rely upon the provision by their parties of technologies for socialization that separate us from the information upon which our social lives rely. Crucial resources for interaction are no longer in our own hands (at least to the extent that they once were), but are stored in servers owned and controlled by commercial entities.

We do not have to go far to figure out *why* people are so willing to use such sites: they provide a ready, convenient, and entertaining way of enriching, extending, and preserving our connections with others. What requires a bit more explanation is how we might discern, in a voluntary and rewarding activity, the traces of exploitation. The result of the form of separation facilitated by Facebook is not the dispossession of users, but rather the alienability of the product of their online social activity: the fact that the fruits of this activity can become a resource whose uses range far beyond their control. Or, given that the extraction of the value of information gathered about users relies on the same logic of resource enclosure and the consequent asymmetry of power relations that structure the "freely" agreed-upon surrender of control over personal information, the more salient question is why should we care?

The notion of exploitation is meant to invoke questions of social justice. From a Marxian-inflected critical perspective, the charge of exploitation is both a term of critique and a call to action: exploitation is, as Holmstrom puts it, "evil" because it "involves force and domination in manifold ways and because it deprives workers of control that should be theirs."[19] The force is not often directly manifested in the compulsion to surrender control over one's labor power, but is built into asymmetrical social relations and manifests itself overtly when these are challenged. Likewise, the privatization and commercialization of much of the digital media infrastructure does not take place by force, but merely reproduces existing property relations by extending them into the digital realm. The background of compulsion is built into the legal structure and regulatory regimes that enable the privatization process. We might note the indirect effects of compulsion by positing that, given the choice, users are more likely to prefer not having to submit to comprehensive forms of monitoring in order to access online and networked resources, as suggested by recent surveys that indicate opposition to monitoring-based profiling and high levels of concern about online information collection.[20] They do not freely choose to exchange their personal information for convenience but do so under conditions structured by the private ownership of network resources and the attendant low level of awareness about actual tracking practices. If what concerns us about workplace exploitation is both the forms of compulsion that underwrite it and the toll it takes on workers in terms of physical immiseration (exhaustion and worse) and loss of control over their creative activity (what Holmstrom calls alienation), do these concerns carry over into critiques of the exploitation of free labor? Here we might note a distinction—free labor does not carry with it the same physical toll as some forms of workplace exploitation, not least because users can stop when they wish without threat of losing their job (at least in some contexts). However, they do lose control of aspects of their productive activity in ways that are, in the terms suggested by the critique of alienation, turned back upon them. The goal of comprehensive surveillance is to discover those levers that allow marketers to channel consumer behavior according to commercial imperatives—to relegate the consumer to the role of feedback mechanism in an accelerating cycle of production and consumption. As the founder of cybernetics put it in an embittered paean to the power of feedback-based marketing:

> A certain precise mixture of religion, pornography, and pseudo-science will sell an illustrated newspaper... To determine these, we have our machinery of fan-ratings, straw votes, opinion samplings and other psychological investigations with the common man as their object.... Luckily for us, these merchants of lies, these exploiters of gullibility have not yet arrived at such a pitch of perfection as to have things all their own way.[21]

The goal of marketers and other exploiters of gullibility is, of course, to realize the implicit threat in Wiener's formulation: to overcome the "not *yet*."

In more concrete terms, the goal of marketers is, as Ian Ayres puts it in his book on data mining, to "predict what you will want and what you will do"—even when you yourself do not know or are unsure.[22] This does not mean predicting some kind of inevitable future; it means learning how to manipulate conditions, appeals, and contexts in order to yield a desired behavior or action. It means using the detailed information gathered about people to accelerate and channel the consumption process. It is only about serving consumers better if that means getting them to believe that they must consume more copiously and expeditiously. The goal is to determine what triggers are most effective in stimulating consumer behavior as well as how to get around the reservations and concerns that might forestall consumption. It is to discover what appeals—whether to one's insecurities, one's anxieties and health concerns—are most effective in driving behavior, and what subconscious factors might influence behavior without consumers realizing what is taking place.

To the extent that consumers participate in generating the information that feeds into the manipulation process, we might level the charge of exploitation to highlight the way in which the capture of personal information turns our own activity against ourselves. Marx describes this as estrangement or alienation:

> The *alienation* of the worker in his product means not only that his labor becomes an object, an *external* existence, but that it exists *outside him,* independently, as something alien to him, and that it becomes a power on its own confronting him. It means that the life which he has conferred on the object confronts him as something hostile and alien.[23]

Although Marx is here talking about the product of wage labor in the context of capitalist social relations, it is a formulation that illuminates the trajectory of information commodities generated by consumers and then turned back upon them for the purposes of manipulating their actions and desires.

The alienated world envisioned by interactive marketers is one in which all of our actions (and the ways in which they are aggregated and sorted) are systematically turned back upon us. It is, in the end, a disturbing vision: an informationalized world in which the very atmosphere through which we move has become privatized and commercialized. Every message we write, every video we post, every item we buy or view, our time-space paths and patterns of social interaction all become data points in algorithms for sorting, predicting, and managing our behavior. Some of these data points are spontaneous, the result of the intentional action of consumers; others are induced, the result of ongoing, randomized experiments. The complexity of the algorithm and the opacity of correlation render it all but impossible for those without access to the databases to determine why they may have been denied a loan, targeted for a particular political campaign message, or saturated with ads at a particular time and place when they have been revealed to be most vulnerable to marketing. Much will hinge on whether the power to predict can be translated into the ability to manage behavior, but this is the bet that marketers are making. Or, more accurately, this is the bet that a society makes when it turns to a monitoring-based system of data mining and predictive analytics as a means for supporting its information and communication infrastructure.

In part, the question of whether exploitation applies to forms of free labor hinges on an attempt to hold separate the realms of leisure, consumption, and domesticity from the workplace proper. Marx's critique of capitalism emerged within the context of a distinctly modern realm of differentiation. The development of wage labor relied on maintaining a clear distinction between the workplace and other realms of social life—not least for the purposes of surveillance and monitoring. Interactive digital technologies facilitate forms of de-differentiation that challenge this clear-cut distinction: we can work from home and socialize in our workplaces, thanks to mobile phones, text messaging, portable computers, and so on. At the same time, the cultural and economic shifts associated with the development of so-called immaterial labor capitalize on the capture of activities that blur clear-cut distinctions between realms of leisure, labor, and domesticity. As Terranova puts it, quoting Toni Negri: "The 'social factory' describes a process whereby 'work processes have shifted from the factory to society, thereby setting in motion a truly complex machine.'"[24] When we help build the value of Facebook with work we do at home, while on the train, or on the beach, we are participating in this social factory.

At the same time, the line between online creativity and the workplace proper is becoming much less clear in many professional contexts. Academics, politicians, and TV producers alike are encouraged to blog, send tweets, and network online to promote themselves and their work. A researcher who studies public broadcasting recently told me that whereas once upon a time television producers put their work in "the can" and could then be elsewhere when it aired, now they are expected to be online, following the online discussion and posting tweets in response to viewer comments when their programs air.

In some cases, the obligation to network online is becoming institutionalized and recognized as a potential source of value. Consider, for example, the development of applications that allow employers to capitalize on contacts harvested from their employees' social networks. The press release for a company called Appirio, for example, outlines the triple value of employee social networking data as a resource for recruiting, sales, and marketing—all of this without having to pay employees extra for providing the data. Appirio's marketing application piggybacks on Facebook to increase the size of a company's "virtual account team" by leveraging relationships that employees might already have:

> The employee can see if a friend has become a lead, bought a product, attended an event...etc. If the employee chooses they can contact their friend through Facebook to make a connection and ultimately help contribute to their company's bottom line (and maybe even their own bonus!).[25]

The same data that can provide leads for potential hires and clients serve treble duty by providing data for targeted marketing appeals: "Based on a search of keywords in friend profiles, the application makes recommendations of friends who might be interested in the offer, which users can then choose to take action on."[26] The application links data from the social networks of individual employees with a proprietary consumer relationship marketing database in order "to track leads, make follow-up offers, and report on campaign success to see how their viral campaigns stack up to other marketing programs."[27]

The future envisioned by such applications is one in which online activities serve as multiple sources of value for employers who seek to capture and monetize the value created by the after-work activities of their employees as well as by commercial entities that harvest detailed personal information online. There is double logic of appropriation at work in this scenario: private ownership of workplace resources and private ownership of communication resources are both used to extract value from activities that take place beyond the workplace. The type of concessions that employers can extract from employees is part of the ongoing struggle over wage labor contracts conditioned by asymmetric control of productive resources. Appirio envisions a future in which submission of one's social network to workplace priorities becomes one of the conditions of earning one's livelihood.

If, as Hesmondhalgh argues, the notion of exploitation is an explanatory concept as well as a historical and analytical one, it is tempting to note the way in which it helps account for the forms of anticipated productivity that characterize the digital economy. The value accruing to the privatization of network resources is, at least in part, dependent upon the ability to extract productive data from users—data that can serve as a resource for advertisers, employers, political campaigns, and policing. Unlike more material commodities, there is no clearly defined saturation point for the consumption of data—as long as automated systems can be developed for sorting and processing it. Individual humans may be limited in their ability to absorb data, but not databases. Nor is there a clear limit on the amount of information that can be extracted, which grows along with the opportunities for interaction, transaction, and communication—even as the cost of data collection continues to drop. It is the anticipated productivity of data collection and mining that serves as justification—at least in some quarters—for refusing to regulate it more aggressively. The threat from companies that prefer so-called self-regulation is that enhanced privacy legislation will put a check on the growing online economy. This threat was invoked by a privacy attorney who claimed that proposals to require websites to include a do-not-track option "may lead to the Internet economy—one of the few economic bright spots—being shackled."[28]

Privacy-based critiques do not quite capture the element of productive power and control at work in the promise of monitoring-based marketing. If privacy violations constitute an invasion—a loss of control over the process of self-disclosure—market monitoring includes an additional element of control and management: the systematic use of personal information to predict and influence. The critique of exploitation addresses this element of power and control. Defenders of market monitoring will argue that individual consumer behavior remains uncoerced. Critical approaches, however, locate coercion not solely at the level of discrete individual decisions, but also in the social relations that structure them. In this regard, the invocation of the notion of exploitation parallels Jonathan Beller's claim in his contribution to this volume that, "an interest in labor should force us to rethink the logistics of media platforms and see them as technologies formed in the struggle between labor and capital and thus by and for the expropriation of labor."

Given the difference between post-Fordist forms of productive consumption and industrial modes of production, a critical approach to exploitation needs to be revisited. This chapter argues for the importance of considering how the components of exploitation (the capture of unpaid surplus labor, coercion, and alienation) operate within the context of technologically facilitated forms of commercial surveillance. While these components are interconnected—alienation, for example, implies the existence of background forms of coercion—they appear in different configurations in the realms of consumer productivity or immaterial forms of collective, social labor. Some critics focus on the element of unpaid labor, others on the element of alienation. The challenge is to think these together against the background of the coercion embedded in relations of control over communication resources and the forms of productive surveillance it facilitates.

Mobilizing the Critique of Exploitation

The potential usefulness of an exploitation-based critique of online monitoring is that it invites us to reframe questions of individual choice and personal pleasure in terms of social relations. In abstract analytic terms, there are structural similarities between the extraction of value in the wage labor exchange and in the convenience-for-personal-information exchange. Both rely on the private enclosure of productive resources to structure the surrender of control over aspects of productive activity. In both cases, this surrender of control returns in the form of alienation—the misrecognition of one's own participation in the very forces that seem to come from elsewhere. Both contribute to the generation of wealth for those who own and control the productive resources. In more concrete terms, exploitation in the social factory looks very different from that in the actual one. It is the sign of a certain kind of material luxury to be able to be exploited online—to have the leisure time and resources to engage in the activities that are monitored and tracked. Both highlight different ways in which the potential of individual and social life is diminished—in which the productive capacities developed by society fall short of their promise of an unalienated existence. The point of running them alongside one another is not to diminish the brutality of the exploitation of industrial capitalism but to add depth and urgency to the critique of exploitation in the emerging information economy.

Notes

1 Byron Acohido, "Online Tracking Takes a Scary Turn," *USA Today,* August 4, 2011, B1.

2 Tanzina Vega, "New Web Code Draws Concern over Privacy Risks," *The New York Times,* October 10, 2010, A1.

3 Acohido, "Online Tracking," B1.

4 Karl Marx, *The Economic and Philosophic Manuscripts of 1844,* http://www.marxists.org/archive/marx/works/1844/manuscripts/preface.htm.

5 Julia Angwin, "The Web's New Gold Mine: Your Secrets," *The Wall Street Journal,* July 30, 2010, http://online.wsj.com/article/SB10001424052748703940090457539507351 2989404.html.

6 Tiziana Terranova, "Free Labor: Producing Culture for the Digital Economy," *Social Text* 63, no. 18 (2000): 37.

7 Michael Hardt, "Affective Labor," *Boundary* 2, no. 26 (1999): 93.

8 Søren Petersen, "Loser Generated Content: From Participation to Exploitation," *First Monday* 13, no. 3 (2008), http://firstmonday.org/htbin/cgiwrap/bin/ojs/index.php/fm/article/viewArticle/2141/1948.

9 George Ritzer and Nathan Jurgenson, "Production, Consumption, Prosumption: The Nature of Capitalism in the Age of the Digital 'Prosumer,'" *Journal of Consumer Culture* 10, no. 1 (2010): 21.

10 Edward Comor, "Contextualizing and Critiquing the Fantastic Prosumer: Power, Alienation and Hegemony," *Critical Sociology* 9, no. 16 (2010): 14.

11 Maurizio Lazzarato, "Immaterial Labor," in *Radical Thought in Italy: A Potential Politics,* eds. Paulo Virno and Michael Hardt (Minneapolis: University of Minnesota Press, 1997), 137.

12 Nancy Baym and Robert Burnett, "Amateur Experts: International Fan Labor in Swedish Independent Music," Paper prepared for the Internet Research 9.0 conference, Copenhagen, Denmark, October 2008, 23.

13 Baym and Burnett, "Amateur Experts," 23.

14 Baym and Burnett, "Amateur Experts," 23.

15 Nancy Holmstrom, "Exploitation," in *Exploitation: Key Concepts in Critical Theory*, eds. Kai Nielsen and Robert Ware (Atlantic Highlands, NJ: Humanities Press International, 1997), 80.

16 Holmstrom, "Exploitation," 79.

17 David Hesmondhalgh, "User-Generated Content, Free Labor and the Cultural Industries," *Ephemera* 10, no. 3/4 (2010): 274. Hesmondhalgh here relies on Erik Olin Wright, *Class Counts: Comparative Studies in Class Analysis* (Cambridge: University of Cambridge Press, 1997).

18 Esther Dyson et al., "Cyberspace and the American Dream: A Magna Carta for the Knowledge Age," *The Information Society* 12, no. 3 (1996): 295.

19 Holmstrom, "Exploitation," 89.

20 See, for example, Joseph Turow, Deidre K. Mulligan, and Chris Jay Hoofnagle, "Research Report: Consumers Fundamentally Misunderstand the Online Advertising Marketplace," University of Pennsylvania Annenberg School for Communication and UC Berkeley Law Samuelson Law, Technology & Public Policy Clinic, October 2007, http://www.law.berkeley.edu/files/annenberg_samuelson_advertising.pdf; and Joseph Turow et al., "Contrary to What Marketers Say, Consumers Reject Tailored Advertising and Three Activities That Enable It," 2010, http://papers.ssrn.com/sol3/papers.cfm?abstract_id=1478214.

21 Norbert Wiener, *The Human Use of Human Beings: Cybernetics and Society* (Boston: Houghton Mifflin, 1954), 185.

22 Ian Ayres, *Super Crunchers: How Anything Can Be Predicted* (London: John Murray, 2007), 44.

23 Karl Marx, *The Economic and Philosophic Manuscripts of 1844*, http://www.marxists.org/archive/marx/works/1844/manuscripts/preface.htm.

24 Terranova, "Free Labor"; the internal quotes refer to Toni Negri, *The Politics of Subversion: A Manifesto for the Twenty-first Century* (Cambridge: Polity Press, 1989).

25 Appirio, "Appirio Referral Management Solution Connects Social Networks with Business Applications to Encourage, Manage and Measure Word-of-Mouth Referrals," February 2, 2009, http://press.appirio.com/2009/02/appirio-referral-management-solution.html. Note that the only compensation for the employee's "voluntary" participation is a *potential* bonus.

26 Appirio, "Appirio Referral Management Solution."

27 Appirio, "Appirio Referral Management Solution."

28 Acohido, "Online Tracking," B2.

References

Acohido, Byron. "Online Tracking Takes a Scary Turn." *USA Today*, August 4, 2011, B1–B2.

Angwin, Julia. "The Web's New Gold Mine: Your Secrets," *The Wall Street Journal*, July 30, 2010, http://online.wsj.com/article/SB10001424052748703940904575395073512989404.html.

Appirio. "Appirio Referral Management Solution Connects Social Networks with Business Applications to Encourage, Manage and Measure Word-of-Mouth Referrals." Press release, February 2, 2009, http://press.appirio.com/2009/02/appirio-referral-management-solution.html.

Ayres, Ian, *Super Crunchers: How Anything Can Be Predicted*. London: John Murray, 2007.

Baym, Nancy, and Robert Burnett. "Amateur Experts: International Fan Labor in Swedish Independent Music." Paper prepared for the Internet Research 9.0 conference, Copenhagen, Denmark, October 2008.

Comor, Edward. "Contextualizing and Critiquing the Fantastic Prosumer: Power, Alienation and Hegemony." *Critical Sociology* 9, no. 16 (2010): 1–19.

Dyson Esther, et al. "Cyberspace and the American Dream: A Magna Carta for the Knowledge Age." *The Information Society* 12, no. 3 (1996): 295–308.

Hardt, Michael. "Affective Labor." *Boundary* 2, no. 26 (1999): 89–100.

Hesmondhalgh, David. "User-Generated Content, Free Labour and the Cultural Industries." *Ephemera* 10, no. 3/4 (2010): 267–84.

Holmstrom, Nancy. "Exploitation." In *Exploitation: Key Concepts in Critical Theory*, eds. Kai Nielsen and Robert Ware, 81–102. Atlantic Highlands, NJ: Humanities Press International, 1997.

Lazzarato, Maurizio. "Immaterial Labour." In *Radical Thought in Italy: A Potential Politics*, eds. Paulo Virno and Michael Hardt, 133–50. Minneapolis: University of Minnesota Press, 1997.

Marx, Karl. *The Economic and Philosophic Manuscripts of 1844*, http://www.marxists.org/archive/marx/works/1844/manuscripts/preface.htm.

Negri, Toni. *The Politics of Subversion: A Manifesto for the Twenty-first Century*. Cambridge: Polity Press, 1989.

Petersen, Søren. "Loser Generated Content: From Participation to Exploitation." *First Monday*, 13, no. 3 (2008), http://firstmonday.org/htbin/cgiwrap/bin/ojs/index.php/fm/article/viewArticle/2141/1948.

Ritzer, George, and Nathan Jurgenson. "Production, Consumption, Prosumption: The Nature of Capitalism in the Age of the Digital 'Prosumer.'" *Journal of Consumer Culture* 10, no. 1 (2010): 13–36.

Terranova, Tiziana. "Free Labor: Producing Culture for the Digital Economy." *Social Text* 63, no. 18 (2000): 33–58.

Turow, Joseph, Deidre K. Mulligan, and Chris Jay Hoofnagle. "Research Report: Consumers Fundamentally Misunderstand the Online Advertising Marketplace." University of Pennsylvania Annenberg School for Communication and UC Berkeley Law Samuelson Law, Technology & Public Policy Clinic, October 2007. http://www.law.berkeley.edu/files/annenberg_samuelson_advertising.pdf.

Turow, Joseph, et al. "Contrary to What Marketers Say, Consumers Reject Tailored Advertising and Three Activities That Enable It." 2010. http://papers.ssrn.com/sol3/papers.cfm?abstract_id=1478214.

Vega, Tanzina. "New Web Code Draws Concern over Privacy Risks." *The New York Times*, October 10, 2010, A1.

Wiener, Norbert. *The Human Use of Human Beings: Cybernetics and Society*. Boston: Houghton Mifflin, 1954.

Wright, Erik Olin. *Class Counts: Comparative Studies in Class Analysis*. Cambridge: University of Cambridge Press, 1997.

10

DIGITALITY AND THE MEDIA OF DISPOSSESSION

Jonathan Beller

Despite everything that's happened—and I think I mean *everything*—some persist in the belief that they live in a world of immediacy: that there is nature and a level playing field, that they see things as they are, that words say what they mean, that you and I are just talking.

We don't just talk anymore, we run programs. Whom do they serve?

Whether we are just talking about the figure in 20th-century Euro-American painting, the integrity of literary form in modernity, Vietnamese bodies trapped in the inexorable logic of the Phoenix project, Iraqi bodies caught in the U.S.-run Abu Ghraib and the sites of Black Hawks and drones, or the recent economic crisis that rendered the nominal values of institutions and commodities obsolete (until the banks were shored up by a desperate expropriation of collective wealth by a government beholden to already-existing entities), one might find a common logic at work—namely, the almost unbearable pressure of social forces on the material signifier. This pressure breaks up prior codifications like so many icebergs. Here, of course, I am speaking simultaneously about signs *and their users.* The pulverization of signs pulverizes some of these users, who, as we know (from Lacan), are also identified via signs. While Volosinov may have been correct when he wrote in the late 1920s in *Marxism and the Philosophy of Language* that language is the most sensitive index of social change, we have, in the last long century, witnessed not just changes within language but changes in the status of language itself. Today, a simultaneous injunction to communicate along with a rapidly shrinking horizon of the kinds of things words as we know them might accomplish seems to prevail. The very power of speech is in question—such is the situation of the writer. His master's voice is just one download among many. In *The Order of Things,* Michel Foucault identified an inflection point for language at the end of the Classical Age. During the late 18th century and throughout the 19th century, he argues there was a generalized "demotion of discourse." In the

20th century and into our own, I would argue that this demotion of discourse has intensified and that it includes the demotion of discoursers.[1]

Let us explore this demotion of discourse as the intensification of capitalism by other, ostensibly extra-economic, means. Allow me to suggest that by examining mediatic shifts (the crisis of representation, the rise of visuality and informatics), by developing new concepts for labor and capital (that is, reconceptualizing the forms of labor, value, accumulation, attention, the wage) in ways that keep pace with changes already being instituted in practice, and by noting transformations in the character and role of language, affect, and utterance, we may pose a set of metrics and tactics attuned to yet opposed to those ventured and imposed by capital. I am suggesting, therefore, that it is possible at once to tell a more precise (if subaltern and subterranean) history of the conditions of possibility for what is known micropolitically as cognitive capitalism and macropolitically as Empire than what has been offered to date and that, in doing so, one is not obliged to give way to the theories of the immeasurability of surplus value as proposed by the autonomists. Which is to say that one may speak rigorously about the expropriation of language and of the linguistic commons by a capitalism that continues to depend upon quantitative metrics and the now computer-mediated calculus of profit.

Disappointingly perhaps, what I have to offer here does not accomplish all of the tasks I just set out; rather, it concentrates on the epistemic shifts that have occurred in relation to the transformation of political economy and language function and leaves the math for another time. But by expanding on a section of "The Digital Ideology"—a talk that I gave at a November 2009 conference on digital labor at The New School called The Internet as Playground and Factory,—I hope to at once extend the history of the digital and shift the locus of the general tenor of thought surrounding it. Figure 10.1 shows the intimate relation between the cognitive and mathematical functions of Empire. The image, one of digitality, is of a handout I passed around in an edition of 100 at that conference. This is all that remains—little, yes, but it is not nothing.

By all appearances, what you see before you is an ordinary one-dollar bill with a red ink stamp of the word *Distributed* on it along with a handwritten # indicating the number in the series. But one could legitimately ask: Was the

FIGURE 10.1

handout a performance, an image, or software? Was it an icon of, or an occasion for, what Trebor Scholz and others call distributed creativity? No doubt, it was already an image of images, but one could not and cannot decide here whether the medium is paper or money or computers. Maybe it was once paper... once gold? But... Oh strange conversion! The handout, which audience members were invited to accept (as payment for their attention to my talk, as ironic critique of their scholarly intentions?) or reject (either as perverse outing of deeply embarrassing relations endemic to contemporary knowledge production that had best remain unconscious or as an act of disidentification with said relations?), gives new resonance to the still-significant formulation, the medium is the message. (For the record, some took a handout, some took several, some ironically asked for them to be signed, others left them in small piles like so much garbage—while taking the memory with them, perhaps.) But what exactly is the medium? The various inks on paper raise numerous questions along the lines of the following series: Value as Writing/Photography as Image as Money as Capital... as Value. It being understood that in its reiteration through the representational-technical-financial network, value becomes not a mere economic determination but an inexorable dimension of representational praxis. It is at once an image among images and an archetypical image—one that all others well could bear a relation to. This distributed dollar then is at once an image of extreme superficiality and of infinite permutation, mediation, regress, and progress. Dialectics at a standstill.

The understanding that emerges from a consideration of the implied series that spans the history of money, writing, photography, printing, and computerization (and, not incidentally, that of colonialism, the rise of corporate power, and U.S. imperialism) would insist that capital informs not only writing and image but their reception. However, this insistence only becomes fully convincing (which is to say realized) in the contemporary, when digital technologies underpin the world media system and when so-called cognitive capitalism, or the expropriation of what Paolo Virno calls the "cognitive-linguistic capacities of the species," reigns.[2] However, given this outcome in which cognition itself is today digitally mediated without question—not a trivial outcome and furthermore one that is often undertheorized where cognitive practices are considered today—we might consider that the substitution of Quantity for Quality (the reconfiguration of quality by quantity), which has been occurring at least since capital's beginnings, informed the first as well as this, our computer-mediated penultimate digital culture. (Optimism of the will requires that we do not consider our current digital the ultimate culture but only a precursor: as Christian Fuchs would have it, the emergence of the digital computer is a necessary precondition to the long-sought arrival of communism.) Nonetheless, we should, and indeed must, wager that the current digitization of cultural form finds its conditions of possibility not in what we most easily recognize as the computer but in the dynamics of an older machine language: that of use value/exchange value imposed by wage labor and the commodity form—which is to say, by capitalism itself. Price was already a snapshot, and a digital one at that.

The role of digitization and its relation to the money form is a central question in both the history of political economy and our own period. The rise not only of Newtonian calculus (a calculus of space and time) but of a calculus of cultural form—and emphatically of a calculus of the image—is paramount. Marx's account of capital was a parsing of the process of integration—the taking of the integral of capitalist production cycles along various points in the trajectories of production. Too, the artist has long used her work as a wager or exploit to gain a foothold in the socius—an effort to convert attention into a means of subsistence that increasingly has meant the cash nexus. Cinema, advertising, and banner ads clearly function in a network of politic-economic relation that convert affect to monetary units and are machines for the mining of attention, but these later forms are the key to the anatomy of their precursors: painting and photography, which must also be grasped as techniques of capture and strategies of control. Taken as whole, we could say that what was once, for the artist at least, only a more or less embarrassing presupposition and but one dimension of visual-cultural production has become the overriding component. Crudely put, these media (what is meant by "the media") convert attention into cash—quality into quantity. Yes, there are many mediations, but the accountants (i.e., bankers) always do their best to have the last say. Just read the papers for their latest take.

Vilém Flusser, in his brief but nonetheless monumental work entitled *Towards a Philosophy of Photography,* sees Descartes as the pivotal figure in which alphabetical writing begins to be displaced by numerical notation. This is a significant development in the already profound disruption occasioned by linear writing. Referring to the camera but also to apparatuses in general he says:

> All apparatuses (not just computers) are calculating machines and in this sense "artificial intelligences," the camera included, even if their inventors were not able to account for this. In all apparatuses (including the camera), thinking in numbers overrides linear, historical thinking. This tendency to subordinate thinking in letters to thinking in numbers has been the norm in scientific discourse since Descartes; it has been a question of bringing thought into line with "extended matter" constructed of punctuated elements. Only numbers are suited to a process of bringing thought into line with "extended matter." Since Descartes at least (perhaps since Nocholas of Cusa) scientific discourse has tended towards the re-encoding of thought into numbers, but only since the camera has this tendency become materially possible. The camera (like all apparatuses that followed it) is *computational thinking flowing into hardware* (italics mine). Hence the quantum (computational) structure of all the movements and functions of the apparatus.[3]

One could obviously trace the overlap between Flusser's idea of the apparatus and Norbert Wiener's understanding of cybernetics in *The Human Use of Human Beings: Cybernetics and Society*—characterized by what I think of as the welding of a set of intentions to future attention through calculated metrics (a principal that, we might note, already inheres in writing). I want to dwell, however, on Flusser's understanding of photography and its *relation* to writing. For here one can observe the consequences of the technical image for writing as well as the digitization of images (and thus discourse) already in the 19th century. Flusser asserts that the photograph, "the first post-industrial image," is a "technical image"—and therefore an abstract image—whose internal mechanics derive from the operation of written concepts. Thus, the photograph is a form of programming. Indeed, for Flusser, despite the appearance of transparency, the technical image is triply abstract. Very briefly, its genealogy is as follows: In what he calls the "pre-historical" era, the pictographic image (think cave painting) is a first abstraction from the visible world, mapping it to a two-dimensional picture plane that can be visually scanned. In the "historical" era, linear writing "tears up the image," organizes its pieces in a linear manner, and imposes a temporal sequence. Flusser has given the example of an image containing stick figurations of a sun, two people, and a dog, which can then be written grammatically in "Mesopotamian tiles" as a linear sequence of these four elements.[4] Linear writing is thus an abstraction of the image, which for Flusser is its "metacode." Where the image is once abstracted from reality (three dimensions into two), writing is doubly abstracted (two dimensions into one). Furthermore, its strict imposition of linearity and temporal process gives rise to a new experience of time, which Flusser calls "history." Thus, historical consciousness and writing are inseparable. The technical image, which for Flusser inaugurates our current "post-historical" era, is made with an apparatus (literally a black box) that is designed vis-à-vis the application of written—that is, abstract—postulates. Linear writing, which for Flusser is now also mathematical notation and therefore science, and which was already an abstraction from images that reduced its two dimensions into a temporal line, writes the program that is then put into operation to build the camera. Thus, while the technical image seems to be a window on the world, it is in fact an image—one that is triply abstract. Each photographic or technical image has as its condition of possibility (and is therefore a result of) this increasingly complex process of abstraction that at this point extended thought into matter via digital notation. From this point of view, no transparency exists in the technical image, and its legibility is a question with radical implications. For his part, the photographer, sometimes referred to by Flusser as "the functionary," is locked in a struggle with the overdeterminations imposed by the programming of the apparatus—an apparatus that clearly takes on cultural dimensions—given the dialectic of usage and innovation in which the apparatus is itself engaged. The camera is an interaction of programs, and the resultant image functions as a social program.[5]

Despite important overlaps between Flusser's work and what, following Alfred Sohn-Rethel, is currently being referred to as "real abstraction," Flusser's philosophical approach to photography cannot, however, be conflated with the economic abstractions decoded by classical Marxism (though Flusser does claim that the innovations of the photographer against the overcoding of the apparatus is the only revolution left open to us).[6] The technical image for Flusser interrupts and indeed breaks with linear history and historical time, putting society into what he identifies as a postindustrial, and therefore postwork and postproletarian, mode in which information dominates, and functionaries—that is, "human beings"—are neither "the fixed nor the variable,"[7] as they were in prior modes of production, but "merge" with the apparatus "into a unity."[8] The increasingly complete incorporation of humans into the apparatus changes the relations of production. Flusser, without presuming to name or identify the meta-systemic principles in operation here, nonetheless acknowledges that the programs that constitute the photographic apparatus are programmed by higher-order programs:

> Beyond these [programs that inhere in the camera] are further programs— that of the photographic industry that programmed the camera, that of the industrial complex that programmed the photographic industry, that of the socio-economic system that programmed the industrial complex; and so on.[9]

Provocatively, Flusser adds, "Of course there can be no 'final' program of a 'final' apparatus since every program requires a meta-program by which it is programmed. The hierarchy of programs is open at the top."[10] For Flusser, there is no ultimately determining instance, and, for all we know, the algorithms that shape informatics may have their higher-order programs in quantum mechanics—an outcome that for—and indeed *in*—all its cosmic neutrality and sublimely naturalistic indifference would be disappointingly *ideological*.[11]

Nonetheless, Flusser does register the overdetermination of the programming of the photographic apparatus by what he calls "the socio-economic system"—or what we would want to call political economy—as a crisis. This crisis involves an immersion in the universe of technical images, which no one knows how to properly interpret, not least of which because the old modalities of meaning that belong to writing (particularly those relying on sequential thinking and historical imagination) no longer function. While endeavoring to remain far aloof of what he calls the "textolatry" of Marxism (which, Flusser claims, it shares with Christianity), Flusser nonetheless also clearly acknowledges that the framework of signification seemingly guaranteed by what elsewhere has been called a logocentric culture (which, in its heyday [remember those days?], proposed human actors and meanings in the form of "man" along with the weighting factors of historical time) now disorganized by "the ritualized and endlessly repeatable movement"[12] of images, creates a tremendous crisis for human beings. While one apparatus among many, the camera, for Flusser, is the apparatus par excellence and, in a quasi-Darwinian mode, has created the conditions for not just its self-reproduction but the exponential multiplication of its functions and expansion of its presence, to the point that "Nothing can resist the force of this current of technical images—there is no artistic, scientific or political activity which is not aimed at it, there is no everyday activity which does not aspire to be photographed, filmed, video-taped."[13] As Flusser puts it elsewhere:

> [W]e are manipulated by photographs and programmed to act in a ritual fashion in the service of a feedback mechanism for the benefit of cameras. Photographs suppress our critical awareness in order to make us forget the mindless absurdity of the process of functionality, and it is only thanks to this suppression that functionality is possible at all. Thus the photographs form a magic circle around us in the shape of the photographic universe.[14]

In a nutshell, the camera's program creates an evolutionary vector that at once incorporates and exceeds human self-definition.

Flusser's account of the quantum character of the apparatus above clearly owes a debt to Turing's conception of the steady-state machine, and might even be said to endeavor to construct the historical conditions of possibility for Turing's still-penetrating insights into the machinic aspects of all orders of information processing, from the simplest information transfer to the highest forms of behavior and cognition—forms that may well include cosmic processes such as galaxy formation. However, while Flusser would not agree, I would argue that when tracking the emergence of digitality, we ignore the rise of the money system and capitalism at our extreme peril. Privileging the emergence of "the apparatus" represses the socioeconomic determinations that provide the ground for its emergence. The rise to social preeminence of the general equivalent—that is, money—alongside the organization of production in accord with the split register of the commodity form (use value/exchange value) inaugurates a transformation whose ultimate consequences have not been drawn. At the origins of capitalism, commodification (use value over exchange value—that is, quality over quantity) already provided a general method for the extension of cognition into matter. Profit, alienated production, and the accumulation of private property was itself a program—one that extended digitality (in the form of exchange value) into the deepest recesses of matter and continues its ramifications to this day. As has been said (by Fredric Jameson, among others), the emergence of the commodity form, the ability to quantitatively and thus abstractly compare specific and otherwise incomparable qualities is similar in historical import to the neolithic revolution. Thus, the Cartesian subject should be understood as exercising the mode of cognition slated by money—the vanishing mediator. Likewise, the Cartesian coordinate system, with its transposable 0 point (0,0,0) and axonometric grid that can be thrown over any space whatever lays the groundwork for the numerical calculus of space and time. We may agree with Sohn-Rethel that the real abstraction that is the money form is the condition of possibility for abstraction in classical philosophy. For Marx, it was clear that the rise of individuality and the modern subject coincided with the emergence of markets in which structurally equivalent owners of commodities came to exchange the qualities of their commodities for quantities of the general equivalent.

Today the so-called vanishing mediator is the computational underpinning of images, thought, information, and form itself. The vanishing mediator is the medium of the media. Which is also to say that labor is the medium of capital. How it underpins and sustains the various layers of mediation is one of the fundamental questions of our times. Subfields and entire fields, as well as start-up and full-blown business models, position themselves in relation to the de rigeur insight that coupling digitization to image/cognition is an investment that generates capital. Somehow, despite the overwhelming evidence, we must continuously remind ourselves of this transformation as well as the dialectical corollary that the changes in capitalist informatics have also transformed political economy and thus politics at every level. Sean Cubitt's brilliant discussion of environmental and nonsubjective agency, Ned Rossiter and Soenke Zehle's challenging insights into the culture of code and of algorithmic futures, and Patricia Clough's incisive consideration of affect and measure in essays included in this volume point to new arenas of political economy, political-economical engagement, and forms of practice. Indeed, it is arguable that there is no easy distinction between financialization and digitization and that all such distinctions, save those that self-consciously endeavor to be politicizing, make political claims in the guise of nominally cultural ones.

Let us pause for a moment to take stock. We began with the problem of discourse in the context of the digital and have arrived at a universal tendency toward digitization that precedes the so-called digital age by at least five centuries. Cartesian mathematics, Newtonian calculus, the rise of capitalism, and the infusion of digital programming into apparatuses of representation all testify to a environment of discursive practice that has been transformed over several centuries. We also see the relative inability of our language-based strategies of meaning making to account for this digital (which is to say, metaphysical) transformation. Let us dwell for a moment on the unperceived operations that have rendered our language far less transparent, far less adequate, than we may have heretofore expected. How are we to solve or even to conceive world-historical problems that have exceeded all categories of knowledge, including history? Humankind sets forth only such problems as it can solve—so said Marx. Given the degradation of language, have we arrived at a problem we cannot even set forth? The imbrication of digitality in all modern media, as well as the subsumption of labor by and in digital media, recasts the moment of conceptualization, of utterance, as a preeminently political one.

Let us say that, for political reasons (reasons still possibly caught within the domain of an epoch that has not come to a complete close and therefore remains susceptible to its foibles, logics, and what may later admittedly appear as misconceptions; but also reasons that recognize capital as something like an event horizon: a present mathematically extended into matter and therefore currently untranscendable), one wanted a counter to all the celebratory hoopla and evangelical hand rubbing with respect to the digital and its correlative posthumanism by dwelling further on the negatives of digitality; one could also look again, in support of a quest for radical disenchantment, at some of the classic critiques of media clustered around the global 1960s (decolonization, revolution)—specifically, McLuhan,

Enzensberger, and Baudrillard. These thinkers, beyond their specific claims, have the merit of showing how little prepared we are to think the problems of history and society. While it may appear tedious to rehearse some of these arguments, my hope is that readers will see this as a kind of affective practice, an attitude adjustment that might occur in relation to cultural analysis and what is known as thought.

The still-underappreciated McLuhan argued in 1964 that new media technologies alter the sense ratios and that the macroeffects of such alteration cannot be easily or quickly apprehended. Indeed, only with the rise of electronic media do we grasp the historical significance of the Gutenberg press. McLuhan drops blazing one-liners such as, "Print created individualism and nationalism in the 16th century," which, of course, implies that the fundamental categories for thinking about agency, history, and geopolitics in the standard historical accounts (i.e., the individual and the nation) miss the mark. Beginning with the famous, but perhaps not famous enough, example of the light bulb as a medium without content (without content, at least until neon lights—McLuhan's example—and perhaps the cinema screen—my example), McLuhan argues that "The medium is the message."[15] In other words, the deep structural and epistemic changes of history and society are media based and take place irrespective of particular content.

In 1970, Hans Magnus Enzensberger could have been writing about this, our current moment:

> Anyone who expects to be emancipated by technological hardware or by a system of hardware however structured, is the victim of an obscure belief in progress. Anyone who imagines that freedom for the media will be established if only everyone is busy transmitting and receiving is the dupe of a liberalism which, decked out in contemporary colors merely peddles the faded concepts of a preordained harmony of social interests.[16]

Cleaving to the belief that content, distribution, and access to the means of production matter, Enzensberger dismisses "the charlatan" McLuhan's formulation that the medium is the message:

> The sentence...tells us that the bourgeoisie does indeed have all possible means at its disposal to communicate something to us, but that it has nothing more to say. It is ideologically sterile. Its intention is to hold on to the control of the means of production at any price while being incapable of making the socially necessary use of them is here expressed with complete frankness in the superstructure. It wants the media *as such* and *to no purpose*.[17]

Enzensberger also dismisses (as bourgeois):

> the symbolical expression by an artistic avant-garde whose program logically admits only the alternative of negative signals and amorphous noise.

> Example: the already outdated "literature of silence," Warhol's films in which everything can happen at once or nothing at all, and John Cage's forty-five minute-long, *Lecture on Nothing.*[18]

Interestingly, for us theorists of cinema, cut 'n' mix and the mash-up, he sees the potential of content and agenda-driven programming and identifies the partisan character of montage, "Cutting, editing, dubbing—these are techniques for conscious manipulation." He describes these techniques as "work processes" and calls the results "proto-types," presumably for the fabrication of reality. In contrast to traditional works of art, Enzensberger writes, "the media do not produce such objects, they create programs." This statement is not too far from Solanas and Gettino's position in their 1969 manifesto "Towards a Third Cinema," which saw the cinematic work as a catalyst of revolution and for the creation of a "new man"; it is also not entirely different from Flusser's ideas of the technical image and of the apparatus, at least in as much as it sees programming and labor as endemic to the logistics of the image.

In his 1972 "Requiem for the Media" (a title shot through with unrequited wish fulfillment), the much-maligned Jean Baudrillard explains that "the media are not *co-efficients,* but *effectors* of ideology."[19] Ideology is not "some Imaginary floating in the wake of exchange value: it is the very operation of exchange value." This thesis is brilliantly elaborated in what, for me anyway, is his most significant work: *For a Critique of the Political Economy of the Sign.* In "Requiem," using the mass-media response to and thus containment of Paris '68, Baudrillard asserts that:

> The mass media are anti-mediatory and intransitive. They fabricate non-communication: they are what always prevent a response, making all processes of exchange impossible (except the various forms of response simulation...). The revolution *tout court* lies in restoring this possibility of response.[20]

The media's power of preventing a response, its irresponsibility, ultimately lies in what Baudrillard calls "the terrorism of the code." The invariable organization of code by the algorithm Encoder-Message-Decoder, an algorithm which we must assume is the result of the history of the practical applications of code and therefore the historical achievement of "communication" as "the code" itself, means that one can only be transmitter or receiver, never both, and that both ambiguity and genuine reciprocity are excluded. Against Enzensberger, Baudrillard writes, "Reversibility has nothing to do with Reciprocity" and concludes that the code institutes "decentralized totalitarianism."

A summary of these late-1960s media negatrons could read as follows: For McLuhan, the nonrecognition of the mediatic basis of society leads to a gross miscategorization of agency and to historical (and therefore political) error. Without a mediatic understanding of the transformation of consciousness by means of the shift in sense ratios, no proper understanding of human agency is possible. For Enzensberger, bourgeois-organized media is liquidated of socialist content/program and therefore divested of content meaningful for anything but the intensification of capitalism; thus, the mass media is counterrevolutionary in its current incarnation, though perhaps not in essence. For Baudrillard, the functioning of the code itself negates the production of noncapitalist values— one must "smash the code." Thus, whether the failure of revolutionary socialism is in misperception of nearly invisible media effects, improper programming, or the historically imposed structure of communication itself, these three thinkers insist that a radical reconsideration of mediatic modes is the sine qua non of social justice.

These critiques of what we are now calling media platforms and their functions or exploits, along with Flusser's understanding of the postindustrial character of photography, should be further linked to the more recent extrapolation and development of what Regis Debray christens mediology. In *Media Manifestos,* Debray, theorist of the *foco* movements, volunteers the mnemonic, "Submission rhymes with Transmission" "because to transmit is to organize, and to organize is to hierarchize. Hence also to exclude and subordinate."[21] Debray suggests, in effect, that the history of sign function is organized by what we might now think of as media platforms and the apparatuses, institutions, and practices that sustain them. "Let us agree on the propriety of calling 'medium' in the strong sense the system of *apparatus-support-procedure,* that which a mediological revolution would unsettle and disturb organically."[22] We see from this text that, in addition to whatever else it may be, sign function is clearly extrasemiotic—in other words, practical-material. Whether thinking about writing and the institutional system of books, libraries, and print media; television with its networks, power grids, and editing suites; or computers with their servers, protocols, and globally disaggregated factories for the assemblage of both the machines and the platforms, Debray allows us to consider more concretely the material operation of the apparatus proper in the organization of what Althusser called "ideological state apparatuses" but also in ostensibly nonstatist media forms.[23] Furthermore, the hypermediation of language (and hence its radical denaturing) is everywhere evident.

In light of these critical—and let's admit it, radically pessimistic—takes on media history (and therefore History), I hope, for the sake of further disenchantment, that it will be worth revisiting and further elaborating my own brief history of visuality as laid out in *The Cinematic Mode of Production,* which understands the highlights of 20th-century intellectual history as inflection points describing the decreasing purchase of sign function (that is, "natural" language) on reality. It is only by examining the codevelopment of sign function and technocapitalism that one can really understand the situation of linguistic function described phenomenologically by the Italian post-Marxists. More importantly still, taking a mediological approach explains how the effective short-circuiting of language function has been a necessary achievement of capital's worldwide suppression of democracy. It requires the world media system to convert nominal democracy into its antithesis. Mass cynicism, irony, farce, and indifference are mere symptoms of this historical transformation.

However, before proceeding to my central thesis here regarding the worldwide foreclosure of democracy through the demotion of discourse, let us return to Foucault regarding the compensatory cultural shifts resulting from the "demotion of language to the mere status of object" during the 19th century. Speaking about the practice of exegesis, he writes:

> [N]ow it is not a matter of rediscovering some primary word that has been buried in [language], but of disturbing the words we speak, of denouncing the grammatical habits of our thinking, of dissipating the myths that animate our words, of rendering once more noisy and audible the element of silence that all discussion carries with it as it is spoken. The first book of *Das Kapital* is an exegesis of "value"; all Nietzsche is an exegesis of a few Greek words; Freud, the exegesis of all those unspoken phrases that support and at the same time undermine our apparent discourse, our fantasies, our dreams, our bodies. Philology, as the analysis of what is said in the depths of discourse, has become the modern form of criticism. Where, at the end of the eighteenth century, it was a matter of fixing the frontiers of knowledge, it will now be one of seeking to destroy syntax, to shatter tyrannical modes of speech, to turn words around in order to perceive all that is being said through them and despite them. God is perhaps not so much a region beyond knowledge as something prior to the sentences we speak; and if Western man is inseparable from him, it is not because of some invincible propensity to go beyond the frontiers of experience, but because his language ceaselessly foments him in the shadow of his laws [quoting Nietzsche]: "I fear that we shall never rid ourselves of God, since we still believe in grammar.[24]

The analysis of the transformed status of language, so meticulously and brazenly undertaken by Foucault, stands as one of the important intellectual achievements of what, until recently, could be said to be "our times." The consequences of the demotion of language from its classical transparency to a medium still has to be reckoned with. Foucault elucidates three compensations: (1) language is understood as a necessary medium for knowledge, (2) there is a critical value bestowed upon the study of language, and (3) "the appearance of literature, of literature as such"[25] a practice in which language "has nothing to say but itself, nothing to do but shine in the brightness of its being."[26] While this last is an arresting, even beautiful, statement, we could well ask for whom does it shine and for whom might it sparkle or flame? And furthermore, why the visual metaphor? Why write laudatory sentences about the literary when the literary as such would mark the diminution of linguistic power in the world? Without really embarking on an argument here, but only suggesting a line of inquiry, could one resituate the work of Foucault in relation to the history of media technology? Would a Kittlerization of Foucault rescue him (or at least us) from remaining as Edward Said said, "the scribe of power?" One who abrogates his agency (and not only in his rejection of Marxism) in the recording of Power's micropolitics? Might an apparatus centered historicization of Foucault's claims potentially transform the aspects of his work that are ideological in Regis Debray's sense of the term "ideology: the play of ideas in the silence of technology." What might become visible if the archeological approach gives way to the mediological approach would be not simply discursive practices—or even, as with biopower, the interface of the body with the technics of the social—but the historico-materiality of mediation: the machines, platforms, techniques, and concrete media of inscription, transmission, and dissemination, and perhaps (above all?), the investments in and complex financialization of these apparatuses. What might then appear is the multiple capitalist bases on which "man" has been invested in and built, and is now meeting his end.

Without skipping too many logical steps in an argument here, then one could go so far as to say that digitization is the necessary precondition of modern humanity. This digital core of humanity is today manifest by even a superficial examination of the contemporary world: as far as global citizenship is concerned, where there is no money, hegemony recognizes no humanity. Or as Solanas and Gettino put it in "Towards a Third Cinema:" "The more exploited a man is, the more he is placed on a plane of insignificance. The more he resists, the more he is viewed as a beast."[27] One can show (and, indeed, it *has* been shown—many times, yet seemingly not often enough) that the very idea of the human, at least as put into practice by the West, depends upon violent racist and culturalist-nationalist exclusions of discursively and materially produced others: non-, in-, and sub-humans. These images of the racial other, grasped by Western(ized) eyes as images of animality, stupefaction, irrationality, and abjection, should be understood as nothing less (if perhaps something more, much more) than representational technologies of capitalist expansion. Discursively speaking, iterations of self and other amount to ideologies in an older idiom, software in a more contemporary one; narratives and images of self/other conform to Foucault's idea of a "techne" for both the making of certain subjects and the disappearance of others. In the Foucaultian paradigm, this organization of knowing is part of an episteme, the archeology of which allows Foucault to ask in all resonant seriousness in *The Order of Things,* "Does man really exist?"

> To imagine, for an instant, what the world and thought and truth might be if man did not exist, is considered to be merely indulging in paradox. This is because we are so blinded by the recent manifestation of man that we can no longer remember a time—and it is not so long ago—when the world, its order, and human beings existed, but man did not. . . . Ought we not remind ourselves—we who believe ourselves bound to a finitude which

belongs only to us, and which opens up the truth of the world to us by means of our cognition—ought we not remind ourselves that we are bound to the back of a tiger?[28]

The epistemic changes *are* bigger than man; we are finally starting to know that. I suppose the question here is whether or not one could say that Foucault's tiger is digital. This would allow us to assert that "Man" was the brand name for a once-popular (if still unspeakably violent) operating system. If contra Foucault and with his ruptures and discrete epistemes, we allow ourselves to be guided by Marx's dictum that "The anatomy of man is the key to the anatomy of the ape," which argues that the later formations reveal the eschatological tendencies incipient in the former, we find ourselves not only collecting animal spirits but confronted by the following paradox: retroactively, the ur-medium of "man," of "humanity" is capital. Thus, "man" was an early symptom of the digital.

At one level, this claim that "man" is capital with a human face seems simple enough, obvious even: the same ur-medium that has produced the human has also produced the radical dispossession of the human. The only other achievement that can be understood to be of the same order as the achievement of humanity is inhumanity. In a refrain of Cesaire's surrealistic query into paradox from *Discourse on Colonialism,* we might also wonder, "Civilization and Colonization?" The charismatic dictator, the great family of man—all symptoms of the dialectic of capital-man. This is not necessarily to take this dialectic as the summation of modernity en toto. My project here is not to identify the ruling trope of an era and even less to offer a totalizing view of world history (really), but rather to explore the bankruptcy of the ruling ideas that continue to structure the cultural inflection of emergent media. Thus, it is significant to critique "man" and "the human" not only because these are still operative but because the emergent considerations of a much-touted posthumanism negatively locate the human remainder as a central investment for Western (that is, Western self-identifying) culture. As critics such as Joel Dinerstein and Alexander Weheleya pointedly demonstrate, not just humanisms but also posthumanisms smuggle the white Western subject of liberalism back in as the metric for the measurement and the enjoyment of the drama of its—that is, *his*—own disappearance. Something similar might also be said of the literary function of the sublime in the work of Foucault: in the words of Walter Benjamin, "man experiences his annihilation as an aesthetic pleasure of the first order." The payoff is in watching the air go out of the bag. Thus, from the Nietzschean nihilism of "Man would rather will nothingness than will nothing at all" to the Benjaminian diagnosis of the aesthetics of fascism, one begins to understand the compensatory pleasures offered an enfranchised if still exploited citizenry: Debord's "gilded poverty" lived in exchange for new forms of marginalization and nonexistence. These relations are distributed through the encroachment of a new sociologistical media paradigm, reiterated at the level of philosophy and savored by theory. One could follow this thread through the contemporary rise of farce, blank irony, simulation, and reality TV, but that would lead us too far afield. The point here is that the demotion of language and the liquidation of the Real is orchestrated in direct relation to the intensive development of the first digital medium of representation.

However, it also needs to be mentioned here that the recession of the Real and the deconstruction of "man" that reached new levels of intensity during the 20th century was not merely the effect of domination; it was also the effect of struggle. In other words, as commodities, images, pirates, and police arrived to dominate, counterimages, counternarratives, countertheories, and counterhistories have been put forward staking claims that either challenged the Real or Deconstructed it. The imposition of various realities in the name of Man and his democracy were countered by their negation. The disintegration of the Real, of the referent, of "being" was, in fact, also a hallmark of struggle. Thus, one must understand the essential but all too often unremarked centrality not only of the self-contradiction of capitalism and fascism (a seemingly internal affair) but of antiracist, anticolonialist, anti-imperialist, postcolonial, feminist, women of color feminist, and queer struggles (the rebellions of the trod upon) and the resultant theories and practices in the making of the 20th-century epistemic shift that I am speaking about. Without exception, these struggles aspire beyond the framework insisted upon by capitalism, even if they are partially recuperated by said framework in a later iteration. Without a clear understanding of insurrectionary work such as that of Hortense Spillers, Frantz Fanon, Gayatri Spivak, Helene Cixous, Angela Davis, and Judith Butler (to put but one, perhaps for today still too provincial, name on each of the endeavors listed above), there is no real possibility of understanding the outrage nor the historical and geopolitical stakes that animate the changes we have been so mechanically (and in fact anachronistically) discussing in terms of "man." The Arab Spring, Los Indignados in Spain, and the worldwide protests of 2011 all transmit a radical disaffection with the capitalist organization of representation and assert the living history and potential of insurrection as a constituent element of a nominally capitalist planet.

To return to the troublesome history of the human sciences and perhaps place Foucault's work in a mediological context, we might propose that the major moments of this history be read as an indexical phenomenologicon of sign function in relation to the capitalist development of technology. Together, these differentiable endeavors, each with its own theory of sign function, offer a periodization of verbal sign effects in relation to an overall trajectory: the *technologically mediated* recession of the Real. It should be taken as axiomatic that the development of technologies of mediation—particularly visual, audiophonic, and digital technologies—does not occur apart from either political economy or the geopolitical forces of colonialism, imperialism, racialization, and the regulation of sexuality and gender.

Beginning in the 19th century with the rise of the world market and the international interstate system (itself, as Benedict Anderson shows, a kind of media phenomenon organized by the newspaper), tendencies toward universal (which is to say, global market) protocols were increasingly pronounced. Linguistics and structuralism institute an inaugural and henceforth unrecoverable split between signifier and signified—the sign shadows the real and vice versa, while arguing that these basic dynamics adhere in all linguistic representation regardless of content. One might say that the shift from what Saussure viewed as classical philology to linguistics marks the final demotion of language to being one medium among many, one record of accounts to a world that may now offer competing versions of itself in other languages and media. Only then can one derive the arbitrary nature of the sign (Foucault reads Schlegel, Cuvier, and Bopp for this, but for me the decisive figure is Saussure). Psychoanalysis and semiotics propose that the world beyond the purview of language churns in accord with logics beyond those of daytime rationality (grammatology) and definitively shifts the whole Marxian notion of the depth-hermeneutic and the symptom from the appearance of things (the commodity) to language itself (the sign). Things and words have subterranean dynamics. The year 1895—roughly the advent of cinema, psychoanalysis, and structuralism—provides a convenient date to mark both this breakdown of language and its strategies to accommodate its newly precipitated dysfunction. Language ruptures to find images—images to which it can only affix more of itself. These ruptures in sign function, signs of the real, turn out to be signs themselves. Parapraxis, a pronounced breakdown in language, through which the unconscious emerges, requires the discourse that will be psychoanalysis to explain it. Signifier/Signified is a generative image of the sign. The dream is a rebus. The *objet petit a* is a name for the gaze. Language notices and endeavors through the proliferation of the humanistic disciplines to accommodate its own displacement by the rising tide of the visual—by the omnipresence of images. Vast amounts of discourse are required to manage the ever-intensifying proliferation of these images.

As I tried to show in "The Unconscious of the Unconscious," the onslaught of the visual and the penetration of the life world by visual technologies can be thought of as the unconscious of the unconscious itself—the repressed media history that provided the template for the new insights into human nature that emerged out of both psychoanalysis and studies of sign function. Likewise semiotics, with its attention to visual texts as well as its meditations on the meaning of meaning that in one branch of its endeavors culminated in the analysis of the structure of myth as a second-order signifying system (Barthes), showed the ways in which signs could be deployed (and therefore denatured) by what we might today recognize as a program. Poststructuralism and deconstruction, despite the latter's intensive emphasis on textuality, amounted to an elaboration of Lacanian aphanasis (the fading of the subject) by placing presence and being itself under erasure. Both the subject and existence could no longer be guaranteed by writing or speech, which, in being understood as moments of a specific technological formation, had become one and the same. One could say that in a visual-becoming-infomatic digital culture, the traditional forms of writing and its subjects were driven to the brink of extinction. Linear time, grand narratives, history, presence, and being itself, all of the once-essential elements of not only human nature but purportedly of nature proper, were shown to be at once discursive formations and formations that were crumbling. One could find the visible, photographic, and electronic light of images pouring through the cracks of the old forms. The subjects who once presided over their objects melted into them, and, as I put it somewhere else, all that is solid melts into film. What's more, this light, once seemingly external but now internal to language and subjectivity itself, was powered by the masses.

With full postmodernism (a new moment of capitalist digitality) and the full emergence of virtuality and simulation, along with the waning of historicity and what I would call not the waning but the repurposing of affect, we enter a world in which not only has language been functionalized by the great political-economic machines of the imagination known as but not limited to cinema, television, digital cameras, and computers, but the productive possibilities and social roles of language have been forever transformed. And, almost incidentally, so, too, has the role of philosophy and, for what (little) it's worth, the definition of our species. A la Kubrick's *2001,* the human drama may have a cosmic scope, but if it does, it is most certainly not humanistic. As it turns out, infinite existentialism when combined with infinite irony produces simulation as the sine qua non of knowledge. From the perspective of the absolute fading of the Real, what could be more nihilistic than the current engagement with a recognized simulation *as if* it were real, it being understood, of course, that today the other name for nihilism is faith?

In this manner then, the discursive frames of the recent human sciences—psychoanalysis, structuralism, poststructuralism, deconstruction—could be borrowed from intellectual history for the staging of the exit of the Real from representation. Indeed, I would say that it is only with Saussure and the arbitrary nature of the sign that language really begins to be understood as a medium among others and embarks on the journey toward a full abrogation of its privileged access to the Real. This exit of the Real from the symbolic is to be correlated, then, with the intensifying penetration of the life-world by technologies of the visual, the audiophonic, and the digital as well as the struggles for decolonization and social justice that further relativize linguistic claims. Incidentally, the 20th-century human sciences should also be correlated with the parametric instrumentalization of the signifier in various capitalist endeavors spanning that not-so-wide gamut that runs from advertising to torture, both of which endeavor to theatrically create for its audience (victim) an existential crisis that shatters the traditional personality so it can be resignified by the domain of power in which it is newly bound. The contest over the Real—its increasing distance from the subjects of civilization—has been continuously reintegrated and transformed as the new ground of encounter. Consequently, the subject has been pulverized. I mention this violent reconfiguration and reprogramming of the concrete individual because it allows us to return to my thesis: that the capitalist development of digitality and informatics served the dual purpose of capture and marginalization, of mobilization and nonrepresentation, writ large, of worldwide massification without worldwide democracy. This program was absolutely essential for the continued concentration of the accumulation of surplus value and, what amounts to the same thing, the preservation and intensification of hierarchical society.

* * *

Marx himself showed that the modern subject—the individual—emerges as the subject of exchange within the framework imposed by market capitalism; Althusser showed how the subject becomes the other side of the capitalist state form—a functional position always already *within* ideology—effectively foreclosed from any breach with ideology. The lessons here are formal as well as political—certain modalities of subjectification and discursive practices are, if not out and out dead ends, then fraught with the paradox of capture—by what Brian Holmes calls "the overcode."[29] The subsequent pulverizing of the subject, the transformed role of discourse under the paradigm of virtuosity, and the reconstruction of state governance as Empire must be closely linked to an understanding of the increasing intimacy—one might even risk saying the *convergence*—of media forms and the logistics of capitalism. Aphanasis and the recession of the real is not only a tragic revolutionizing of the forces of production, it is also necessarily an opportunity: aesthetic, political, social.

In considering mediation of the terrain of our struggle, we have seen that it involves *the refusal of the commandeering of all mediations for the purposes of capitalist production and reproduction;* however, we have also seen that everywhere and in all cases just such a commandeering of the means of production is at hand, and indeed *in mind.* For the logical conclusion of our discussion of sign function implies that *our very thought is the thought of capital.* How, then, to reconcile such a totalizing view of expropriation and its necropolitics (one that is largely in accord with the current claims surrounding cognitive capitalism and virtuosity) with what would appear to be the bourgeoning of life all around? Perhaps, given Turing's brilliant dismissal of the idea that there simply could not be a program for human behavior, we cannot dismiss an account that strives to be adequate to the history and as it were aspiration of capital's enclosure on the mere grounds that sheer planetary difference "could never be" subsumed by a universal Turing machine of financialization? Nonetheless, we might will a different fate.

Here, in the face of informatic subsumption, we could say with Flusser that the hierarchy of programs is open at the top and satisfy ourselves with the cosmic indifference of digitality, or we could wager that this indifference or indeterminacy itself appears through a sociohistorical lens that is not indifferent—that our cognition, in its very formation, is being bent to conform to capitalist process. Such an assertion (for that's what it is) would be political (before it was ethical) and aware that it was bound to a conceit that could well be rendered moot (for example, if thought became utterly impossible, or if the environment collapsed and consciousness as we know it ceased). A *political* and thus politicizing approach to media studies would insist upon the materiality of mediation as well as a reckoning of the material consequences of even the most ostensibly immaterial and abstract mediations. In other words, the indeterminacy regarding the nature of our program is our best hope and hence a call to arms.

A mediatic approach to the sphere of operations would restore the technical and economic components—the *realia*—of affective dispensations. Media platforms are not merely technologies in the sense of being objects or machines or practices that have an objective character; rather, they are social formations and, more particularly, gender and racial formations. For example, the geopolitical emergence and role of photography during the violent racialization processes of slavery and colonialism tells us not simply about the visual sculpting of racial formations but about the *coevolution* of two ostensibly separate technologies for graphing people(s) by their external appearances. Which is to say that, as surely as the camera and the photograph have had a role in the transmission and productive (for capital) development of the various racisms, *intrinsic* to the camera and the photograph is the history of racial exploitation. This is part of the Program that Flusser does not see.

Just as an interest in labor should force us to rethink the logistics of media platforms and see them as technologies formed in the struggle between labor and capital and thus by and for the expropriation of labor, we must understand that the flesh, in Hortense Spillers's sense of the word, is now the surface of inscription, the medium in the last instance, for all transmissions. Which is to say that for the 2 billion people who live on two dollars or less per day, it is their labor of survival that bears the burden of the messages considered to be worthy of transmission.[30] The medium is the flesh of the world. Dialectically, the flesh is the other side of the vanishing mediator called money and, hence, necessarily, the other side of the digital.

A rigorous mediological approach would also attend closely to the politics of the utterance. Is it really possible to talk anymore as if race, class, nation, and gender were issues that were marginal or have been surpassed? Even though it is fair to say that the meaning of these terms has shifted—moreover that the very forms of racial and class oppression are being reimagined and repurposed to fit the emergent exigencies of domination—these terms remain at the very least the names for technologies of violence and expropriation that are brought to bear in full force upon, to use an old-fashioned term, the masses. The fragmentary character of the multitudes, such that each of us has the multitude within, and the monadic character of geopolitics, such that each of us bears the signature of the globopolitical *jetzeit,* cannot license the emergence of a purportedly value-neutral, degree-zero, commonsensical, highly civilized speaking subject that a/ effects a deafness to the call of the enslaved, the savaged, the raped, and the expropriated even as it claims to listen. If the enormity of the crimes that make us what we are, if the unspeakable violence and unendurable pain of history does not haunt our words, then we have said too much and not enough. This invocation of the myriad agonies (past and present) against the pat presentation of the iterations of capital logic (cynically or ironically self-conscious or not) is not a mere poetic gesture; it is the informing call to which liberatory work must be offered in response. Answering this spectral calling would endeavor to reanimate all the sedimented dead labor that is the condition of possibility for the living labor of this day's utterances; these calls as the eternal return of the oppressed are the very principle of organization (a subterranean genealogy) that might inform our cognitive-linguistic labor such that it is not merely the productive reproduction of yesterday's unheralded violence.

Notes

1 For example, "In his acceptance speech of the Bruno Kreisky Prize for the advancement of human rights on March 9, 2006 Habermas said that the 'use of the Internet has both broadened and fragmented the contexts of communication. This is why the Internet can have a subversive effect on intellectual life in authoritarian regimes. But at the same time, the less formal, horizontal cross-linking of communication channels weakens the achievements of traditional media. This focuses the attention of an anonymous and dispersed public on select topics and information, allowing citizens to concentrate on the same critically filtered issues and journalistic pieces at any given time. The price we pay for the growth in egalitarianism offered by the Internet is the decentralized access to unedited stories. In this medium, contributions by intellectuals lose their power to create a focus.'" (http://ejournalist.com.au/v6n2/ubayasiri622.pdf, editor's note)

2 Paolo Virno, *A Grammar of the Multitude: For an Analysis of Contemporary Forms of Life* (n.p.: Semiotext(e), 2004).

3 Vilém Flusser, *Towards a Philosophy of Photography* (London: Reaktion Books, 2000), 31–2.

4 Vilém Flusser, "The Codified World," in *Writings,* ed. Andreas Strohl, trans. Erik Eisel (Minneapolis: University of Minnesota Press, 2002), 37–8.

5 It is worth interjecting that the rise of photography coincides with the early writings of Marx—not just the invocation of the camera obscura (which dates from much earlier) that Marx uses to figure the ideological inversion of the world image that makes it appear that ideas ground material relations, but more emphatically, the triple abstraction that Flusser claims for photography might also be claimed for use value/exchange value and money/capital. But that would be another essay.

6 Alfred Sohn-Rethel, *Intellectual and Manual Labour: A Critique of Epistemology* (Macmillan, 1983).

7 Vilém Flusser, *Towards a Philosophy of Photography,* trans. Anthony Matthews (London: Reaktion Books, 2000), 27.

8 Ibid.

9 Flusser, *Towards a Philosophy,* 29.

10 Ibid.

11 A clue to Flusser's cosmologistics can be gleaned from his remarks on the criticism of the photographic program, which he laments "serves the suspension of the critical faculties [and] the process of functionality." Flusser writes:

> Of course, critical awareness can still be awakened so as to make the photograph transparent. Then the photograph of Lebanon becomes transparent as regards its newspaper program and the program behind it belonging to the political party

programming the newspaper. Then the photograph of the toothbrush becomes transparent as regards the program of the advertising agency and the program behind it belonging to the toothbrush industry. And the powers of "imperialism," "Zionism," "terrorism" and "tooth-decay" are revealed as concepts contained within these programs. But this critical exercise does not necessarily lead to a disenchantment of the images. That is, it can itself have been put under a magic spell, thereby becoming "functional." The cultural criticism of the Frankfurt School is an example of such a second-order paganism: Behind the images it uncovers secret, super-human powers at work (e.g. capitalism) that have maliciously created all these programs *instead of taking for granted that the programming proceeds in a mindless automatic fashion* (italics mine). A thoroughly disconcerting process in which, behind the ghosts that have been exorcized, more and more new ones are summoned up. (63–4).

Aren't we to conclude from this that capitalism is not to be considered among the programs and much less the operating system of the current juncture of computations that currently constitute the clutch of the species?

12 Flusser, *Towards a Philosophy,* 20.
13 Ibid.
14 Flusser, *Towards a Philosophy,* 64.
15 Marshall McLuhan, "The Galaxy Reconfigured" in *The New Media Reader,* pp. 195–209. This, it should be noted, is diametrically opposed to the methodology of Foucault, for whom not just God, but power is in the details. McLuhan was not averse to a consideration of the details, but for him it was the standpoint of the platform that allowed for the clearest understanding of the reorganization of the sensorium. When all inputs were affected by emergent media, the very disposition of the species was transformed.
16 Originally published as Hans Magnus Enzensberger, "Constituents of a Theory of Media," *New Left Review* 64 (November/December 1970): 13–36; republished in *The New Media Reader,* 267.
17 Hans Magnus Enzensberger, "Constituents of a Theory of Media," in *The New Media Reader,* 271.
18 Ibid.
19 Jean Baudrillard, "Requiem for the Media," in *The New Media Reader,* 280.
20 Baudrillard, "Requiem for the Media," 281.
21 Regis Debray, *Media Manifestos* (London: Verso, 1996), 46.
22 Debray, *Media Manifestos,* 13.
23 Louis Althusser, "Ideology and Ideological State Apparatuses" in *Lenin and Philosophy,* trans. Ben Brewster, Monthly Review Press, 1971.
24 Michel Foucault, *The Order of Things: An Archaeology of the Human Sciences* (London: Routledge, 1996), 298.
25 Foucault, *The Order of Things,* 299.
26 Foucault, *The Order of Things,* 300.
27 Fernando Solanas and Octavio Gettino, "Towards a Third Cinema," http://documentary isneverneutral.com/words/camasgun.html.
28 Foucault, *The Order of Things,* 322.

29 Brian Holmes, *Escape the Overcode,* http://brianholmes.wordpress.com/2007/07/20/ escape-the-overcode/. Additionally, Wlad Godzich, in an important essay called "Language, Images, and the Postmodern Predicament," charts the increasing alienation of the subject of language over the long *durée* of European modernism, linking its existential crisis to the decreasing purchase of language on reality orchestrated by the rise of mechanically reproducible images. And Nicholas Mirzoeff finds that the term *visuality* is first employed by Thomas Carlyle in "On Heroes and Hero Worship" to describe the perspective of the conservative hero who will save the republic from the rising power of the hordes. The suggestion is that the technomediated perceptions that are in the contemporary at once unavoidable and constitutive—perceptions that we now identify under the rubric of visuality—continue to be tinged with this reactionary perceptual modality, in short, a suppression of the masses. Put another way, we could say that the contemporary formation of visuality continues to conspire against the progressive forces of history. Here I would also include my own work on the cinematic mode of production as the emergence of a technology for the industrialization of visual perception and the transformation of the form of both work and the wage.

30 For more on this issue of inscription on the flesh of the global-social body, see my essay, "Paying Attention," in *Cabinet 24* (New York: Distributed Art Publishers, 2007). The essay was republished for Documenta XII. (Documenta is the largest contemporary art exhibition in Europe—similar to the Venice Biennial but curated by a single curator. http://d13.documenta.de/)

11

DON'T HATE THE PLAYER, HATE THE GAME

The Racialization of Labor in World of Warcraft

Lisa Nakamura

Cartman: "I am the mightiest dwarf in all of Azeroth!"
Kyle: "Wow, look at all these people playing right now."
Cartman: "Yeah, it's bullcrap. I bet half of these people are Koreans."
South Park, Season 10, Episode 8, "Make Love Not Warcraft"[1]

Where did all the doggies and kitty cats go
Since the gold farmers started to show
Don't want to know what's in the egg roll
And they keep comin' back
Cuz you're giving them dough
Take one down and I felt inspired
Corpse camp until
This China-man gets fired
That's one farmer they'll have to replace
Not supposed to be here in the first place.
I don't know any other way to convey
How much we wish you'd all just go away
Server economy in disarray
Guess I'll just fear your mobs around all day.
Ni Hao (A Gold Farmer's Story), warcraftmovies.com

Massively multiplayer online role-playing games (MMOs) such as World of Warcraft (WoW), Lineage II, and Everquest are immensely profitable, skillfully designed, immersive, and beautifully detailed virtual worlds that enable both exciting game play and the creation of real-time, digitally embodied communities. In 2011, World of Warcraft surpassed 10 million users, confirming games economist Edward Castronova's (2005) predictions for exponential growth, and these players are intensely interested in and protective of their investments in the virtual world of Azeroth. This stands to reason: as Alexander Galloway (2006) writes, "virtual worlds are always in some basic way the expression of utopian desire." One of players' primary rallying points as a group has been to advocate strongly that American video game developer and publisher Blizzard Entertainment regulate cheating within the game more stringently. However, the definition of cheating is unclear, despite the game's end-user license agreement, since many players break these rules with impunity, a state of affairs that is actually the norm in MMOs.[2] As Mia Consalvo (2007) argues, it makes much less sense to see cheating within games as a weakness of game design or a problem with player behavior than to see it as an integral part of game culture, a feature that keeps players from getting stuck and quitting. Cheating thus benefits players and the game industry alike. However, cheating is as varied in its forms as is game play itself, and some varieties are viewed by players as socially undesirable, while others are not.

Though Consalvo (2007) stresses the extremely subjective ways that MMO players define cheating, asserting that "a debate exists around the definition of cheating and whether it actually hurts other players [and] players themselves see little common ground in what constitutes cheating" (Consalvo 2007: 150), real-money trading—or buying and selling in-game property for real money—is widely considered the worst, more morally reprehensible form of cheating. The practice of gold farming, or selling in-game currency to players for real money, usually through resellers such as the International Gaming Exchange (IGE) or eBay, is especially disliked. Leisure players have been joined by player-workers from poorer nations such as China and Korea, who are often subject to oppression as both a raciolinguistic minority and as undesirable underclassed social bodies in the context of game play and game culture.[3] These "farmers," as other players dismissively dub them, produce and sell virtual goods such as weapons, garments, animals, and even their own leveled-up avatars or virtual bodies to other players for real-world money. As Consalvo (2007: 164) writes, the "gill-buying practice is viscerally despised by some players."

Constance Steinkuehler's (2006) analysis of Lineage II, a Korean MMO, discovered this to be true as well and, more importantly, uncovered some of the ways in which the condemnation of virtual currency buying is far exceeded by a visceral hatred of gold sellers or farmers. This hatred is strongly articulated to race and ethnicity: many (though by no means all) gold farmers are Chinese, and there is a decidedly anti-Asian flavor to many player protests against Chinese gold farmers. As Steinkuehler notes, hatred of gold farmers has given rise to polls querying players on North American servers: "Is it OK to Hate Chinese Players?" (32% of players responded yes; the majority, 39%, replied, "I don't hate China, just what they stand for in L2"; and 10% checked "I am CN and you should mind yourself, you racist pig"). Though she notes "calling someone 'Chinese' is a general insult that seems aimed more at one's style of play than one's real-world ethnicity" (Steinkuehler 2006: 200), the construction of Chinese identity in MMOs as abject, undesirable, and socially contaminated racializes the culture of online games, a culture that scholars such as Castronova (2005) have claimed are unique (and valuable) because they are exempt from real-world problems such as racism, classism, "looksism," and other types of social inequality.[4] Though, as T. L. Taylor (2006) notes, MMOs are distinguished by their "enormous potential in a fairly divisive world," the "fact that people play with each other across regions and often countries" as often as not results in ethnic and racial chauvinism: "as a tag the conflation of Chinese with gold farmer has seemed to come all too easy and now transcends any particular game" (Taylor 2006: 321). Robert Brookey (2007) expands upon this claim; in his analysis of gaming blogs, he discovered "overt racist attitudes" toward Chinese farmers; most importantly, that "some players, who harbor negative feelings toward Chinese farmers, do not believe that these feelings denote racial discrimination." Thus, although it is the case that players cannot see each others' bodies while playing, specific forms of gamic labor, such as gold farming and selling, as well as specific styles of play, have become racialized as Chinese, producing new forms of networked racism that are particularly easy for players to disavow.

Unlike the Internet itself, MMOs have *always* been a global medium, with many games originating in Asia.[5] Korea has been a major player in the industry from its beginning, but Asian players are numerous even in U.S.-run MMOs such as Blizzard's WoW; in 2008, the number of simultaneous players on Chinese WoW servers exceeded 1 million, the most that have ever been recorded in Europe or the United States ("Blizzard" 2008). Thus, although gold farmers are typecast as Chinese, most Asian players are leisure players, not player-workers. WoW sells Chinese, European, Japanese, and U.S. versions of its game software and also organizes its players into groups once they are signed on. MMOs support thousands, sometimes millions, of players from all over the world simultaneously in a live environment; therefore, to make the game playable and pleasurable and take pressure off of resources and space, players sign up to play on a specific "shard" or "server" when they create their user accounts. These servers are divided by region and language to facilitate efficient connections and handshaking as well as to promote social discourse between players who speak different languages, but users can choose to play on any server they wish. Blizzard disables virtual currency transfers between servers, which means that each server contains its own economy. Thus, players who engage in real-money trading can be found on every server—MMO virtual property resellers such as IGE offer level-ups, gold, and other property on every server in WoW.

Like the biblical poor, in the world of MMOs, gold farmers are and will probably always be with us. Perhaps because most digital game scholars are players themselves, the economics of gold farming are usually discussed in the scholarly literature in terms of their negative impact upon the world of leisure players, who buy gold because they lack the time to earn virtual capital through "grinding" or performing the repetitive and tedious tasks that are the basis of most MMOs.

However, as Toby Miller (2006) has advocated, digital games scholars need to attend to its medium's political economy, and to "follow the money" to its less glamorous, less virtual places, such as games console and PC manufacturing plants, gold farmer sweatshops, and precious metals reclamation sites—in short, to China. Yet while many players are fairly unaware that their computer hardware is born and dies, or is recycled, in China, they are *exceptionally* aware of the national, racial, and linguistic identity of gold farmers. Gold farmers are reviled player-workers whose position in the gamic economy resembles that of other immigrant groups who cross national borders to work, but, unlike other types of "migrant" workers, their labors are offshore, and thus invisible—they are "virtual migrants" (see Aneesh 2006). However, user-generated content in and around MMOs actively visualizes this process. Machinima fan-produced video production racializes this reviled form of gameplay as "Oriental" in ways that hail earlier visual media such as music videos and minstrel shows. Gold farming, a burgeoning gray-market labor practice in a disliked and semi-illegal industry that, as Consalvo (2007) notes, may soon outstrip the primary games market as a source of revenue, has become racialized as Asian—specifically as Chinese. The impact this racialization has had upon the medium and culture of gaming is tremendous and echoes earlier examples of online community such as MUDs (multiplayer real-time virtual world) and MOOs (text-based online virtual reality system), which also encouraged the development of racialized personae in a supposedly race-free medium.[6]

A Short History of Racial Identity in Virtual Worlds: From Public to For-Profit

While early text-only online social environments such as MUDs and MOOs enabled users to adopt virtual personae or avatars across the lines of race, gender, and sexuality in order to experience pleasure, their contemporary counterparts, MMOs, put users to work to create profit. Earlier online environments such as LambdaMOO were usually run by volunteers and academic institutions such as Xerox PARC at Stanford and were accessed free of charge by users. Though these virtual worlds are the direct ancestors of MMORPGs, there is at least one major difference: MMORPGs are heavily capitalized entertainment media and are rapidly converging with other digital forms, such as cinema, online commerce, and advertising (Mortensen 2006). Cross-media franchises such as the *Lord of the Rings, Star Trek,* and *Star Wars* have all produced successful digital games as well as action figures, spin-off novels, and other officially licensed media products. MUDs and MOOs employed narratives and imagery from licensed media such as science fiction novels and films but were not owned or developed for profit. However, as Jenkins (2006) notes, participatory media technologies like the Internet, digital video, and video game engines have permitted fans to broadcast their own, unofficial, unlicensed additions to these franchises, thus changing the political economy of media irrevocably and for the better. The Internet takes pride of place among these technologies; it is the distribution channel that has permitted fans to broadcast their work for minimal cost and with maximum impact. The mass adoption of the Internet in recent years has led to both an increase in user production and the increased licensing of digital media products, creating a delicate balance between media industries' desire to control their products and fans' desires to contribute to them. While many scholars have noted the democratic, empowering effects of participatory media upon media for users, it can also provide fans with a powerful vector for distributing racializing discourses that reflect the concerns of an online culture obsessed with determining identity online through virtual profiling.[7]

MUDs—virtual communities based upon gift economies that were distinguished by their key differences from the real world of capital, labor, and profit— have given way to for-profit virtual worlds that increasingly dominate the media landscape. This has created an increasingly polarized social environment; one divided into leisure players and player-workers, virtual property buyers and laborer/ sellers, and Asians and non-Asians. Asian "farmers" or virtual capital laborers have a significant cultural and social impact on MMOs. Though not all farmers, or for-profit workers, are Asian by any means, the image of the farmer has come to include race as part of the package. This racialization of the player-worker in online social spaces is actively constructed by WoW fans, who have produced an extensive body of writing and digital cinema that cybertypes Asian farmers as unwanted, illegal, and antisocial workers (Nakamura 2002).

In an essay on the social lives of guilds in WoW, Dmitri Williams (2006: 358) asks, "How is race being managed within the anonymity of avatar space?" While Castronova (2005) and Julian Dibbell (2006) have produced excellent book-length treatments of digital economies in online gaming spaces, there is little scholarship on the way that the rapidly expanding economies of MMORPGs are creating differentially racialized profiles, images, and behaviors (see Chan 2006; Yee 2006). While WoW and other MMOs do permit users to choose their own avatars within the range offered by the game's protocols, they are far from anonymous spaces for avatars. Race is indeed managed in MMOs, both by the affordances or rules of the game and by the game's players. While others have noted that the game narrative is structured around the notion of racial conflict between distinct races that players must choose, my focus here is upon the racializations that players bring to the game (Gotanda 2004). Player resentment against Asian player-workers results in a continual process of profiling other avatars to determine their status as legitimate leisure players or as unwanted farmers. Player class (as Yee 2005 notes, rogues and hunter class avatars are often chosen by player-workers because they can accumulate saleable property without needing to group with other players), language use or unwillingness to speak to other players, equipment type, and repetitive behaviors are noted by other players as evidence that a player is a Chinese gold farmer. Although these behaviors, player classes, uses of language, and equipment types are often employed by other leisure players, prejudice against farmers who are "ruining the game" results in the production of media texts that reproduce familiar tropes from earlier anti-Asian discourse. Though players cannot detect other play-ers' races by looking at their physical bodies, they constantly produce a taxonomy of behaviors that create new racializations of avatar bodies in digital space. A player who speaks either Chinese or ungrammatical or broken English, who refuses to speak at all, or who repetitively harvests the game's prizes or "mobs" is often as-sumed to be a Chinese gold farmer and may be targeted for ill treatment or even virtual death. This profiling activity is the subject of the fan-produced machinima that I will discuss in this essay and is part of a larger biometric turn initiated by digital culture's informationalization of the body (Hammonds 2006; Chun 2007).

The Racialization of Player-Workers in MMOs

Gold farmers were a fairly mysterious, almost mythic group while Dibbell (2006) was conducting much of the research for *Play Money;* however, as Yee (2006) notes, since 2005, a surge of information about Chinese farmers has become available in the popular press as well as online. Gold farmers, or workers who are paid to "play online all day, every day, gathering artificial gold coins and other virtual loot that, 'as it turns out, can be transformed into real cash,'" were the topic of a *New York Times* story on December 9, 2005 (Barboza 2005). They are also a major source of controversy and division among players. As Dibbell writes, the rise in WoW's pop-ularity gave rise to a flourishing economy in virtual loot, such that "millions now spoke knowledgeably of the plague of 'Chinese gold farmers'" (Dibbell 2006: 294).

In his *New York Times* magazine article, "The Life of a Chinese Gold Farmer," Dibbell (2007) writes quite sympathetically of their plight, noting that, while play-ers complain vociferously about the way that gold selling has plagued or "ruined" the game economy,

> as a matter of everyday practice, it is the farmers who catch it in the face. . . . In homemade *World of Warcraft* video clips that circulate on You-Tube or GameTrailers, with titles like "Chinese gold farmers must die" and "Chinese farmer extermination," players document their farmer-killing expeditions through that same Timbermaw-ridden patch of *WoW* in which Min does his farming—a place so popular with farmers that Western players sometimes call it China Town. (Dibbell 2007: 40).

Their position as virtual service workers mimics that of illegal immigrants and other low-end workers in service economies in the global South. They are rou-tinely racially profiled and harassed by other players in MMORPGs, producing a climate of anti-Asian sentiment.

WoW and other virtual worlds have been touted for their democratic potential:

> People entering a synthetic world can have, in principle, any body they desire. At a stroke, this feature of synthetic worlds removes from the social

calculus all the unfortunate effects that derive from the body... all without bearing some of the burdens that adhere to the Earth bodies we were born with. (Castronova 2005: 25–6)

The social calculus of race, nation, and class are burdens borne by Chinese gold farmers, Chinese leisure players, and, ultimately, the gaming community as a whole. Hatred of Chinese gold farmers drives WoW users to produce visual and textual media that hews closely to earlier anti-Asian discourses, media that they broadcast to other users through forums, general chat in-game, and homemade videos.

World of Warcraft is a virtual world where significant numbers of people are conducting their psychic, financial, and social lives. This massively multiplayer online game continues to roll out content for its users in the form of expansion packs, frequent software updates, action figures and a feature film in development, and an extensive content-rich and frequently updated website for its community of users. Users are invited by Blizzard to get involved in some aspects of this world's production by contributing interesting screen shots, machinima, personal narratives, and advice on game play to its site, and even in cases when they are not, players actively produce in defiance of its wishes. Topics that the game industry may wish to avoid because they may seem divisive or may reflect badly on the virtual world are confronted frequently in participatory media created by its users.

Machinima as User-Generated Racial Narrative: The Media Campaign against Chinese Player-Workers in WoW

Machinima is a crucial site of struggle over the meaning of race in shared digital space, and it is a central part of the culture of MMOs such as World of Warcraft. Machinima has recently become the object of much academic interest because it exemplifies the notion of participatory media, an influential and useful formulation that is the basis for Jenkins's (2006) book *Convergence Culture*. In it, Jenkins describes how machinima are prime examples of users' seizing the right to contribute to media universes in defiance of industry wishes, standards, and control; their value lies in the ability to produce counternarratives whose impact lies in their active subversion of the narrow messages available in many dominant media texts. Machinima literally extend the story space of the games upon which they are based, and the most interesting of these actively work to reconfigure their original meanings in progressive, socially productive ways. Jenkins explains that transmediated story spaces that exist across media platforms permit increased opportunities for engaged users like fans to insert their own content into these "synthetic worlds," to use Castronova's (2005) phrase—while game developers like Blizzard provide limited, licensed, and fairly tightly controlled virtual space for players to navigate, users extend this space by writing fan fiction, creating original artwork, and making their own movies or machinima using images, narratives, and tropes from the game.

While part of the pleasure of World of Warcraft consists in navigating its richly imaged, beautifully rendered spaces, users must rely upon the company to provide more of this valuable commodity in the form of expansion packs such as "The Burning Crusade" and "The Wrath of the Lich King," eagerly anticipated and extremely profitable products for which users are willing to stand in line for days. Machinima permits users to expand this space for free; while navigable space is still tightly controlled by the company—unlike in Second Life, where users are unable to build their own structures or objects to insert in the world—machinima allows users to extend its representational or narrative space, creating scenarios that are genuinely new because they depict activities or behaviors impossible in the space of the game. This is a fascinating area of study and one that is a thriving and integral part of WoW in particular. The struggle for resources integral to the structure of MMOs can also be re-envisioned as the struggle to own or claim virtual space and to police national boundaries as well.[8] Player-produced machinima accessed from warcraftmovies.com make arguments about race, labor, and the racialization of space in World of Warcraft.[9] These highly polemical texts employ the visual language of the game, one of the most recognizable and distinctive ever created for shared virtual play, to bring into sharp relief the contrast between the privileges of media production available to empowered players with the time and inclination to create machimina and those who are shut out of this aspect of WoW by their status as player-workers. Participatory media is a privilege of the leisure class; active fandom is too expensive a proposition for many digital workers, who, as Dibbell explains poignantly, can't afford to *enjoy* the game that they have mastered, much less produce media to add to it.[10]

Not surprisingly, there are two tiers of this type of user production—Blizzard frequently solicits screen shots, holds art contests, and showcases user-produced machinima that become part of the official canon of the game. However, there is extensive traffic in content that is not endorsed by the developer but that is nonetheless part of the continuing rollout of the world. Racial discourse is a key part of this rollout. If the official World of Warcraft game is a gated community that users pay to enter, its covenants consist in its end-user license agreement. However, part of Jenkins's (2006) argument is that media technologies such as the Internet have made it impossible to gate media in the same way. The underground machinima I will discuss in this essay build and expand the world of WoW in regard to representations of race in just as constitutive a way as its official content. As Lowood (2006) notes, WoW players have been creating visual moving image records as long as, or perhaps even longer than, they have been playing the game. Thus, machinima is anything but a derivative or ancillary form in relation to WoW, for its history runs exactly parallel, and in some sense, slightly in advance of the game itself—as Lowood notes, users were employing the beta version of WoW to make machimina before the game was available to the public. Lowood claims, "*WoW* movies, from game film to dance videos, have become an integral part of the culture shared by a player community" (Lowood 2006: 374).

If indeed machinima extend the world of game play, how are players cocreating this world? Antifarmer machinima produces overtly racist narrative space to attach to a narrative that, while carefully avoiding overt references to racism or racial conflict in our world, is premised upon a racial war in an imaginary world—the World of Azeroth. While Jenkins (2006) celebrates the way that fans, particularly female fans, have extended the worlds of *Star Trek* in truly liberatory ways, inserting homosexual narratives between Captain Kirk and Spock that the franchise would never permit or endorse, a closer look at user-produced content from warcraftmovies.com reveals a contraction and retrenchment of concepts of gender, race, and nation rather than their enlargement.

Warcraftmovies.com, the most popular World of Warcraft machinima website, organizes its user-generated content under several categories. "Underground" machinima deals with topics such as "bug/exploit," "exploration," and "gold farming." *Ni Hao (A Gold Farmer's Story)*, by "Nyhm" of "Madcow Studios," has earned a "4x Platinum" rating, the highest available, from warcraftmovies.com, and the video is also available on YouTube, where it has been viewed 533,567 times, has been favorited 1,998 times, and has produced 981 comments from users (*Ni Hao*). This extremely popular, visually sophisticated machinima music video features new lyrics sung over the instrumental track of Akon's hit hip-hop song "Smack That." This polemical anti-Asian machinima's chorus is:

> I see you farmin primals in Shadow moon Valley, 10 cents an hour's good money when you are Chinese, I buy your auctions you sell my gold right back to me, feels like you're bendin' me over, you smile and say "ni hao" and farm some gold, "ni hao" it's getting old, ni hao, oh. (see Figure 11.1)

The claim that "10 cents an hour's good money when you are Chinese" displays awareness that the farmers' incentive for exploiting or "bending over" better-resourced players comes from economic need. Another part of the video shows a farmer shoveling gold into a vault, with the subtitled lyric "IGE's making bank now." The International Gaming Exchange is one of the largest resellers of gold, avatar level-ups, and other virtual property, and it is a U.S. business, not an Asian one. Nonetheless, this commentary on the gold farming economic system resorts to the full gamut of racial stereotypes, including a Chinese flag as the background for a video scene of a sexy singing female troll in a scanty outfit flanked by the human farmers wielding pickaxes and shovels.

Later in the video, a Chinese gold farmer is killed by another player, who comments as he kneels next to the corpse that "this China-man gets fired, that's one farmer they'll have to replace, not supposed to be here in the first place" (see Figure 11.2). Clearly, Asian players—specifically those suspected of being farmers but, as can be seen in this image, all "China-men"—have a diminished status on WoW: many American players fail to see them as "people." As Cartman notes in the Emmy Award–winning "Make Love Not Warcraft" episode of *South Park,*

FIGURE 11.1 "10 cents an hour's good money when you are Chinese."

Asians don't count as other players, or as people. In this sense, they are nonplayer characters, or NPCs, which are typically artificial intelligence modules, or AIs, that give players information or missions. NPCs can also refer to the game's monsters, or "mobs." This characterization of Asian farmers as either automated service workers or monsters fits neatly into their racialization within *Ni Hao,* for the video depicts them as all owning exactly the same avatar, a man wearing a red and gold outfit and wielding a pickax. This dehumanization of the Asian player—they "all look the same" because they all *are* the same—is evocative of earlier conceptions of Asian laborers as interchangeable and replaceable.

As Robert Lee (1999) notes, language, food, and hair were all privileged sites of boundary crises set up between Chinese and whites in minstrel shows in nineteenth-century America. Player-produced videos such as *Ni Hao* mock Chinese food ways, implying that Chinese eat dogs and cats. This is a nonsensical accusation, since there are no dogs or cats in WoW, nor any egg rolls. But, of course, neither are there real-world races in WoW, until they are actively produced and shaped in visual form by fans' media production. In addition, the exoticism and supposed unintelligibility of the language is highlighted by the use of a spiky-looking, irregular font that spells out the title *Ni Hao.* The management of race within the virtual worlds of MMOs is reflective of earlier methods of managing race in U.S. history, but it also offers some new twists. Though gold farming is not a form of labor that is exclusively practiced by Chinese player-workers, it has become racialized, partly through the dissemination of texts such as these. This has been well documented in other MMOs as well; as Steinkuehler (2006) notes, the player class of female dwarf was tainted by its association with Chinese gold farmers, and thus became an unplayable class because female dwarfs became racialized as Chinese.[11]

FIGURE 11.2   Screen shot from *Ni Hao.*

Avatarial Capital: The Disenfranchisement of Player-Workers and the Neoliberal Discourse of Colorblindness in MMOs

Nick Yee (2006) has written eloquently about the resonances between anti-Chinese rhetoric during the gold rush and some of WoW's anti-Chinese farmer discourses, resulting in a lively discussion on his blog that contains in miniature some key neoliberal positions on race. His excellent article, "Yi Shan Guan," yielded over a hundred comments from readers as of October 30, 2007, many of whom dismissed anti-Chinese gold farmer racism as not really racism, but rather a result of legitimate anger over player-workers ruining other players' immersion in the game as well as creating in-game inflation. These positions are mirrored in the lively discussion forums for *Ni Hao* on warcraftmovies.com. After one poster left a comment saying simply "racist," another replied:

> g2 lv love people who consider things racism when in actuallity they are rascist for making the diffrence in their head, if every one just veiwed every one else as "people" theyd be no problem belvie i rated alrdy also.

Another remarked:

> what's rasict, no we are only one race the human race, now if there where another species and he was making fun of them, then it would be rasict. no he is only being anticultural, not rascist. anyway good job with the song Nyhm but the movie wasn't as good.

This last comment is an excellent example of the liberal position, an ideology that eschews outright racism based on bodily characteristics, favoring instead a "liberal democratic state where people of color could enjoy equal rights and upward mobility" (Lee 1999: 145) if they could succeed in assimilating to American culture. As Lee writes, the triumph of liberalism and the racial logic of the Cold War produced an "emergent discourse of race in which cultural difference replaced biological difference as the new determinant of social outcomes" (1999: 145). Asian Americans became the "model minority" after the Cold War because they could be pointed to as successfully assimilated to American capitalism but also, as Lee points out, because they were not black.

Neoliberalism is premised on the notion of colorblindness. The first comment cited above advocates exactly this position: racism is not the result of an individual's bad behavior, but rather the result of the person who identifies it, for they are they ones who see race, or "make the difference in their head." As is also evident in the readers' comments to Yee's essay, posters are eager to prove that their hatred of Chinese gold farmers isn't racist, is not a prejudice against "biological difference," but is rather a dislike of unsuccessful assimilation to American social norms, what the poster calls the "anticultural" position. The problem with gold farmers isn't that they *are* Chinese; it is that they *"act* Chinese." The characterization of American WoW player behavior as self-sufficient, law-abiding, noncommercial, and properly social is belied by their role as gold buyers within WoW's server economy: the purchasing of virtual property lies within the bounds of American gaming behavior while selling it does not. But this is only the case if one is Chinese—IGE is not targeted in racialized terms, if at all. The notion that it is permissible to condemn someone for how they behave rather than what they are is a technique for avoiding charges of racism, for culture is seen as something that can be changed, hopefully through assimilation to American norms, but race is not. However, as Yoshino (2006) notes, this neoliberal position results in a compulsion to cover one's identity, to behave in ways that are normatively colorless or sexless, in order to take one's unchangeable race, gender, or sexuality out of play.

Ni Hao is one of many examples of machinima that demonstrate that anti-Asian racism is both common within the game and that the problems with the server economy are attributed to Chinese gold farmers. Judging from its popularity on YouTube, this is a widespread belief. It also employs an unusual technique to stress the equivalence between Chinese culture and gold farming: one episode depicts a WoW avatar entering a Chinese restaurant whose image is *not* taken from in-game, but rather is a photographic image featuring several Chinese people eating. The next scene depicts a Chinese fortune cookie opening up to reveal the words "Buy gold" as the title proclaims "it's another gold farm ad from Beijing." This insertion of photographs of actual people within the world of WoW machinima violates a generic convention—generally, machinima makers stick to in-game images. This exceptional moment invokes images of real Chinese people to make clear the connection between their racialized bodies and gold farmers in-game. WoW allows players to hide their race during game play, and an enormous amount of player energy goes into outing gold farmers. Though, as noted earlier, WoW and other MMOs are populated by as many legitimate or leisure players who are Asian as those who are European or American, it is clear that being profiled as Korean or a "China-man" in-game can be dangerous. *Ni Hao*'s introduction asks, "I see you there, could you be the farmer?" It is crucial to note that online anonymity makes it impossible to verify whether a player is Chinese and whether he or she is, by extension, a gold farmer. Many WoW forums and video clips such as "Chronicles of a Gold Farmer" address this problem by sharing strategies for profiling Chinese worker players.

Ni Hao depicts the killing of gold farmers in-game amid a mise-en-scène of gongs, dog-filled egg rolls, fortune cookies, Chinese flags, and photographs of Chinese people dining in a restaurant. Even in a theoretically body-free space such as an MMO, the calculus of race, nation, and class result in user-produced algorithms based on player behaviors, equipment type, language use, and player class that result in racist discourse, both in real-time interaction and in the construction of WoW's transmedited synthetic world.[12]

As Dibbell (2007) notes, WoW isn't a *game* for everyone in a literal sense: for player-workers, it is a virtual sweatshop. Player-workers in MMOs produce informationalized property that they can neither consume themselves nor sell directly to those who can—in this sense, their high-tech labor in low-tech conditions more closely resembles maquiladora factory laborers' conditions than it does other recreational or professional software-based activities. Farmers work in shifts, playing WoW in 12-hour sessions and sleeping on pallets—their work exemplifies "flexible accumulation's strategy of mixing nonmodern and modern forms of production," which, as Hong (2006: 115) explains, "depends on and reproduces racialized and gendered exploitation." Gold farming is an example in extremis of informationalized capitalism, for the avatar is a form of property that is composed of digital code yet produced by the sweat of a worker's brow.

Castronova (2005) makes the excellent point that much of the attraction of MMOs lies in the pleasure of accumulating "avatarial capital." Like the notion of cultural capital or human capital to which it refers, avatarial capital is a "soft" form of accumulation; as Castronova puts it, "things like education and on-the-job experience that enhance earning power... are intangible and inalienable" (2005: 110). Unlike the physical capital that is linked to both in-game currencies and real world economies, avatarial capital is a different but equally compelling scale of value based on the virtual accumulation of "experience points and skills and attributes" that "allow people to make investments, investments whose returns are in the form of increases in their ability to do and see things in the world" (Castronova 2005: 110). This is precisely the style of capital accumulation that player-workers are denied; the repetition of value-producing labor in WoW greatly curtails their movements within the game as well as the range of activities available to them. The Timbermaw area in WoW nicknamed China Town that Dibbell (2007) describes is favored by farmers not because of its beauty, exciting activities, or opportunities for exploration and creative social play, but rather because it is a good source of saleable virtual property.

While scholars such as Greg Lastowka (2007) have done an excellent job describing the rules and constraints that govern the creation and movement of physical capital within the server economy, less research has been done on avatarial capital within WoW (see also Balkin and Noveck 2006). Though as Castronova (2005: 45) notes and most gamers already know, "coming to own the avatar, psychologically, is so natural among those who spend time in synthetic worlds that it is barely noticed." This emotional investment in avatars is relatively little studied in MMOs, and certainly not from the perspective of player-workers. Filiciak's (2003) psychoanalytically informed scholarship on avatar creation and ownership posits an intimate relation between a player's real-life bodily identity and his or her avatarial body. He writes, citing Reid, "avatars 'are much more than a few bytes of computer data—they are cyborgs, a manifestation of the self beyond the realms of the physical, existing in a space where identity is self-defined rather than pre-ordained" (Filiciak 2003: 91). However, while Chinese gold farmers create and deploy avatars, they are unable to accumulate avatarial capital since their jobs consist in selling level-ups as well as gold and equipment. Thus, the notion that avatars are manifestations of the self when applied to gold farmers neatly sums up the problematics of informationalized capitalism. The privilege of avatarial self-possession is, like capital itself, unevenly distributed across geopolitical borders. Though emotional investment is an unavoidable side effect of avatar usage, the luxury of either hard or soft capital accumulation is denied player-workers in virtual worlds. If late capitalism is characterized by the requirement for subjects to be possessive individuals, to make claims to citizenship based on ownership of property, then player-workers are unnatural subjects in that they are unable to "come to own an avatar." The painful paradox of this dynamic lies in the ways that it mirrors the dispossession of information workers in the Fourth Worlds engendered by ongoing processes of globalization.[13]

Conclusion

The anti-Asian racial discourse in *Ni Hao,* as well as that noted in Brookey's (2007), Steinkuehler's (2006), and Taylor's (2006) research, are not necessarily representative of the WoW population as a whole (though it must be said that, while YouTube and warcraftmovies.com are full of machinima or trophy videos of farmer-killing replete with racist imagery, there are no pro-farmer user-produced machinima to be seen).[14] Machimina is a breakthrough medium because it differs from previous mass forms of media or performance; it is the product of individual users. However, like the minstrel shows that preceded it, it shapes the culture by disseminating arguments about the nature of race, labor, and assimilation. As a *Ni Hao* commenter on YouTube on October 31, 2007, notes: "GO MADCOW!! lol kick gold-farmer's asses;) the place in nagrand where u cant get witout fly mount is nice for china-man killing." Similarly, it is certainly not the case that games must be entirely free of racist discourse in order to be culturally important or socially productive—in short, to be "good." No multiplayer social game could meet that criterion at all times. On the other hand, if we are to take games seriously as synthetic worlds, we must be willing to take their racial discourses, media texts, and interpersonal conflicts seriously as well. As Dibbell (2006) claims, it is constraint and scarcity—the challenge of capital accumulation—that makes MMOs pleasurable, even addictive. Game economies based on cultures of scarcity engender real-money trading, and as long as this form of player-work is socially debased and racialized, it will result in radically unequal social relations, labor types, and forms of representation along the axes of nation, language, and identity. Asian player-workers are economically unable to accumulate avatarial capital and thus become persons; they are the dispossessed subjects of synthetic worlds. As long as Asian farmers are figured as unwanted guest workers within the culture of MMOs, user-produced extensions of MMO space such as machinima will most likely continue to depict Asian culture as threatening to the beauty and desirability of shared virtual space in the World of Warcraft.

Notes

1 Air date October 4, 2006, Comedy Central Network.

2 Players of WoW regularly use an arsenal of "mods" and "add-ons" that are circulated on player boards online. Although these are technically in violation of the end-user license agreement, many players consider the game unplayable without them, especially at the terminal or "end game" levels. Blizzard turns a blind eye to this, and in fact tacitly condones it by posting technical updates referring to the impact of add-ons on game performance.

3 See T. L. Taylor (2006), in-game language chauvinism and the informal enforcement of English-only chat in WoW, even by players of non-Anglophone nationalities.

4 Castronova writes that avatar use in MMOs creates new bodies for users, and that they "erase, at a stroke, every contribution to human inequality that stems from body differences" (2005: 258).

5 See Chan (2006) as well as the January 2008 special issue of *Games and Culture* on Asia, volume 3, number 1, in particular Hjorth's (2008) introductory essay, "Games@Neo-Regionalism: Locating Gaming in the Asia-Pacific."

6 See Nakamura (2002), in particular chapter 2, "Head Hunting on the Internet: Identity Tourism, Avatars, and Racial Passing in Textual and Graphic Chatspaces."

7 Machinima has been credited with enormous potential as a means by which users can create their own cinematic texts and is often seen as an ideal means for fans to make new, socially progressive meanings out of old texts. See Lowood (2006) and Jenkins (2006).

8 As Brookey (2007) argues:

> national boundaries have been reproduced in cyberspace, and the location of the servers that generate these virtual environments are used to demarcate the borders. These respondents claim that if Chinese players experience discrimination on US servers, it is because they have crossed the border into territory where they do not belong and are not welcome.

9 The phrase "player-produced machimina" is in some sense a redundant one, since machinima is from its inception an amateur form; however, it is becoming an increasingly necessary distinction as professional media producers appropriate it. *South Park*'s "Make Love Not Warfare" was coproduced with Blizzard Entertainment, and Toyota has aired a 2007 commercial made in the same way. See http://www.machinima.com/film/view&id=23588. In an example of media synergy, *South Park* capitalized on the success and popularity of the episode by bundling a World of Warcraft trial game card along with the DVD box set of its 2008 season.

10 See Dibbell for an eloquent account of "Min," a highly skilled player-worker who took great pride in being his raiding party's "tank," a "heavily armed warrior character who...is the linchpin of any raid" (2007: 41). Min's raiding team would take "any customer" into a dangerous dungeon, where a lower-level player could never survive alone, and let them pick up the valuable items dropped there—thus acting like virtual African *shikaris* or Nepalese porters. Min greatly enjoyed these raids but was eventually forced to quit them and take up farming again when they proved insufficiently profitable.

11 As Steinkuehler writes, because adena farmers often play female dwarves, they

> have become the most despised class of character throughout the game....Girl dwarfs are now reviled by many players, systematically harassed, and unable to find anyone that will allow them to hunt in their groups...it seems as if a whole new form of virtual racism has emerged, with an in-game character class unreflectively substituted for unacknowledged (and largely unexamined) real-world difference between China and America. (2006: 208)

12 Interestingly, gender is not part of this profiling practice. This may have to do with the depiction of Chinese farmers as male in both the popular press and in photo essays depicting MMO game players and their avatars. See Cooper (2007).

13 As Castells (2000: 60) writes of the Fourth World, "the rise of informationalism at the turn of the millennium is intertwined with rising inequality and social exclusion throughout the world.

14 University of California, San Diego, doctoral candidate Ge Jin's distributive filmmaking project on the lives of Chinese player-workers in MMOs can be viewed at www.chinesegoldfarmers.com. His films, which can also be viewed on YouTube, contain documentary footage of Chinese player-workers laboring in gaming workshops in Shanghai. His interviews with them make it clear that these player-workers are well aware of how despised they are by U.S. and European players, and that they feel a sense of inferiority that is articulated to their racial and ethnic identity.

References

Aneesh, A. (2006). *Virtual migration: The programming of globalization*. Durham, NC: Duke University Press.

Balkin, J. M., and B. S. Noveck. (2006). *The state of play: Law, games, and virtual worlds*. New York: New York University Press.

Barboza, D. (2005, December 9). Ogre to Slay? Outsource It to Chinese. *The New York Times*. http://query.nytimes.com/gst/fullpage.html?res=9A04E7DD1131F93AA35751C1A9639C8B63.

Blizzard Entertainment's World of Warcraft: The Burning Crusade surpasses one million peak concurrent player milestone in mainland China. (2008). *PR Newswire: United Business Media.* http://www.prnewswire.com/news/index_mail.shtml?ACCT=104&STORY=/www/story/04-11-2008/0004790864&EDATE=.

Brookey, R. A. (2007, November). *Racism and nationalism in cyberspace: Comments on farming in MMORPGS.* Paper presented at the National Communication Association Annual Convention, Chicago, IL.

Castells, M. (2000). *End of millennium* (2nd ed.). Oxford: Blackwell.

Castronova, E. (2005). *Synthetic worlds: The business and culture of online games.* Chicago: University of Chicago Press.

Chan, D. (2006). Negotiating Intra-Asian games networks: On cultural proximity, East Asian games design, and Chinese farmers. *Fibreculture* 8. http://journal.fibreculture.org/issue8/issue8_chan.html.

Chun, W. (2007). Race and software. In M. T. Nguyen and T.L.N. Tu (Eds.), *Alien encounters: Popular culture in Asian America* (305–33). Durham, NC: Duke University Press.

Consalvo, M. (2007). *Cheating: Gaining advantage in videogames.* Cambridge, MA: MIT Press.

Cooper, R. (2007). *Alter ego: Avatars and their creators.* London: Chris Boot.

Dibbell, J. (2006). *Play money.* New York: Basic Books.

Dibbell, J. (2007, June 17). The life of the Chinese gold farmer. *The New York Times Magazine,* 36–41.

Filiciak, M. (2003). Hyperidentities: Postmodern identity patterns in massively multiplayer online role-playing games. In M.J.P. Wolf and B. Perron (Eds.), *The video game theory reader* (87–102). New York: Routledge.

Galloway, A. (2006). Warcraft and utopia. *1000 days of theory.* http://ctheory.net/printer.aspx?id=507.

Gotanda, N. (2004, October). *Virtual world identity panel.* Panel presented at State of Play II, New York. http://terranova.blogs.com/terra_nova/2004/10/state_of_play_2.html.

Hammonds, E. (2006). Straw men and their followers: The return of biological race. *Is race "real"?* http://raceandgenomics.ssrc.org/Hammonds/.

Hjorth, L. (2008). Games@Neo-regionalism: Locating gaming in the Asia-Pacific. *Games and Culture* 3, no. 1: 3–12.

Hong, G. K. (2006). *The ruptures of American capital: Women of color feminism and the culture of immigrant labor.* Minneapolis: University of Minnesota Press.

Jenkins, H. (2006). *Convergence culture: Where old and new media collide.* New York: New York University Press.

Lastowka, G. (2007). *Rules of play.* terranova.blogs.com/RulesofPlay.pdf.

Lee, R. G. (1999). *Orientals: Asian Americans in popular culture.* Philadelphia: Temple University Press.

Lowood, H. (2006). Storyline, dance/music, or PvP? Game movies and community players in World of Warcraft. *Games and Culture* 1, no. 4: 362–82.

Miller, T. (2006). Gaming for beginners. *Games and Culture* 1, no. 1: 5–12.

Mortensen, T. E. (2006). WoW is the new MUD: Social gaming from text to video. *Games and Culture* 1, no. 4: 397–413.

Nakamura, L. (2002). *Cybertypes: Race, identity, and ethnicity on the Internet.* New York: Routledge.

Ni Hao (A Gold Farmer's Story). http://youtube.com/watch?v=0dkkf5NEIo0.

Steinkuehler, C. (2006). The mangle of play. *Games and Culture* 1, no. 3: 199–213.

Taylor, T. L. (2006). Does WoW change everything? How a PvP server, multinational player base, and surveillance mod scene cause me pause. *Games and Culture* 1, no. 4: 318–37.

Williams, D. (2006). From tree house to barracks: The social life of guilds in World of Warcraft. *Games and Culture* 1, no. 4: 338–61.

Yee, N. (2005). Introduction: The RL demographics of World of Warcraft. *The Daedalus Project* 3–4. http://www.nickyee.com/daedalus/archives/001364.php.

Yee, N. (2006). Yi-Shan-Guan. *The Daedalus Project* 4–1. http://www.nickyee.com/daedalus/archives/001493.php.

Yoshino, K. (2006). *Covering: The hidden assault on our civil rights* (1st ed.). New York: Random House.

PART IV

Organized Networks in an Age of Vulnerable Publics

12

THESIS ON DIGITAL LABOR IN AN EMERGING P2P ECONOMY

Michel Bauwens

Peer-to-peer (P2P) is the ideology of the new cognitive working class. The majority of workers in Western countries are no longer involved in factory work but are either cognitive or service workers. There are strong connections between peer-to-peer values such as openness, participation, commons orientation, and the structural conditions of this new working class.

First, peer-to-peer responds to the ideal conditions for cognitive work. For cognitive work to progress, it needs participation of all those who can contribute, and the knowledge needs to be freely shared and available to all who will need the same material in the future. It is no accident that peer production was born among the developers of software code, who are uniquely dependent on access to shareable code to progress in their work.

Under structural conditions of exploitative and intellectual property-constrained wage-based knowledge work, peer production is the modality of life and work that cognitive workers aspire to and engage in whenever they can either escape voluntarily from waged labor, or are obliged to engage in because of a precarious exodus outside of wage labor in the context of conditions of temporary or permanent economic crisis.

Peer-to-peer corresponds to the objective needs of the new craft structure of cognitive labor. Cognitive workers are no longer primarily engaged in long-term factory work but have very flexible career paths, by choice or necessity, which require them to change from being wage laborers to independent freelance consultants to entrepreneurs and back again. Under conditions of chosen or forced flexibility, workers have an objective interest in being networked to gain practical experience, social and reputational capital, and access to networks of exchange and solidarity. Networked peer production is the best avenue to obtain these advantages.

Peer-to-peer, and engagement with peer production, is the objective condition of participation into networks and therefore affects and engages all network users to the degree that they are engaged in online collaboration and knowledge exchange and the eventual creation of common value through such free aggregation of effort. All work, however, has cognitive aspects, and so today all workers are exposed to networks and the peer-to-peer value system. The peer-to-peer value system and peer production as a social dynamic are therefore *not* constrained to full-time knowledge workers, but to the totality of the working class and working people.

Because of the hyperproductive nature of peer production, which allows for broader participation and input, passionate engagement, and universal distribution of its benefits (conditioned by network access), it attracts the participation and engagement of capital through the activities of netarchical capitalists. Netarchical capital is that sector of capital that understands the hyperproductive nature of peer production and therefore enables and empowers social production to occur, but it is conditioned by the possibility of value extraction to the benefit of the holders of capital.

Peer production is both immanent and transcendent vis-à-vis capitalism, because it has features that strongly decommodify both labor and immaterial value and institute a field of action based on peer-to-peer dynamics and a peer-to-peer value system. Peer production functions within the cycle of accumulation of capital but also within the new cycle of the creation and accumulation of the commons. Netarchical capital uses peer production for its own accumulation of capital; peer producers naturally strive for the continued existence and protection of their commons.

The creation of commons under the rule of capital is *not* a zero-sum game. This means that the fact or objective relation between the commons and capital does not automatically constitute a hard and fast distinction between capitalist and anticapitalist commons. Workers associated with peer production have a natural interest to maintain and expand the commons of knowledge, code, and design, and under conditions of capital, the role of wage labor and capitalist investment contributes to the sustainability of both the commons and the commoners.

However, under conditions of capitalist crisis, commoners have an objective interest in maintaining commons and conditions of participation that create maximum independence from capital and aim for its eventual replacement as the dominant system. We propose that this can happen through the creation of noncapitalist, community-supportive, benefit-driven entities that participate in market exchange without participating in capital accumulation. Benefit-driven institutions are responsible for the financial sustainability and social reproduction of the commoners as well as for the protection and strengthening of the commons.

Through the use of a new type of peer production license, commoners can freely share the commons with commons-friendly entities while charging for-profit entities that do not reciprocate to the commons, thereby creating a positive feedback loop that creates a commons-centered countereconomy. Crucial for phase transition under conditions of capitalist crisis is to combine the emergent countereconomy and its working solutions to issues of social reproduction to the broad social movements that emerge to protect the life conditions of working people.

Traditional labor and its organizations have an objective interest, under conditions of declining capitalism, to adopt the idea of global and shared innovation commons and thereby ally themselves with the emergence and deepening of peer production. Under conditions of social strife, capitalist corporations can be transformed into worker-owned, self-managed entities that create their own commons of shared knowledge, code, and design.

Farmers and agricultural workers have a similar interest in the creation of shared innovation commons to transform soil-depleting industrial agriculture into smart eco-agriculture based on shared innovation commons uniting farmers and agricultural knowledge workers.

Commons-oriented peer production can both strengthen netarchical capital, and hence the system of capital accumulation, and the reproduction of the commons. Peer producers can benefit from corporate platforms while struggling for their own rights as the real value creators and, in conditions of social strength, could potentially take over such platforms as common or publicly owned utilities.

Participants in commoner-owned for-benefit entities can significantly transcend purely competitive market dynamics while avoiding authoritarian central planning through the adoption of open-book management, adaptation to publicly available signaling, and negotiated coordination of production and distribution. This does not obviate the possible need for democratic planning through citizen participation whenever this is needed and wished for. However, it creates broad areas for mutual alignment of productive capacities.

The traditional ideologies and movements of the industrial labor movement became largely associated with collective property. Peer production opens the avenue for more distributed property, whereby individuals can freely aggregate not only their immaterial productive resources but their material productive resources. Under those conditions, possible abuse of collective property is balanced by the individual freedom of forking productive resources.

Peer production is vital for sustainability and biosphere-friendly production methods, as open design communities design naturally for sustainability but also transform the production process itself—for example, to ensure participation and more distributed access to productive resources. Combined with the development of more distributed machinery as well as more distributed capital allocation, peer production can lead to a new system that combines smart material relocalization with global cooperative innovation and the existence of global phyles uniting peer production entities on a global material scale. Phyles are transnational, community-supportive entities that create a new layer of postcapitalist material cooperation.

Free labor is only problematic under conditions of precarity and nonreciprocal value capture by (netarchical) capital. Under conditions of social solidarity, the freely given participation to common value projects is a highly emancipatory activity.

Because of its hyperproductive nature and inherent ecological sustainability, peer production becomes the condition for transcending capitalism. Its own logic—that is, free contributions to a commons managed by for-benefit associations and made sustainable through for-benefit entrepreneurship of the commoners themselves—creates a seed for a new social and economic form centered on the core value creation of the commons, managed and contributed to by both for-benefit associations and entrepreneurial coalitions and sustained by participatory collective services, which form the basis of a new model of the partner state, which enables and empowers social production as the core reason of its existence.

The hyperproductivity of peer production makes it conform to the dual conditions for phase transitions—that is, the crisis of the old model of production and the availability of a working alternative that can perform better while solving a number of systemic problems plaguing the current dominant form of production. The task of the movements of cognitive and other forms of labor is to create a new hegemony and a new commons-based alliance for social change that challenges the domination of capital, the commodity form, and the biospheric destruction that is inherent to it.

13

CLASS AND EXPLOITATION ON THE INTERNET

Christian Fuchs

The term *social media* has been established to characterize World Wide Web platforms such as social networking sites, blogs, wikis, and microblogs. Such platforms are among the most accessed websites in the world and include Facebook, YouTube, Wikipedia, Blogger, Twitter, LinkedIn, and WordPress. All online platforms and media are social in the sense of providing information that is a result of social relations. The notion of sociality underlying the now frequently employed term social media is based on concepts such as communication, community, cooperation, collaboration, and sharing. All too often, the term is used without differentiation or grounding in social theory.

This chapter challenges techno-optimistic versions of social media analysis by pointing out its limits. First, the notion of a participatory Internet is questioned by conducting an analysis of the political economy of selected corporate social media platforms. Next, an alternative theorization of social media that is based on Marx's class theory is offered. Finally, some thoughts about the need for an alternative Internet are presented.

Critical Internet studies is an emerging field of research. Trebor Scholz's conference The Internet as Playground and Factory has shown how important critical thinking about the contemporary Internet is and that there is a huge interest in critical political economy and theory relating to the Internet. Today, we are experiencing times of capitalist crisis, and it is no surprise that critical studies and critical political economy are celebrating a comeback after decades of postmodern, culturalist, and neoliberal domination of academia. Questions relating to class, labor, exploitation, alienation, and ideology have become paramount. The critical analysis of social media requires a critique of both ideology and exploitation. It also calls for practical proposals. Trebor Scholz (2008) has stressed that "the suggestion of sudden newness of social media is aimed at potential investors" and that web 2.0 is therefore primarily a marketing ideology. Jodi Dean argues that the Internet and other forms of communication in "communicative capitalism [are] rooted in communication without communicability" (Dean 2004: 281). Dean suggests that the Internet becomes a technological fetish that advances post-politics. Mark Andrejecvic (2002: 239) speaks of "the interactive capability of new media to exploit the work of being watched." He argues that "accounts of exploitation do not necessarily denigrate the activities or the meanings they may have for those who participate in them rather than the social relations that underwrite expropriation and alienation" (Andrejevic 2011: 283). These and other contributions are characteristic of the emergence of the field of critical Internet studies.[1]

In this chapter, we explicitly propose to re-actualize and "reload" Marxian theory. The task is to create a Marxist theory of the Internet.

Participatory Web as Ideology

Henry Jenkins argues that, increasingly, "the Web has become a site of consumer participation" (Jenkins 2008: 137). He argues that blogs and other social media bring about a "participatory culture." Benkler (2006), Shirky (2008), and Tapscott and Williams (2007) have made similar arguments.

Answering the question of whether the web is participatory requires an understanding of the notion of participation. In democracy theory, the term *participation* is mainly used and most prominently featured in participatory democracy theory (Held 2006). The earliest use of the term *participatory democracy* that I could trace in the literature is in an article by Staughton Lynd (1965) that describes the grassroots organization of the student movement. Two central features of participatory democracy theory are the broad understanding of democracy as encompassing areas beyond voting, such as the economy, culture, and the household, and the questioning of the compatibility of participatory democracy and capitalism.

A participatory economy requires a "change in the terms of access to capital in the direction of more nearly equal access" and "a change to more nearly equal access to the means of labor" (Macpherson 1973, 71). "Genuine democracy, and genuine liberty, both require the absence of extractive powers" (Macpherson 1973: 121). A participatory economy involves the democratizing of industrial authority structures. Consequently, an Internet platform can only be participatory if it involves participatory ownership structures. Such participatory economy is a necessary, although not a sufficient, condition for participatory democracy. Further factors include participatory learning and decision making. Platforms that are not built on a participatory economy model cannot be participatory.

Can Google, YouTube, and Facebook be considered participatory? Google is a corporation that is specialized in Internet search, cloud computing, and advertising technologies. It is one of the largest transnational companies in the world. Common points of criticism of Google are that the page rank algorithm is secret and that the search results are personalized, which is facilitated through close surveillance of the search behavior of users. Google also exploits and monitors users

TABLE 13.1 Search Results for "Political News" on Google, August 19, 2011

Rank	Website	Type	Owner
1	politico.com	Corporate	Allbritton Communications
2	cnn.com	Corporate	Time Warner
3	foxnews.com	Corporate	News Corporation
4	msnbc.com	Corporate	NBC Universal
5	realclearpolitics.com	Corporate	RealClear Holdings
6	nytimes.com	Corporate	New York Times Company
7	reuters.com	Corporate	Thompson Reuters
8	bbc.co.uk	Public service	BBC
9	politics.co.uk	Corporate	Adfero
10	cbcnews.go.com	Corporate	Walt Disney

by selling their data to advertising clients. Half (50.12%) of all people using the Internet access Google,[2] and that is roughly 1.05 billion people, or almost 15% of the world population.[3] Google would not exist without these users, because its profits are based on ads targeted to searches, which means that the search process is value-generating. Google's more than 1 billion users are, however, largely lacking financial compensation. They perform unpaid, value-generating labor.

The stratification of the visibility of Google search results becomes evident if one searches for the term *political news* on Google: the main search results are news sites owned almost exclusively by big corporate media companies (see Table 13.1)

Facebook is the most popular social networking service in the world.[4] Some points of criticism of the service are that it has a complex and long-winded privacy policy, and it is nontransparent to users which data are collected about them and how the data are used. Facebook users are not involved in decisions. Facebook fan groups are dominated by popular culture, with politics being a sideline. Oppositional political figures are marginalized (see Table 13.2). Facebook is dominated by entertainment. Politics on Facebook is dominated by established actors. Alternative political views are marginalized, and especially critical politics is not often found on Facebook. It is a more general feature of the capitalist culture industry that focuses more on entertainment because it promises larger audiences and profits.

Owned by Google, YouTube is the third most trafficked web platform in the world.[5] There have been some well-known political uses of YouTube, such as the video of the death of Neda Soltani in the 2009 Iranian protests and the video of the death of Ian Tomlinson at the London anti-G20 protests. YouTube is also a known haven for videos by human rights activists that would be censored elsewhere. However, the question arises about how much visibility YouTube really provides to progressives, at least compared to the numbers of views of other material that is shared on YouTube. The list of the ten most viewed videos on YouTube (shown in Table 13.3) exemplifies how the corporate exploiters of surplus

TABLE 13.2 The Most Popular Facebook Groups

Rank	Website	Type	Number of fans
1	Facebook	Technology	50.7 million
2	Texas Hold 'Em Poker	Computer game	48.6 million
3	Eminem	Pop star	45.4 million
4	YouTube	Technology	43.6 million
5	Rihanna	Pop star	43.4 million
6	Lady Gaga	Pop star	42.4 million
7	Michael Jackson	Pop star	39.7 million
8	Shakira	Pop star	39.0 million
9	*Family Guy*	TV series	36.4 million
10	Justin Bieber	Pop star	34.8 million
41	Barack Obama	Politician	22.4 million
	Michael Moore	Socialist filmmaker	495,866
	Noam Chomsky	Socialist intellectual	325,325
	Karl Marx	Communist intellectual	186,722

Source: http://statistics.allfacebook.com, August 19, 2011.

TABLE 13.3 The Most-Viewed YouTube Videos

Rank	Video	Type	Ownership	Views (in millions)
1	Justin Bieber, *Baby*	Music	Universal	607
2	Lady Gaga, *Bad Romance*	Music	Universal	407
3	Shakira, *Waka Waka*	Music	Sony	383
4	Eminem, *Love the Way You Lie*	Music	Universal	371
5	*Charlie Bit My Finger—Again!*	Entertainment	Private user	367
6	Jennifer Lopez, *On the Floor*	Music	Universal	350
7	Eminem, *Not Afraid*	Music	Universal	266
8	Justin Bieber, *One Time*	Music	Universal	260
9	Justin Bieber, *Never Say Never*	Music	Universal	248
10	Thigh massage video	Entertainment	Private user	244

Source: http://www.youtube.com, August 19, 2011.

value-generating labor control YouTube's political attention economy. At first sight, YouTube's video category "News & Politics," which is one of fifteen categories, seems to be the bright political star on the YouTube firmament. A closer look, however, shows that the most viewed video in this category is one in which children sing the song "If You're Happy and You Know It, Clap Your Hands."[6] It is an open question whether politics really does make many people very happy today. Entertainment is sought after on YouTube and Facebook, whereas more overtly political clips are far less visible.

Based on participatory democracy theory, we argue that scholars who suggest that today's Internet is participatory advance an ideology that simply celebrates capitalism without taking into account how capitalist interests dominate and shape the Internet. Web 2.0 is not a participatory system, and it would be better understood in terms of class, exploitation, and surplus value.

Class and the Web

In 1994, Dallas W. Smythe called for a "Marxist theory of communication" (Smythe 1994: 258). Graham Murdock and Peter Golding (2005: 61) have argued that "Critical Political Economy of Communications" is critical in the sense of being "broadly Marxisant." Given the dominance of the Internet through capitalist structures, Marxist critical political economy and Marxist theory seem to be suitable approaches for the analysis of Internet prosumption in contemporary capitalism. Such an analysis is grounded in Marx's model of the expanded reproduction process of capital accumulation.

In the three volumes of *Capital,* Marx analyzes the accumulation process of capital. This process, as described by Marx, is visualized in Figure 13.1.

In the accumulation of capital, capitalists buy labor power and means of production such as raw materials and technologies to produce new commodities,

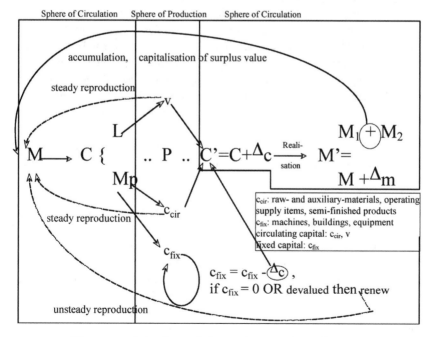

FIGURE 13.1 The accumulation/expanded reproduction of capital

which are later sold with the expectation to make profit, which is partially re-invested. Marx distinguishes two spheres of capital accumulation: the circulation sphere and the sphere of production. In the circulation sphere, capital transforms its value form: First, money M is transformed into commodities (from the stand-point of the capitalist as buyer), the capitalist purchases the commodities labor power L and means of production Mp. M–C is based on the two purchases M–L and M–Mp. This means that, due to private property structures, workers do not own the means of production, the products they produce, and the profit they gen-erate. Capitalists own these resources. In the sphere of production, a new good is produced: the value of labor power and the value of the means of production are added to the product. Value takes on the form of productive capital P. The value form of labor is variable capital v, which can be observed as wages, the value form of the means of production constant capital c that can be observed as the total price of the means of production and producer goods.

In the sphere of production, capital stops its metamorphosis so that capital cir-culation comes to a halt. A new value V' of the commodity is produced, which contains the value of the necessary constant and variable capital and surplus value Δs of the surplus product. Surplus value is generated by unpaid labor. Capital-ists do not pay for the production of surplus; therefore, the production of surplus value can be considered as a process of exploitation. The value V' of the new com-modity after production is $V' = c + v + s$. The commodity then leaves the sphere of production and again enters the circulation sphere, in which capital conducts its next metamorphosis: By being sold on the market, it is transformed from the com-modity form back into the money form. Surplus value is realized in the form of money value. The initial money capital M now takes on the form $M' = M + \Delta m$; it has been increased by an increment Δm. Accumulation of capital means that the produced surplus value is partly reinvested/capitalized. The end point of one pro-cess M' becomes the starting point of a new accumulation process. One part of M', M_1, is reinvested. Accumulation means the aggregation of capital by invest-ment and exploitation in the capital circuit M–C. P. C'–M', in which the end product M' becomes a new starting point M. The total process makes up the dynamic character of capital. Capital is money that is permanently growing due to the exploitation of surplus value.

Commodities are sold at prices that are higher than the investment costs so that profit is generated. For Marx, one decisive quality of capital accumulation is that profit is an emergent property of production that is produced by labor but owned by the capitalists. Without labor, no profit could be made. Workers are forced to enter class relations and to produce profit in order to survive, which enables capital to appropriate surplus. The notion of exploited surplus value is the main concept of Marx's theory, by which he intends to show that capitalism is a class society. "The theory of surplus value is in consequence immediately the theory of exploi-tation" (Negri 1991: 74) and, one can add, the theory of class is a consequence of the political demand for a classless society.

Many Marxist class concepts are wage labor–centric (see, e.g., Wright 1997). Marxist feminism has argued that unpaid reproductive labor can be considered as an inner colony and milieu of primitive accumulation of capitalism (Mies 1986; Mies, Bennholdt-Thomsen, and von Werlhof 1988; Werlhof 1991) and is a class in itself. Antonio Negri uses the term *social worker* to argue that there is a broadening of the proletariat that is "now extended throughout the entire span of production and reproduction" (Negri 1982: 209). Later, Hardt and Negri (2000, 2004) transformed the notion of the social worker into the concept of the multitude. These approaches remind us that, given the complexity of capitalism, we need a multifaceted and dynamic class concept that, in addition to wage labor, also includes groups such as the unemployed, house workers, migrants, people in developing countries, precarious workers, students, public servants, and precarious self-employees in the concept of class. All of them create the commons of society, and users of corporate social media are part of this expanded notion of the proletarian class.

Dallas Smythe suggests that, in the case of media advertisement models, the audience is sold as a commodity to advertisers: "Because audience power is produced, sold, purchased and consumed, it commands a price and is a commodity. . . . You audience members contribute your unpaid work time and in exchange you receive the program material and the explicit advertisements" (Smythe 1981/2006: 233, 238). With the rise of user-generated content, freely accessible social networking platforms that yield profit through online advertisement, the web seems to come close to accumulation strategies employed by capital on traditional mass media such as television or radio. Individuals who upload images, write wall posts or comments, send messages to their contacts, accumulate friends, or browse profiles constitute an audience commodity that is sold. The difference between the audience commodity on traditional mass media and on the Internet is that, in the latter case, the users are also content producers; they engage in constant, often creative, activity, communication, community building, and content production. Alvin Toffler introduced the notion of the prosumer in the early 1980s, which refers to the "progressive blurring of the line that separates producer from consumer" (Toffler 1980: 267). Due to the permanent activity of the recipients and their status as prosumers, we can say that, in the case of corporate social media, the audience commodity is an Internet prosumer commodity. The conflict between cultural studies and critical political economy of the media about the question of the activity and creativity of the prosumer has been resolved in relation to web 2.0: On Facebook, Twitter, and blogs, users are fairly active and creative, which reflects cultural studies insights about recipients, but this active character is the very source of exploitation, which reflects the emphasis of critical political economy on class and exploitation.

That people are more active on the Internet than they are in their reception of TV or radio content is due to the decentralized structure of the Internet, which allows many-to-many communication. Due to the permanent activity of the recipients and their status as prosumers, we can say that, in the case of corporate social media, the audience commodity is an Internet prosumer commodity. The conflict between cultural studies and critical political economy of the media about the question of the activity and creativity of the audience has been resolved in relation to web 2.0: on Facebook, Twitter, and blogs, users are active, which confirms insights of cultural studies about recipients, but this engaged and dynamic behavior of the audience is the very source of exploitation, which reflects critical political economy's stress on class and exploitation.

Figure 13.2 shows the process of capital accumulation on corporate social media platforms that are funded by targeted advertising. Social media corporations invest money (M) for buying capital: technologies (server space, computers, organizational infrastructure, etc.) and labor power (paid employees). These are the constant capital (c) and the variable capital v_1 outlays. The outcome of the production process P_1 is not a commodity that is directly sold, but rather social media services that are made available without payment to users. The waged employees who create social media online environments that are accessed by users produce part of the surplus value. The audience makes use of the platform for generating content that they upload (user-generated data). The constant and variable capital invested by social media companies (c, v_1) that is objectified in the online environments is the prerequisite for their activities in the production process P_2. Their products are user-generated data, personal data, and transaction data about their browsing behavior and communication behavior on corporate social media. They invest a certain labor time v_2 in this process. Corporate social media sell the users' data commodity to advertising clients at a price that is larger than the invested constant and variable capital. The surplus value contained in this commodity is partly created by the users and partly by the corporations' employees. The difference is that the users are unpaid and therefore infinitely exploited. Once the Internet prosumer commodity that contains the user-generated content, transaction data, and the right to access virtual advertising space and time is sold to advertising clients, the commodity is transformed into money capital, and surplus value is realized into money capital.

For Marx (1867), the profit rate is the relation of profit to investment costs: $p = s / (c + v)$ = surplus value / (constant capital (= fixed costs) + variable capital (= wages)). If Internet users become productive web 2.0 prosumers, then, in terms of Marxian class theory, this means that they become productive laborers who produce surplus value and are exploited by capital, because, for Marx, productive labor generates surplus. Therefore, not only are those who are employed by web 2.0 corporations for programming, updating, maintaining the software and hardware, and performing marketing activities exploited surplus value producers, but also the users and prosumers, who engage in the production of user-generated content. New media corporations do not (or hardly) pay the audience for the production of content. One accumulation strategy is to give them free access to services and platforms, let them produce content, and accumulate a

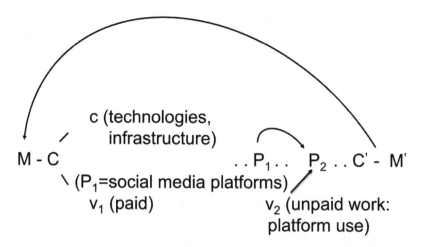

C' = **Internet prosumer commodity** (user-generated content, transaction data, virtual advertising space and time) most social media services are free to use, they are no commodities.
User data and the users are the social media commodity.

FIGURE 13.2 Capital accumulation on corporate social media platforms that are based on targeted advertising

large number of prosumers that are sold as a commodity to third-party advertisers. A product is not sold to the users, but, rather, the users are sold as a commodity to advertisers. The more users are on a platform, the higher the advertising rates can be set. The productive labor time that is exploited by capital involves the labor time of the paid employees and all of the time that is spent online by the users. For the first type of knowledge labor, new media corporations pay salaries. The second type of knowledge is produced completely for free. The formula for the profit rate needs to be transformed for this accumulation strategy:

$$p = s / (c + v_1 + v_2),$$

where s = surplus value, c = constant capital, v_1 = wages paid to fixed employees, and v_2 = wages paid to users.

The typical situation is that $v_2 = > 0$ and that v_2 substitutes v_1 ($v_1 = > v_2 = 0$). If the production of content and the time spent online were carried out by paid employees, the variable costs would rise and profits would therefore decrease. This shows that prosumer activity in a capitalist society can be interpreted as the outsourcing of productive labor to users (in management literature, the term *crowdsourcing* has been established to describe this phenomenon; see Howe

2008), who work completely for free and help maximize the rate of exploitation ($e = s / v$ = surplus value / variable capital) so that profits can be raised and new media capital may be accumulated. This situation is one of infinite exploitation of the users. The wages paid to users for their surplus value generation equal zero, so that the rate of exploitation converges toward infinity. This means that capitalist prosumption is an extreme form of exploitation, in which the prosumers work completely for free. Marx (1867) distinguishes between necessary labor time and surplus labor time. The first is the time a person needs to work in order to create the money equivalent for a wage needed for buying goods that are needed for her or his survival. The second is all additional labor time. Users are not paid on corporate social media (or for consuming other types of corporate media); therefore, they cannot generate money for buying food. All time spent on corporate social media services is surplus labor time.

Students and Scholars Against Corporate Misbehaviour (SACOM) reported that Chinese Foxconn workers who produce iPhones, iPads, iPods, MacBooks, and other information and communication technologies face the withholding of wages, forced and unpaid overtime, exposure to chemicals, harsh management, low wages, unsafe work environments, and lack of basic facilities.[7] In 2010, eighteen Foxconn employees attempted suicide, and fourteen of them succeeded.[8] SACOM describes Foxconn workers as "iSlave Behind the iPhone."[9] In February 2012, Foxconn announced a 25% salary increase.[10] This shows, on the one hand, that civil society pressure and struggles can improve working conditions and, on the other hand, that corporations, due to the drive to raise profits immanent to capitalism, do not automatically care about the lives of their employees, which presents an ongoing challenge for civil society and watchdog groups to monitor corporate irresponsibility and corporate crime. Given the frequent lack of resources among such groups, the monitoring is cumbersome and incomplete and shows the limits of and inhumanity built into the capitalist system. This example shows that the exploitation and surveillance of digital labor—labor that is needed for capital accumulation with the help of Internet communication technologies—is in no way limited to unpaid user labor but includes various forms of labor—user labor, wage labor in Western companies for the creation of applications, and slavelike labor that creates hardware and some software in economic developing countries under inhumane conditions. Digital labor is based on the surveillance, blood, and sweat of superexploited labor in economic developing countries. Post-Fordism does not substitute Taylorism, but it looks more like an even bloodier form of Taylorism.

Toward a Communist Internet in a Communist Society

We are living in times of crisis, unrest, and global transformations. Some observers have argued that understanding and mastering these times requires the "renaissance of Marxist political economy" (Callinicos 2007: 342). "Once again the time has come to take Marx seriously" (Hobsbawm 2011: 419). Göran Therborn has argued that the "new constellations of power and new possibilities of resistance" in the 21st century require retaining the "Marxian idea of human emancipation from exploitation, oppression, discrimination" (Therborn 2008: 61).

Luc Boltanski (2011: 11) argues that critique in the era of neoliberalism lacked an alternative political project, but that today it is time for critique to discuss capitalism's "replacement by less violent forms of utilization of the earth's resources and ways of organizing the relations between human beings that would no longer be of the order of exploitation. It could perhaps then restore the word communism" (Boltanski 2011: 159). Looking for an alternative mode of organizing social relations is the context for the discussion of an alternative Internet. Like Boltanski, also Slavoj Zizek (2010) and Alain Badiou (2010) have argued for the establishment of democratic communism as alternative to crisis capitalism.

Raymond Williams argued that there is an inherent connection of commons, communism, and communication. To communicate means to make something "common to many" (Williams 1983: 72). Communication is part of the commons of society. Denying humans the ability to communicate is like denying them the right to breathe fresh air; it undermines the conditions of their survival. Therefore the communicative commons of society should be available without payment or other access requirements for all and should not be privately owned or controlled by a class.

The era of neoliberalism has been based on the privatization and commodification of the commons. Capital exploits the commons for free (without payment), whereas all humans produce the commons and are thereby exploited. To achieve a just society, one needs to strengthen the commons of society. A democratic communication infrastructure requires strengthening the communication commons. The task is to advance communist media and a communist Internet in a democratic and participatory communist society.

Both Wikipedia and WikiLeaks are shining beacons of a commons-based Internet and a political, networked public sphere. In contrast to corporate social media, the exploitation of free labor is substituted by voluntary user labor, the profit imperative by nonprofit organizations, the provision of advertising by common knowledge accessible to the world for free, and depoliticized content by a certain degree of political information and debate. WikiLeaks is not as popular as established mainstream media. It is ranked at position 28,016 in the list of the world's most accessed web platforms.[11] It therefore depends on corporate mass media such as the *New York Times* or *Spiegel* for news distribution, which are prone to manipulation and political as well as economic censorship. Political economy poses limits for alternative media.

Communism, for Marx and Engels, has three central elements: (1) cooperative forms of production, (2) common control of the means of production, and (3) well-rounded individuality. These three qualities can also be found on the communist Internet. On the communist Internet, humans cocreate and share knowledge; they are equal participants in the decision-making processes that concern the platforms and technologies they use; and the free access to and sharing of knowledge, the remixing of knowledge, and the cocreation of new knowledge creates and reproduces well-rounded individuality. A communist Internet requires a communist society.

Communism is not a condition in the distant future; it is present in the desires for alternatives expressed in struggles against the poverty in resources, ownership, wealth, literacy, food, housing, social security, self-determination, equality, participation, expression, health care, and access that are caused by a system of global stratification that benefits some at the expense of many. Communism is "not a state of affairs which is to be established, an ideal to which reality [will] have to adjust itself" but rather "the real movement which abolishes the present state of things" (Marx and Engels 1844: 57). It starts to exist as movement everywhere, where people resist capitalism and engage in struggles for alternatives. On the Internet, Wikipedia and the Diaspora Project can, to a certain extent, be communist cells entangled into antagonistic relations with capitalism. The communist potentials of such projects are often not consciously seen by those working in them and often have a mystified character, but they are potentials nonetheless that if consciously pursued can lead to significant struggles. Communism starts in struggles that can eventually lead to a revolution of those who do not own property, by those who do not own the economy, politics, culture, nature, themselves, their bodies, their minds, their knowledge, technology, and so on. Communism needs spaces to materialize itself as a movement. Struggles can manifest themselves in the form of noncommercial Internet projects, watchdog projects, public search engines, the legalization of file sharing, or the introduction of a basic income. The context of contemporary struggles is the large-scale colonization of the world by capitalism. A different world is necessary, but whether it can be built remains uncertain. It will be solely determined by the outcome of our struggles. Contemporary struggles are an indication that the world is dreaming of something that it needs to become conscious of in order to possess communism in reality.

Notes

1 For an explanation of the foundations of this field, please see Fuchs (2008, 2009, 2011).
2 In a three-month period, according to alexa.com, accessed on September 13, 2011.
3 Data source for global Internet users is from Internetworldstats.com, accessed on September 13, 2011.
4 "Facebook, Inc.," *New York Times,* June 22, 2012, http://topics.nytimes.com/top/news/business/companies/facebook_inc/index.html.
5 alexa.com, accessed on September 13, 2011.
6 "If You Are Happy," http://www.youtube.com/watch?v=FrsM9WggCdo, accessed September 13, 2011.
7 Students and Scholars Against Corporate Misbehaviour, *iSlave Behind the iPhone: Foxconn Workers in Central China,* September 24, 2011, http://sacom.hk/wp-content/uploads/2011/09/20110924-islave-behind-the-iphone.pdf.

8 "Foxconn Suicides," Wikipedia, http://en.wikipedia.org/wiki/Foxconn_suicides.
9 SACOM, "iSlave Behind the iPhone."
10 David Barboza, "Foxconn Plans to Lift Pay Sharply at Factories in China," *New York Times,* February 18, 2012, http://www.nytimes.com/2012/02/19/technology/fox-conn-to-raise-salaries-for-workers-by-up-to-25.html.
11 According to alexa.com, August 19, 2011.

References

Andrejevic, Mark. 2002. The Work of Being Watched: Interactive Media and the Exploitation of Self-Disclosure. *Critical Studies in Media Communication* 19, no. 2: 230–48.

Andrejevic, Mark. 2011. Surveillance and Alienation in the Online Economy. *Surveillance & Society* 8, 3: 278–87.

Badiou, Alain. 2010. *The Communist Hypothesis.* London: Verso.

Benkler, Yochai. 2006. *The Wealth of Networks.* New Haven, CT: Yale University Press.

Boltanski, Luc. 2011. *On Critique. A Sociology of Emancipation.* Cambridge: Polity Press.

Callinicos, Alex. 2007. *Social Theory.* Cambridge: Polity Press.

Dean, Jodi. 2004. The Networked Empire: Communicative Capitalism and the Hope for Politics. In *Empire's New Clothes. Reading Hardt and Negri,* ed. Paul A. Passavant and Jodi Dean, 265–88. New York: Routledge.

Fuchs, Christian. 2008. *Internet and Society: Social Theory in the Information Age.* New York: Routledge.

Fuchs, Christian. 2009. Information and Communication Technologies and Society: A Contribution to the Critique of the Political Economy of the Internet. *European Journal of Communication* 24, no. 1: 69–87.

Fuchs, Christian. 2011. *Foundations of Critical Media and Information Studies.* New York: Routledge.

Hardt, Michael, and Antonio Negri. 2000. *Empire.* Cambridge, MA: Harvard University Press.

Hardt, Michael, and Antonio Negri. 2004. *Multitude.* New York: Penguin.

Held, David. 2006. *Models of Democracy.* 3rd ed. Cambridge: Polity Press.

Hobsbawm Eric. 2011. *How to Change the World: Marx and Marxism 1840–2011.* London: Little, Brown.

Howe, Jeff. 2008. *Crowdsourcing: Why the Power of the Crowd Is Driving the Future of Business.* New York: Three Rivers Press.

Jenkins, Henry. 2008. *Convergence Culture.* New York: New York University Press.

Lynd, Staughton. 1965. The New Radicals and "Participatory Democracy." *Dissent* 12, no. 3: 324–33.

Macpherson, Crawford Brough. 1973. *Democratic Theory.* Oxford: Oxford University Press.

Marx, Karl. 1867. *Capital.* Vol. 1. London: Penguin.

Marx, Karl, and Friedrich Engels. 1844. *The German Ideology.* Amherst, NY: Prometheus Books.

Mies, Maria. 1986. *Patriarchy and Accumulation on a World Scale.* London: Zed Books.

Mies, Maria, Veronika Bennholdt-Thomsen, and Claudia von Werlhof. 1988. *Women: The Last Colony.* London: Zed Books.

Murdock, Graham, and Peter Golding. 2005. Culture, Communications and Political Economy. In *Mass Media and Society,* eds. James Curran and Michael Gurevitch, 60–83. London: Hodder.

Negri, Antonio. 1982. Archaeology and Project: The Mass Worker and the Social Worker. In *Revolution Retrieved: Selected Writings on Marx, Keynes, Capitalist Crisis and New Social Subjects 1967–83,* 199–228. London: Red Notes.

Negri, Antonio. 1991. *Marx beyond Marx.* London: Pluto.

Scholz, Trebor. 2008. Market Ideology and the Myths of Web 2.0. *First Monday* 13, no. 3.

Shirky, Clay. 2008. *Here Comes Everybody.* London: Penguin.

Smythe, Dallas W. 1981/2006. On the Audience Commodity and Its Work. In *Media and Cultural Studies,* eds. Meenakshi G. Durham and Douglas M. Kellner, 230–56. Malden, MA: Blackwell.

Smythe, Dallas W. 1994. *Counterclockwise.* Boulder, CO: Westview Press.

Tapscott, Don, and Anthony D. Williams. 2007. *Wikinomics: How Mass Collaboration Changes Everything.* London: Penguin.

Therborn, Göran. 2008. *From Marxism to Post-Marxism?* London: Verso.

Toffler, Alvin. 1980. *The Third Wave.* New York: Bantam.

Werlhof, Claudia von. 1991. *Was haben die Hühner mit dem Dollar zu tun? Frauen und Ökonomie.* Munich: Frauenoffensive.

Williams, Raymond. 1983. *Keywords.* New York: Oxford University Press.

Wright, Erik Olin. 1997. *Class Counts.* Cambridge: Cambridge University Press.

Zizek, Slavoj. 2010. How to Begin from the Beginning. In *The Idea of Communism,* eds. Costas Douzinas and Slavoj Zizek, 209–26. London: Verso.

14

ACTS OF TRANSLATION

Organized Networks as Algorithmic
Technologies of the Common

Ned Rossiter and Soenke Zehle

Exodus from the General Intellect

Defined by the informatization of life and labor, the networked condition is characterized by the comprehensive connection of users to circuits of capital via predominantly corporate communication and information infrastructures. The economic value of these engines of entry into a world of communicative commerce is largely determined by the very acts of communication they elicit, structure, and sustain. And as the proliferation of proprietary mobile devices separates a new generation of users from previous, more localized generations of personal computing, the corresponding establishment of cloud computing as the primary infrastructural paradigm of storage and service delivery aimed at efficient datamining establishes a new technocentralism that should give the evangelists of decentralization-as-democratization pause for thought. At stake is, once again, the "authority to act" and, with it, the question of action itself.[1]

A mere political economy of digital media cannot grasp this enmeshment of individual and institutional forms of affective articulation, expression, and inscription that fuels the production of value in today's information economies. Why not? Because political economy cannot handle elusiveness terribly well, which makes it difficult for this approach to register subjectivity and affect as holding economic potential. By contrast, Paolo Virno has suggested that in contemporary 'bio-linguistic capitalism…the capitalist organization of work takes on as its raw material the differential traits of the species" and raises anew the question of human nature, thus returning us to the perspective of political anthropology.[2] While we find this vision too grand to offer much analytical advice to the very actors whose transnational organizing efforts are all-too-quickly conflated into global movements and endowed with epochal agency, it is this primacy given to the communicative constitution of relations as the core element of labor and life that has also increased interest in conceptualizations of the common and the specific relation the common holds to the political as one of its contemporary iterations.

Transversal relations immanent to the media of communication underscore the production of the common—a form of relation that holds substantive conceptual and material distinctions from that which it is often confused and conflated with: the commons, which serve as a central resource for the information economy and are a defining feature of the network condition. If we understand *the commons* to refer both to the material context and the consequence of practices of peer production, *the common* is the political potential immanent in such practices. Such an understanding of the common situates it conceptually as the latest iteration of the political; just as there exists an "excess of the political over politics,"[3] the affirmation of the common is offered as a condition of possibility for collaborative constitution; for the sharing of affects of love, solidarity, and wrath; and for the translation of such affects and experiences across the "irreducible idiomaticity" of ethico-political practices and the production of subjectivity.[4]

Frequent slippage occurs between the invocation of the terms *the common* and *the commons*. The latter is often understood as a collaboratively produced, open yet scarce resource to be protected from regimes of enclosure, as seen in the rise of intellectual property rights as the politico-juridical instrument for governing the circulation of cultural commodities within information economies. As we have noted elsewhere, "The common is not given as a fragile heritage to be protected against the ravages of new forms of primitive accumulation and enclosure. Rather, it is something that must be actively constructed, and this construction involves the creation of 'subjects in transit.'"[5] What strikes us as significant about what Hardt and Negri phrase as the "commonality of a potential community" is the question of form as it relates to the production of the common understood as a community to come, a potentiality held in common that may include but is not exclusive to the commons.[6] How, in other words, does the common reveal itself if it is to manifest in more concrete, less elusive ways? Is there a materiality to *potentia* beyond sensation and affect (keeping in mind that sensation and affect are composed in acutely material ways)? We suggest that the multiple forms of movement, occupation, and encampment that intervene in public, state, and corporate spaces in recent months and years can be seen as material iterations of a political potential that distinguishes the common from the commons.

In proposing an exodus from the general intellect, we are calling not for an abandonment of the common. Such a force of *potentia* refuses any singular action, since the *potentia* is situated within the field of immanence and thus refuses capture or control, yet is modulated and revealed through the singularity of the event and the instantiation of expression. Again, the history of movements illustrates this point well. No matter how much news media is compelled by its form—column inches, airtime, and updates—to contain dissenting voices and reduce heterogeneity, the dispersed energies and interests of movements themselves are always in the process of transformation. While the production of the commons as an open resource is something to be welcomed, and even celebrated, we wish to sound a note of caution. Coextensive with the proliferation of open access systems (publishing, software, code) is the social production of value, which frequently becomes exploited as a resource or data set in the reproduction of capital. Within network societies, the general intellect is an informational mode of primitive accumulation or social production of value, and, as such, living labor is subjugated as labor-power without the classical exchange of a wage.[7] Instead, a symbolic economy prevails at best and very rarely for most. The social-political challenge within such a horizon is to appropriate the means of biopolitical production.

Our interest is to question the valorization of the common less by drawing attention to the more obvious register of political economy and the exploitation of free labor than by highlighting the role of the common as a political potential in biopolitical assemblages organized around logistics industries and the politics of the human. As Fiona Jeffries maintains, "One place where we find the common and the commons converge is in globalizing communication infrastructures."[8] It is from within this conceptual context that we want to raise the possibility of alternative cartographies of the political. The question of translation is a crucial element in the conceptual elaboration of these emergent configurations.

The Task of the Translator

Boris Buden has suggested that

> culture has not, as it is often believed, simply pushed away the notion of society from the political stage and taken its leading role in theoretical debates and practical concerns of political subjects. The change is more radical. Culture has become this very stage, the very condition of the possibility of society and of our perception of what political reality is today.[9]

This centrality of culture has given the practice of cultural translation new significance and a political purpose. From within the horizon of multiculturalism, its "political purpose is the stability of the liberal order, which can be achieved only on the grounds of non-conflictual, interactive relations between different cultures in terms of the so-called multicultural cohabitation." Understood in the more radical (if still liberal) sense Buden derives from Walter Benjamin, Homi Bhabha, and Judith Butler, cultural translation refers to "the process by which the excluded within the universality is readmitted into the term," which implies that "cultural translation—as a 'return of the excluded'—is the only promoter of today's democracy. It pushes its limits, brings about social change and opens new spaces of emancipation. It does so through the subversive practices, which change everyday social relations." Over and against what remains an essentially liberal articulation of cultural translation, Buden turns to Spivak's "strategic essentialism" to acknowledge that "she simply admits that there is no direct correspondence between these two languages" since the language of antiessentialist theory and of essentialist political practices "cannot be sublated in an old dialectical way by a third universal term which could operate as a dialectical unity of both. Therefore, the only possible way of a communication between them is a kind of translation." Cultural translation is, then, the mise-en-scène that brings new visions of the political onto the stage of culture.

Such translation, at least in the sense of Walter Benjamin—translation is the "afterlife" of the original—necessarily does away with any notion of originality. In the case of universalism, "what is irretrievably lost in the translation, what died with the original and can therefore no longer be grasped in the translation, is the revolutionary meaning of the old concept of universalism, its practical aspiration to change the world."[10] Here, Buden adopts Paul Gilroy's notion of a strategic universalism, which "was developed to close the non-reducible gap between two languages of our historical experience, between the language of reflexive critique and the language of political practice." For Buden, this is an eminently practical question:

> Is it not time now, after all the attempts to articulate a leftist political engagement in the sense of strategic essentialism, to try out the other, universalist strategy? The best that one can do in this dilemma is probably to make a decision for the dilemma itself. That means lingering in the gap that neither of the concepts can close. It would not mean evading all the extorted decisions and foul compromises once and for all, but rather recognizing them as such.

Lingering in the gap of a new politics of the universal is, then, our point of departure for reflections on alternative articulations of the global—understood as the "afterlife" of the universal, over and against which new visions of the political have to be created.

A politics of the universal is not, of course, always-already a politics beyond liberalism. Quite the contrary:

> Universalization is conventionally understood as a proto-democratic and thus also a proto-political event. An inherently particular position suddenly raises a universalist claim, thus evoking a new antagonism, which divides and newly articulates the given political field.... Strategic universalism... always remains bound to the hegemonic liberal-democratic order—and not its critique.

What strategic essentialism and strategic universalism "have in common is the vision of a gradual progress of emancipation that takes place as a clever balancing between the two poles of the existing political world order, the particular essentialist and the universal constructivist world order." The task of critique, however, is different:

> Today it is actually impossible to offer resistance against global power that is politically effective at the same level. In the same way, it is impossible to articulate a reflexively effective critique at the local level. Local, political essentialism makes all critical thinking mute, just as reflexively universalist critique leaves every locally effective political act untouched. Seeking to overcome this division can be a noble task, but it is not the task of critique. It is not there to balance a world again that has lost its balance, but rather to probe the depth of the crisis in which this world finds itself.

To probe the depth of the crisis is, it turns out, to return to the question of culture; if culture is to be the stage for new productions—of subjectivity, of modes of relation—we need a better sense of the scope of scenography, of collaborative choreographies, of performative practices. And indeed of dominant articulations of the global over and against which a different politics of the universal (such as the common) could be articulated.

In his reflections on a politics of the universal, Étienne Balibar turns to the question of "the institution of the universal, or even the institution of the universal as truth."[11] What complicates the task of critique is that "certain forms of universality at least derive their institutional strength not from the fact that the institutions in which they are embodied are absolute themselves, but rather from the fact that they are the site of endless contestations on the basis of their own principles, or discourse." Balibar, following Hannah Arendt, proposes "equaliberty"—the right to have rights—not as another institution of the universal but as "the *arch-institution,* or the institution that precedes and conditions every other institution" in modern democracies. But if equaliberty, democracy, civic universality as the pursuit of equality and liberty are the horizon of a democratic politics of the universal, their "simultaneous realization is rarely seen or only visible as a tendency, as exigency."

In the current call for democratic control of financial markets and processes of financialization, arguably the most influential figure of the global and perhaps the most dominant dynamic of universalization today, activists not only call the self-universalization of regimes of financialization into question but quite literally interrupt it through occupations that establish a cartography of sites through which the institution of financialization as the dominant figure of the global occurs.[12] Financialization is an instance of the global whose advocates have not failed to present it in the terms of the inevitability of a progressive universalization of its practices and policies, of the universal as truth. In the course of a series of financial crises, these truth claims have been visibly unmade, giving rise to contestations that are perhaps endless only insofar as they don't envision a politics beyond a reconfiguration of the relationships between states and markets. But to conduct critique in and on exclusively these terms, retranslating it as a mere negotiation within the ontopolitical matrix of states, markets, and everybody else is to already cede the terrain of culture; instead, we want to reclaim a more radical sense of translation that takes seriously the return of the machine.

Labor, Code, Logistics

Contemporary social-technical arrangements are defined by ubiquitous media and their distinct formats of communication. Coupled with new geopolitical configurations of space shaped by the rise of what we call "logistical cities" and their infrastructural components,[13] the predominance of supply chain and workplace software along with technologies such as RFID, GPS, and voice picking marks the inception of new systems of measure that govern labor performance across a range of trade sectors and service industries.[14] This is the new horizon of politics and labor organization today.

The global logistics industry is an emergent regime of what Alexander Galloway terms "protocological control" that already shapes the conditions of labor and life for many[15] and increasingly affects how knowledge production is governed and undertaken now and in the future.[16] With military origins, logistics emerged as a business concept in the 1950s concerned with the management of global supply chains. The primary task of the global logistics industry is to manage the movement of bodies and brains, finance and things in the interests of communication, transport, and economic efficiencies. There is an important prehistory to the so-called logistics revolution to be found in cybernetics and the Fordist era following World War II. Logistics is an extension of the "organizational paradigm" of cybernetics. Both belong to what Foucault terms the "machine stream ensemble" of neoliberal economics as it emerged following the war.[17] Common to neoliberal economics, cybernetics, and logistics is the calculation of risk. And to manage the domain of risk, a system capable of reflexive analysis and governance is required. This is the task of logistics.

Logistics, as it emerged in the period of the so-called Second Cold War (1979–1985),[18] operates as a kind of third force or articulating device that, on the one hand, negotiates the economic and structural demand for secure national and increasingly global supply chains, while, on the other hand, serves as an adjunct to the arms race by advancing new organizational systems aimed at efficiently managing labor, mobility, and the accountability of things. Logistics was later consolidated as a business management practice as the Cold War began to thaw in the 1980s, and Western economic interests began to penetrate the new markets and, more particularly, harness the surplus labor of ex-Soviet states. For Brian Holmes, "The 1980s were the inaugural decade of neoliberalism, which brought new forms of financialized wealth-creation and motivational management into play, alongside the militaristic technologies of surveillance and control that had been inherited from the Cold War."[19]

Edna Bonacich and Jake Wilson date what they call the "logistics revolution" from the 1970s, with a particular emphasis on the Reagan and Thatcher eras of market and institutional deregulation along with neoliberal international free trade agreements.[20] They characterize this organizational revolution in terms of changes in production (flexibility and outsourcing), logistics ("intermodalization"), and labor (intensification of contingency, weakening of unions, racialization of labor, lower labor standards). Contemporary logistics aims to minimize inventory build-ups, or overaccumulation, which leads to overproduction by manufacturers and retail overstocking (or understocking, as the case may be).[21] In both instances, manufacturers and retailers strive for efficiency in communications to minimize overinvestment in stocks that decline in economic value over time.

The software applications special to logistics visualize and manage the mobility of people, capital, and things, producing knowledge about the world in transit. The political challenge today is to devise techniques and strategies that operate outside the territory of control exerted by logistics technologies and their software algorithms that shape how practices of knowledge production are organized, which in turns shapes the conditions and experiences of contemporary labor. As much as the emergent field of software studies celebrates the collective innovation of open source initiatives and radical gestures of hacker cultures, there is a much more profound and substantive technological impact exerted upon labor-power in the formal and informal economies concomitant with the global logistics industries that has not yet received critical attention in analyses of the cultures of code. The challenge of political organization within the logistics industries is steep. Not only are unionized forms of labor organization marginal, where they do exist—in the maritime industries of some countries, for instance—there is great pressure for workers and their representatives to conform to ever-increasing demands for greater workplace productivity and enhanced efficiency modulated by computational systems that manage key performance indicators.[22]

Against these pressures for increased labor productivity is the savage collapse of labor-power as economies across the world are saddled with the blowout of sovereign debt passed on by massive corporate welfarism in the form of state bailouts of financial institutions—the health of which politicians, shareholders, economists, and traders argue is necessary if consumer life is to continue on its merry path of planetary annihilation. Yet the very model of such institutional-social organization is never questioned—except by the people now mobilizing in urban squares and financial districts across the world. Do we understand this in terms of a politics of action, however, or can we gain greater analytical traction and organizational insight by seeing these movements as a politics *beyond the actionable,* foregrounding nonrepresentational practices rather than repowering the politics of representation?[23] Here, we need to return to the work of translation and collaborative constitution as social-political practices immanent to media of communication.

From Generation to Seriality

Reapproached from within the horizon of logistics and the assemblages organized according to its systems of measure, the work of translation as a social-technical *dispositif* and modality of organization shifts from generation to seriality. What is the generative role of communications media in the production of politics beyond the actionable and invention of the common? Jonathan Zittrain's analysis indicates that *generative technologies* are typically found in their nascent phase, where the rules of operation can be built upon to contribute innovative adaptations to the population of the common. Stand-alone technologies such as the PC and iPhone, by contrast, are defined by proprietary, static, and preprogrammed systems that lock out any generative potential, at least according to Zittrain's argument. The social technology of occupation and encampment indexes a generative capacity for political intervention across geocultural scales. Proprietarization or enclosure can go beyond juridical architectures and take the form of net-cultural practices that become absorbed into mainstream social-political organization. Look what happened to flash mobs: very quickly they became empty gestures of commercial stunts and lost whatever political potency they may have harbored in their gestation phase. TED Talks and Pecha Kucha could be seen as equivalents of net-cultural absorption into the mainstream, except they never even went through a generative stage of producing political subjectivities and new modes of expression.

How, then, are generative political technologies and their concomitant practices distributed across networks? In a recent opinion piece, Hardt and Negri draw a long line of affiliation from Seattle to Cairo to Wall Street, indicating what, in effect, is the *seriality* of political organization as interventions across time and space.[24] Some of the connecting devices along the way to Occupy Wall Street and the thousand or so affiliated occupations in cities across the world include WikiLeaks, Anonymous, and the Arab Spring—itself a *series* of connective devices that encourages us to invoke theories of assemblage despite frequent criticism of their unwieldiness as heuristic, let alone analytical, instruments.[25] Across these disparate, even incommensurate spaces of occupation and encampment we see the production of the common through the mobilization of desire and a seriality of formats. The tipping point registered once a critical mass has galvanized itself into and then beyond action appears crucial in each instance. In these occupations, the emergence of organized networks as proto-institutional forms becomes manifest. Whether they can sustain themselves over time is a question we have asked ourselves repeatedly. Shortly after its political victories, the Arab Spring was confronted with a problem Foucault identified as common to revolution: how to maintain the production of difference when inheriting the political architecture of the state?[26] This is why we speak of organized networks as new institutional forms, bracketing the statist conceptualization of the political not to ignore the actuality of state apparatuses and their geocultural reconfiguration, the material dis- and rearticulation of elements of state sovereignty at sub- and suprastate levels, but to create figures of the universal capable of grasping the political dimension of processes of collaborative constitution at an unprecedented scale.

The network practice of seriality should not be mistaken for the Frankfurt School critique of standardization, which relegated cultural production as an industrialized output of the assembly line. While seriality assumes an element of repetition, the differential work of translation bestows upon network practices a set of social-technical contours specific to the situation, event, and production of desire. When seen in terms of seriality, the uncertain capacity to sustain network politics and culture appears less of an issue. There is a passage of communicating tactics, strategies, and concepts across network settings. In this sense, seriality is best understood as an iterative process over time and space that corresponds loosely with the remix logic of digital culture and the shift toward strategies of a stream-based sharing of serialized content.[27] Both in social and technological terms, it is the work of translation that indicates organized networks are much more robust new institutional forms than their often short-term, even ephemeral, composition suggests. The political and organizational question, therefore, becomes less one of whether Occupy Wall Street can transform into a social movement or whether the Arab Spring can produce state-based forms of governance and more a case of how the techniques and concepts from any particular network instantiation will move in time and across space to another situation. What sort of social-technical transformation and production of new organizational concepts, subjectivities, and desires will define this grammar of iteration, of its constitutive practices and modes of relation?

Algorithmic Futures

If, as we believe, culture in the networked condition must be understood as "algorithmic culture," cultural translation and the politics it may articulate must include the cultures of code.[28] To affect a politics of the universal on its computational terrain is to take this condition of variational territories and topologies of code seriously. Such an action goes beyond the organizational capacity of social media to help oust authoritarian political regimes, and intervenes instead at the algorithmic level. We have already seen the tendency toward such a politics of the universal in the practices of Anonymous and WikiLeaks, even if the rise of pirate parties founded in response to governmental interventions in the technosocial fields of peer-to-peer culture seems to fold such dynamics back into the mechanisms of representation.

Yet to return to the question of code as the terrain of organization is not simply a reaffirmation of the politics of free software as the dominant—indeed, paradigmatic—net-cultural dynamic.[29] Instead, we see the question of algorithmic interventions as linked in a more concrete, substantive sense to the new geopolitical and geocultural configurations of information, labor, and economy wrought by the force of infrastructure associated with the global logistics industries. The year 2009 saw not only the initial peak of the ongoing financial crisis, it also occasioned the entry of Chinese state-owned shipping and logistics company COSCO into a 35-year lease agreement with Greek authorities to access and manage port space at Piraeus, one of the largest shipping ports in Southern Europe.[30] Along with upgrading port facilities and dramatic increases in productivity, local Greek workers have found themselves confronted by employers with substantially different ideas about working conditions, pay rates, and safety. As Greece cedes its sovereign authority to more powerful economic actors, Greek citizens and organizations such as unions have diminished ground upon which to contest perceived and experienced inequalities. With software programs devised to manage key performance indicators and global value chains, algorithmic cultures are key agents that govern subjects and things in logistical operations such as those found at Piraeus, among countless other global sites.

This does not mean that political organization within a logistical world ipso facto submits to algorithmic technologies of control. As Galloway puts it, "What is an algorithm if not a machine for the motion of parts?"[31] WikiLeaks has shown it can handle the U.S. arm of the military-industrial complex, so what might it do to scramble the system of more socially and economically pervasive powers embodied by the logistics industries? We imagine a WikiLeaks or Anonymous raid not on modern institutions of control (the state, firm, military, union, etc.), but rather on the algorithmic architecture that increasingly determines the experience and conditions of labor and life.

At the same time, the concerns of a more conventional politics of representation are never far away, suggesting that the seriality of emergent political forms may translate across a representation/nonrepresentation divide whose enthusiastic conceptual affirmation in the name of a "post-representative politics" has rarely done justice to the ontological heterogeneity of actually existing political assemblages. In the end, the same processes of informatization that support and sustain the becoming-cultural of labor and life are the material conditions of possibility for contemporary regimes of financialization. As big data—data sets too large to be processed in small-scale infrastructures—becomes the new watchword of stock markets and governments alike, a new brand of "cultural analytics" has already emerged, waiting to be harnessed for activist ends.[32] These new encounters between data analysis and information visualization once again call on us to restage aesthetic interventions in emerging publics and engage, above and beyond the demand for transparency and the investigative heroism of freedom of information inquiries, in the algorithmic constitution of new publics.[33]

If new figures of globality emerge in the realm of financial politics, so be it—it is perhaps no accident that the peer-to-peer currency Bitcoin (money without banks) offers us a political metaphor not unlike that of Virno's "republic without a state."[34] We are still waiting for data hacks tracking the money hidden in "secrecy jurisdictions."[35] And a new politics of multimodality brings reverse engineering to the latest generation of motion capture devices, signaling the autonomous creation of multidimensional data and the possibility of a tactical relationship to the "sentient city."[36] Because in the end, "It is the body, and the body alone, that can act as a libidinal force breaking through the containment of the virtualised 'circuits of drive' that attempt to capture the restless desire of the contemporary subject for the encounter in public with the unknown other."[37] These open spaces are not simply spheres of unmediated free speech and democratic deliberation but are structured by algorithmic medialities.

Finally, a misunderstanding perhaps exists—that new technologies call for radically new forms of political organization. Needless to say, this is not the case, and the exaggeration of the role of real-time social media has justly been ridiculed.[38] Instead, we want to stress the archival dimension of contemporary figures of the collective, not in the sense of a straight lineage but in the affirmation of the "will to connect" (Stuart Hall). Encouraging and sustaining a wide range of practices of relation, communication, and organization are part of a dynamic transcultural archive, stored and reproduced in a decentralized fashion, protected by its redundancy. We should not, therefore, allow the metaphor of the cloud to be understood exclusively in terms of corporate server networks and software as service economies. We are the cloud, and in acknowledging the forces of seriality we can invent new logistical protocols to draw more widely on this archive. And as we engage in the work of cultural translation—of relating, for instance, the codes that drive the algorithmicization of our communicative practices, to the social codes that emerge across new cartographies of the political—we may already find ourselves on different terrain, ready to once again reinvent our relationships to the political.

Notes

1 For an example of such a gloomy extrapolation of contemporary trends, see Jonathan Zittrain, *The Future of the Internet—And How to Stop It* (New Haven, CT: Yale University Press, 2008). Needless to say, such an explicit exaggeration of contemporary trends is not meant to obscure the many creative uses to which such infrastructures have been put, or deny that corporate and military infrastructures can also provide public goods, but to counter the unbearable evangelism of decentralization-as-democratization. As Benkler notes:

> For the first time since the industrial revolution, the most important inputs into the core economic activities of the most advanced economies are widely distributed in the population. Creativity and innovation are directly tied to the radical decentralization of the practical capability to act, on the one hand, and of the authority to act, on the other. The critical policy questions of the networked environment revolve round the battles between the decentralization of technology and the push of policy to moderate that decentralization by limiting the distribution of authority to act.

Yochai Benkler, "For the First Time Since the Industrial Revolution," in Richard N. Katz (ed.), *The Tower and The Cloud: Higher Education in the Age of Cloud Computing* (Boulder, CO: EduCause, 2008), 52, http://www.educause.edu/thetowerandthecloud. On the transformation of action, see the discussion on Arendt and Lazzarato in Soenke Zehle and Ned Rossiter, "Organizing Networks: Notes on Collaborative Constitution, Translation and the Work of Organization," *Cultural Politics* 5, no. 2 (2009): 237–64.

2 "Human nature returns to the centre of attention not because we are finally dealing with biology rather than history, but because the biological prerogatives of the human animal have acquired undeniable historical relevance in the current productive process." Paolo Virno, "Natural-Historical Diagrams: The 'New Global' Movement and the Biological Invariant," in Lorenzo Chiesa and Alberto Toscano (eds.), *The Italian Difference: Between Nihilism and Biopolitics* (Melbourne: Re.Press, 2009), 131–47, 142. On the role of language in contemporary capitalism, see Christian Marazzi, *Capital and Language: From the New Economy to the War Economy,* trans. Gregory Conti (New York: Semiotext(e), 2008). See also Jon Solomon's critique of human speciation vis-à-vis translation and the differential production of knowledge:

> When repetition is required, it is called "translation"; where failure is present, it is attributed to exteriority. Today, the historicity of these assumptions is becoming ever clearer. Needless to say, the fact that human beings are disposed to share signs does not guarantee successful communication anymore than sharing itself produces homogeneous community; neither can such sharing be reduced or equated to the notion of an individuated collective intentionality. Yet this is precisely what forms the basic presupposition for the modern thought of community, crystallized in the nation-state.

And:

> To approach the problem of the trans/national study of culture without addressing the way in which knowledge, as it is embedded in various social practices of language, labor, and life, is intrinsically part of the speciation of the human is to continue to blindly defer to the defining search of colonial/imperial modernity for the ultimate technology of human population engineering.

Jon Solomon, "The Trans/National Study of Culture and the Institutions of Human Speciation," *Construction des savoirs en mondialisation. Changements de paradigmes cognitifs: Une révolution épistémologique?* Colloque coorganisé par le Collège international de philosophie (www.ciph.org), la revue Transeuropéennes (www.transeuropeennes.eu), Paris, November 7–8, 2011.

3 Jacques Rancière, "A Few Remarks on the Method of Jacques Rancière," *Parallax* 15, no. 3 (2009): 122.

4 See, for example, the central role of the common in Negri's antinaturalist ontology of liberation, in which the common and the multitude exist in a relationship of mutual constitution. Cesare Casarino and Antonio Negri, *In Praise of the Common: A Conversation on Philosophy and Politics* (Minneapolis: Minnesota University Press, 2008). We think it makes sense to maintain such a conceptual distinction rather than conflate them; for a different approach, see, for example, Michael Hardt, "The Politics of the Common," *ZNet,* 2009, http://www.zmag.org/znet/viewArticle/21899.

For reflections on "irreducible idiomaticity" in the context of translation, see Gayatri Chakravorty Spivak, "Questioned on Translation: Adrift," *Public Culture* 13, no. 1 (2001): 13–22. For a more elaborate typology of the commons, see David M. Berry, *Copy, Rip, Burn: The Politics of Copyleft and Open Source* (London: Pluto Press, 2008), 79ff.

5 Brett Neilson and Ned Rossiter, "Precarity as a Political Concept, or, Fordism as Exception," *Theory, Culture and Society* 25, no. 7/8: 55–66. See also Sandro Mezzadra, "Living in Transition: Toward a Heterolingual Theory of the Multitude," 2007, http://roundtable.kein.org/node/653, and Naoki Sakai, *Translation and Subjectivity: On "Japan" and Cultural Nationalism* (Minneapolis: University of Minnesota Press, 1997).

6 Hardt and Negri state: "Protection and oppression can be hard to tell apart. This strategy of 'national protection' is a double-edged sword that at times appears necessary despite its destructiveness. The nation appears progressive in the second place insofar as it poses the commonality of a potential community." Michael Hardt and Antonio Negri, *Empire* (Cambridge, MA: Harvard University Press, 2000), 106.

7 Christian Marazzi, "The Privatization of the General Intellect," trans. Nicolas Guilhot (n.d.). See also Tiziana Terranova, "Another Life: The Nature of Political Economy in Foucault's Genealogy of Biopolitics," *Theory, Culture and Society* 26, no. 6 (2009): 234–62; and Solomon, "The Trans/National Study of Culture and the Institutions of Human Speciation."

8 Fiona Jeffries, "Communication Commoning Amidst the New Enclosures: Reappropriating Infrastructures," *Journal of Communication Inquiry* 35, no. 4 (2011): 349–55.

9 Boris Buden, "Cultural Translation: Why It Is Important and Where to Start with It?" *transversal: under translation* (June 2006), http://eipcp.net/transversal/0606/buden/en. All quotations hereafter from Buden.

10 Boris Buden, "Strategic Universalism: Dead Concept Walking on the Subalternity of Critique Today," *transversal: under translation* (February 2007), http://eipcp.net/transversal/0607/buden/en. All quotations hereafter from Buden.

11 Étienne Balibar, "On Universalism: In Debate with Alain Badiou," *transversal: on universalism* (February 2007), http://eipcp.net/transversal/0607/balibar/en. All quotations hereafter from Balibar.

12 http://occupywallst.org. It has often been remarked that the Occupy movement has failed to articulate specific demands. This is not where we see its greatest strength; rather, it reaffirms the centrality of physical performative practices in any cartography of the political.

13 Brett Neilson and Ned Rossiter, "The Logistical City," *Transit Labour: Circuits, Regions, Borders,* Digest 3, August 2011, http://transitlabour.asia/documentation/.

14 See Anja Kanngieser, "Tracking and Tracing Bodies: New Technologies of Governance and the Logistics Industries," *Development, Logistics, Governance,* Fourth Critical Studies Conference, Calcutta Research Group, Calcutta, September 8–10, 2011.

15 See Alexander Galloway, "Protocol," *Theory, Culture and Society* 23, no. 2–3 (2006): 317. See also Alexander R. Galloway, *Protocol: How Control Exists after Decentralization* (Cambridge, MA: MIT Press, 2004).

16 See Ned Rossiter, "Logistics, Labour and New Regimes of Knowledge Production," *Transeuropéenes: International Journal of Critical Thought* 8 (August 2011), http://www.transeuropeennes.org/en/76/new_knowledge_new_ epistemologies.

17 Michel Foucault, *The Birth of Biopolitics. Lectures at the Collège de France, 1978–1979,* ed. Michel Senellart, trans. Graham Burchell (Basingstoke: Palgrave Macmillan, 2008), 225.

18 See Fred Halliday, *The Making of the Second Cold War* (London: Verso, 1983).

19 Brian Holmes, "Guattari's Schizoanalytic Cartographies, or, the Pathic Core at the Heart of Cybernetics," *Continental Drift: The Other Side of Neoliberal Globalization,* February 27, 2009, http://brianholmes.wordpress.com/2009/02/27/guattaris-schizoanalytic-cartographies. See also David Harvey, *A Brief History of Neoliberalism* (Oxford: Oxford University Press, 2005).

20 Edna Bonacich and Jake B. Wilson, *Getting the Goods: Ports, Labor, and the Logistics Revolution* (Ithaca, NY: Cornell University Press, 2007), 5.

21 Ibid., 4–5.

22 See Brett Neilson and Ned Rossiter, "Still Waiting, Still Moving: On Migration, Logistics and Maritime Industries," in David Bissell and Gillian Fuller (eds.), *Stillness in a Mobile World* (London: Routledge, 2010), 51–68.

23 On Arendt and the contemporary dissolution of the borders between labor, action, and intellect, see Paolo Virno, *A Grammar of the Multitude,* trans. James Cascaito Isabella Bertoletti, and Andrea Casson (New York: Semiotext(e), 2004), 49–51. See also Zehle and Rossiter, "Organizing Networks": "How, then, to account for a politics *beyond the actionable?* Such work requires a conceptual constellation that foregrounds translation as a conflictual dynamic and social practice immanent to networks of collaborative constitution" (258, note 1).

24 Michael Hardt and Antonio Negri, "The Fight for 'Real Democracy' at the Heart of Occupy Wall Street: The Encampment in Lower Manhattan Speaks to a Failure of Representation," *Foreign Affairs,* October 11, 2011, http://www.foreignaffairs.com. For a different account of such filiation, see Paul Mason, *Why It's Kicking Off Everywhere: The New Global Revolutions* (New York: Verso, 2011).

25 Arguably the most consistent articulation of assemblage as a social ontology scalable beyond analytical micro-/macrodichotomies can be found in the work of Manuel DeLanda. See *A New Philosophy of Society: Assemblage Theory and Social Complexity* (New York: Continuum, 2006). See also Manuel DeLanda, *Philosophy and Simulation: The Emergence of Synthetic Reason* (New York: Continuum, 2011).

26 Michel Foucault, "On Popular Justice: A Discussion with Maoists," in *Power/Knowledge: Selected Interviews and Other Writings, 1972–1977,* trans. Colin Gordon, Leo Marshall, John Mepham, and Kate Soper (New York: Pantheon Books, 1972), 1–36.

27 See David M. Berry, *The Philosophy of Software: Code and Mediation in the Digital Age* (Hampshire: Palgrave Macmillan, 2011).

28 See Alexander R. Galloway, *Gaming: Essays on Algorithmic Culture* (Minneapolis: University of Minnesota Press, 2006). See also Wendy Hui Kyong Chun, *Programmed Visions: Software and Memory* (Cambridge, MA: MIT Press, 2011); Matthew Fuller, *Software Studies: A Lexicon* (Cambridge, MA: MIT Press, 2008); and Konrad Becker and Felix Stalder, *Deep Search: The Politics of Search Beyond Google* (Innsbruck: Studien Verlag, 2009).

29 The sociotechnological process of free and open-source software development has long been considered a paradigmatic net-cultural dynamic—to understand the web is to understand free software. See Samir Chopra and Scott Dexter, *Decoding Liberation: The Promise of Free and Open Source Software* (New York: Routledge, 2007); Joseph Feller, Brian Fitzgerald, Scott A. Hissam, and Karim R. Lakhani (eds.), *Perspectives on Free and Open Software* (Cambridge, MA: MIT Press, 2005); Chris Kelty, *Two Bits: The Cultural Significance of Free Software* (Durham, NC: Duke University Press, 2008). Free software continues to serve as a foil for critiques of alternative licensing schemes such as creative commons; see Berry, *The Philosophy of Software.*

30 See, for example, Louisa Lim, "In Greek Port, Storm Brews over Chinese-Run Labor,"
    NPR, June 8, 2011, http://www.npr.org/2011/06/08/137035251/in-greek-port-
    storm-brews-over-chinese-run-labor. See also Ferry Batzoglou and Manfred Ertel,
    "'Good Friends Are There to Help': Chinese Investors Take Advantage of Greek
    Crisis," *Spiegel,* November 16, 2011, http://www.spiegel.de/international/europe/
    0,1518,797751,00.html.

31 Galloway, *Gaming,* xi.

32 http://lab.softwarestudies.com.

33 Michael Warner, *Publics and Counterpublics* (New York: Zone, 2002). Warner develops a
    taxonomy of reflexive practices around a notion of the public as an "ongoing space of
    encounter" (90) but fails to engage the constitutive dynamic of hybrid online/offline
    publics.

34 Bitcoin remains subject to speculation like any other currency. See Benjamin Wallace,
    "The Rise and Fall of Bitcoin: Inside the Virtual Currency You Can Actually Spend,"
    Wired 12.01 (January 2012), http://www.wired.co.uk/magazine/archive/2012/01/
    features/the-rise-and-fall-of-bitcoin.

35 See Paul Shaxson, *Treasure Islands: Uncovering the Damage of Offshore Banking and Tax
    Havens* (New York: Palgrave Macmillan, 2011), as well as reports by organizations such
    as Publish What You Pay (http://www.publishwhatyoupay.org), Tax Justice Network
    (http://www.taxjustice.net), and Global Witness (http://www.globalwitness.org).

36 See http://www.kinecthacks.com. On the sentient city, see Mark Shepard (ed.), *Sentient
    City: Ubiquitous Computing, Architecture, and the Future of Urban Space* (Cambridge, MA:
    MIT Press, 2011), as well as http://survival.sentientcity.net.

37 Eric Kluitenberg, *Legacies of Tactical Media,* Network Notebooks 05 (Amsterdam: Insti-
    tute of Network Cultures, 2011), 10.

38 See Malcolm Gladwell, "Small Changes: Why the Revolution Will Not Be Tweeted,"
    New Yorker, October 24, 2010, http://www.newyorker.com/reporting/2010/
    10/04/101004fa_fact_gladwell. While we do not necessarily second Gladwell's call
    for a return of (and to) hierarchical forms of organization, we share the concern that
    "[t]he instruments of social media are well suited to making the existing social order
    more efficient" (ibid.).

FURTHER READING

This list was compiled by participants of the Internet as Playground and Factory conference.

Adorno, Thedor W. "Adorno T (1991) 'Free Time,' in Adorno T (1991) *The Culture Industry: Selected Essays on Mass Culture,* (edited and with an Introduction by J Bernstein), London: Routledge." first published 1977. Web. May 13, 2012.

Anderson, Chris. *Free: The Future of a Radical Price.* Hyperion, 2009. Print.

Andrejevic, M. "Exploiting YouTube: Contradictions of User-generated Labor." *The YouTube Reader* 413 (2009): n. pag. Print.

Andrejevic, Mark. *iSpy: Surveillance and Power in the Interactive Era.* University Press of Kansas, 2009. Print.

Andrejevic, Mark. *Reality TV: The Work of Being Watched.* Rowman & Littlefield Publishers, 2003. Print.

Aneesh, A. *Virtual Migration: The Programming of Globalization.* Duke University Press Books, 2006. Print.

Anzaldúa, Gloria, and AnaLouise Keating, eds. *This Bridge We Call Home: Radical Visions for Transformation.* 1st ed. Routledge, 2002. Print.

Aranda, Julieta, Anton Vidokle, and Brian Kuan Wood. *E-Flux Journal: Are You Working Too Much? Post-Fordism, Precarity, and the Labor of Art.* Sternberg Press, 2011. Print.

Arendt, Hannah. *Responsibility and Judgment.* 1st ed. Schocken, 2003. Print.

Arvidsson, Adam. "Ethical Economy." Web. May 10, 2012.

Baker, Stephen. "Will Work for Praise: The Web's Free-Labor Economy." *Businessweek: Technology* 28 Dec. 2008. Web. May 14, 2012.

Barbrook, Richard. *The Class of the New.* Mute, 2006. Print.

Barbrook, Richard. *Imaginary Futures: From Thinking Machines to the Global Village.* Pluto Press, 2007. Print.

Bauman, Zygmunt. *Consuming Life.* 1st ed. Polity Press, 2007. Print.

Beck, John C., and Mitchell Wade. *Got Game: How the Gamer Generation Is Reshaping Business Forever.* Harvard Business Press, 2004. Print.

Beller, Jonathan. *The Cinematic Mode of Production: Attention Economy and the Society of the Spectacle.* Dartmouth, 2006. Print.

Benkler, Yochai. *The Wealth of Networks: How Social Production Transforms Markets and Free-dom.* Yale University Press, 2007. Print.

Berardi, Franco "Bifo." *The Soul at Work: From Alienation to Autonomy (Semiotext(e)).* Trans. Francesca Cadel & Giuseppina Mecchia. Semiotext(e), 2009. Print.

BookRags.com. *The Soul of a New Machine by Tracy Kidder | Summary & Study Guide.* 2010. Print.

Braverman, Harry. *Labor and Monopoly Capital: The Degradation of Work in the Twentieth Century.* Anv. Monthly Review Press, 1998. Print.

Calabrese, Andrew, and Colin Sparks, eds. *Toward a Political Economy of Culture: Capital-ism and Communication in the Twenty-First Century.* Rowman & Littlefield Publishers, 2003. Print.

Carpignano, Paolo. "[iDC] Intro and Response to Ross/Terranova." *iDC Mailing List,* Oct. 20, 2009. Web. May 13, 2012.

Castells, Manuel. *Communication Power.* Reprint. Oxford University Press, USA, 2011. Print.

christianfuchs. "Class and Exploitation on the Internet." The Internet as Playground and Factory. 2009. Technology.

Clough, Patricia Ticineto, and Jean Halley, eds. *The Affective Turn: Theorizing the Social.* 1st ed. Duke University Press Books, 2007. Print.

Coleman, E. Gabriella. "Three Ethical Moments in Debian." *SSRN eLibrary* (2005): n. pag. Web. May 13, 2012.

Corneliussen, Hilde G., and Jill Walker Rettberg, eds. *Digital Culture, Play, and Identity: A World of Warcraft® Reader.* The MIT Press, 2011. Print.

Crary, Jonathan. *Suspensions of Perception: Attention, Spectacle, and Modern Culture.* The MIT Press, 2001. Print.

Crawford, Matthew B. "The Case for Working With Your Hands." *The New York Times,* May 24, 2009. Web. May 10, 2012.

Crawford, Matthew B. *Shop Class as Soulcraft: An Inquiry into the Value of Work.* Reprint. Penguin (Non-Classics), 2010. Print.

Dean, Jodi. *Blog Theory: Feedback and Capture in the Circuits of Drive.* 1st ed. Polity, 2010. Print.

DeNardis, Laura. *Protocol Politics: The Globalization of Internet Governance.* The MIT Press, 2009. Print.

DeNardis, Laura, ed. *Opening Standards: The Global Politics of Interoperability.* 1st ed. The MIT Press, 2011. Print.

Dibbell, Julian. "The Life of the Chinese Gold Farmer." *The New York Times,* 17 June 2007. Web. May 13, 2012.

Dibbell, Julian. *Play Money: Or, How I Quit My Day Job and Made Millions Trading Virtual Loot.* Basic Books, 2006. Print.

Van Dijck, José, and David Nieborg. "Wikinomics and Its Discontents: A Critical Analysis of Web 2.0 Business Manifestos." *New Media & Society* 11.5 (2009): 855–74. Web. May 13, 2012.

Doctorow, Cory. *For the Win.* 1st ed. Tor Teen, 2010. Print.

Dyer-Witheford, Nick. *Cyber-Marx: Cycles and Circuits of Struggle in High Technology Capital-ism.* University of Illinois Press, 1999. Print.

Elkin-Koren, Niva. "Governing Access to Users-Generated-Content: The Changing Nature of Private Ordering in Digital Networks." *SSRN eLibrary,* n. pag. Web. May 13, 2012.

Fish, Adam, and Ramesh Srinivasan. "Digital Labor Is the New Killer App." *New Media & Society* 14.1 (2012): 137–52. Web. May 17, 2012.

FORA.tv—Democratization and the Public Sphere. The New School, 2007. Film.

Foucault, Michel. *The Birth of Biopolitics: Lectures at the Collège De France, 1978–1979*. 1st ed. Picador, 2010. Print.

Fuchs, Christian. *Internet and Society: Social Theory in the Information Age*. Routledge, 2008. Print.

Fuchs, Christian. "Labor in Informational Capitalism and on the Internet." *The Information Society* 26.3 (2010): 179–96.

Galloway, Alexander R., and Eugene Thacker. *The Exploit: A Theory of Networks*. University of Minnesota Press, 2007. Print.

Gill, Rosalind, and Andy Pratt. "In the Social Factory? Immaterial Labour, Precariousness and Cultural Work." *Theory, Culture & Society* 25.7–8 (2008): 1–30. Web. May 11, 2012.

Goffman, Erving. *Behavior in Public Places: Notes on the Social Organization of Gatherings*. Free Press, 1966. Print.

Gregg, Melissa. *Work's Intimacy*. 1st ed. Polity, 2011. Print.

Guy, Mary E., Meredith A. Newman, and Sharon H. Mastraci. *Emotional Labor: Putting the Service in Public Service*. M. E. Sharpe, 2008. Print.

Hippel, Eric Von. *Democratizing Innovation*. The MIT Press, 2006. Print.

Hochschild, Arlie Russell. *The Managed Heart: Commercialization of Human Feeling, Twentieth Anniversary Edition, With a New Afterword*. 2nd ed. University of California Press, 2003. Print.

Huws, Ursula, and Colin Leys. *The Making of a Cybertariat: Virtual Work in a Real World*. Monthly Review Press, 2003. Print.

Kane, Pat. "[iDC] Notes Toward a Theory of Ludocapitalism (O Rly?)." *IDC Mailing List* Sept. 25, 2007. Web. May 13, 2012.

Kane, Pat. *The Play Ethic: A Manifesto for a Different Way of Living*. Macmillan UK, 2004. Print.

Kitcher, P. "The Division of Cognitive Labor." *The Journal of Philosophy* 87.1 (1990): 5–22. Print.

Kücklich, Julian. "FCJ-025 Precarious Playbour: Modders and the Digital Games Industry." *The FibreCulture Journal* 5 (2005) n. pag. Web. May 11, 2012.

Lazzarato, Maurizio. "Immaterial Labor." *Generation Online*. Web. May 13, 2012.

Lessig, Lawrence. *Remix: Making Art and Commerce Thrive in the Hybrid Economy*. Penguin Press HC, 2008. Print.

Liu, Alan. *The Laws of Cool: Knowledge Work and the Culture of Information*. 1st ed. University of Chicago Press, 2004. Print.

Lovink, Geert. *Networks Without a Cause: A Critique of Social Media*. 1st ed. Polity, 2012. Print.

Malaby, Thomas. *Making Virtual Worlds: Linden Lab and Second Life*. Cornell University Press, 2009. Print.

Marazzi, C. *Capital and Language: From the New Economy to the War Economy*. 2008. Print.

Marazzi, Christian. *The Violence of Financial Capitalism (Semiotext(e)/Intervention series)*. Trans. Kristina Lebedeva. Semiotext(e), 2010. Print.

Martin, Randy. *Financialization of Daily Life*. Temple University Press, 2002. Print.

"Michel Bauwens—The Social Web and Its Social Contracts: Some Notes on Social Antagonism in Netarchical Capitalism | Re-public: Re-imagining Democracy–English Version." *Re-public* Special Issue, n. pag. Web. June 13, 2012.

Mills, C. Wright. *The Power Elite*. Oxford University Press, USA, 2000. Print.

Mitchell, Robert, and Catherine Waldby. "National Biobanks: Clinical Labor, Risk Production, and the Creation of Biovalue." *Science, Technology & Human Values* (2009): n. pag. Web. June 13, 2012.

Mosco, Vincent. *The Political Economy of Communication*. 2nd ed. Sage Publications Ltd, 2009. Print.

Mosco, Vincent, and Catherine McKercher. *The Laboring of Communication: Will Knowledge Workers of the World Unite?* Lexington Books, 2009. Print.

Moulier-Boutang, Yann. *Cognitive Capitalism.* 1st ed. Polity, 2012. Print.

Murdock, Graham, and Janer Wasko, eds. *Media in the Age of Marketization.* Hampton Press, 2007. Print.

Nissenbaum, Helen. *Privacy in Context: Technology, Policy, and the Integrity of Social Life.* Stanford Law Books, 2009. Print.

Niva Elkin-Koren. "Net-Ordering: Conceptualizing Governance in Social Media." Web. May 13, 2012.

Oldenburg, Ray. *The Great Good Place: Cafes, Coffee Shops, Bookstores, Bars, Hair Salons, and Other Hangouts at the Heart of a Community.* 3rd ed. Marlowe & Company, 1999. Print.

"The Paradox of Labor, Property, Privacy on the Core Sites of the Sociable Web—Trebor Scholz 'Journalisms'—Collectivate.net." Web. May 11, 2012.

Pariser, Eli. *The Filter Bubble: What the Internet Is Hiding from You.* 1st ptg. Penguin Press HC, 2011. Print.

Pasquinelli, Matteo. *Animal Spirits: A Bestiary of the Commons.* NAi Publishers, 2009. Print.

Perlin, Ross. *Intern Nation: How to Earn Nothing and Learn Little in the Brave New Economy.* 1st ed. Verso, 2012. Print.

Peters, Michael A., and Ergin Bulut (eds.). *Cognitive Capitalism, Education and Digital Labor.* First printing. Peter Lang Publishing, 2011. Print.

Peters, Thomas Atzert, translated by Frederick Peters. "About Immaterial Labor and Bio-power." *Capitalism Nature Socialism* 17.1 (2006): 58–64. Print.

Postigo, Hector. "America Online Volunteers Lessons from an Early Co-Production Community." *International Journal of Cultural Studies* 12.5 (2009): 451–469. Web. May 13, 2012.

Qiu, Jack Linchuan. *Working-Class Network Society: Communication Technology and the Information Have-Less in Urban China.* The MIT Press, 2009. Print.

Rosen, Jeffrey. *The Naked Crowd: Reclaiming Security and Freedom in an Anxious Age.* Random House Trade Paperbacks, 2005. Print.

Ross, Andrew. *Nice Work If You Can Get It: Life and Labor in Precarious Times.* 1st ed. NYU Press, 2009. Print.

Ross, Andrew. *No-Collar: The Humane Workplace and Its Hidden Costs.* Temple University Press, 2004. Print.

Ross, Andrew. "On the Digital Labor Question." *IDC Mailing List* 16 (2009). Web. May 11, 2012.

Rossiter, Ned. *Organized Networks: Media Theory, Creative Labour, New Institutions.* NAi Publishers, 2006. Print.

Rushkoff, Douglas. *Life Inc: How Corporatism Conquered the World, and How We Can Take It Back.* Random House Trade Paperbacks, 2011. Print.

Scholz, Trebor. "[iDC] Documents from The Internet as Playground and Factory (Trebor Scholz)." Web. May 13, 2012.

Scholz, Trebor. "Internet as Playground and Factory: Introduction." Web. May 11, 2012.

Scholz, Trebor. "Market Ideology and the Myths of Web 2.0." *First Monday* 13.3 (2008): n. pag. Web. May 27, 2012.

Scholz, Trebor. "What the MySpace Generation Should Know About Working for Free | Re-public: Re-imagining Democracy—English Version." Web. May 11, 2012.

Scholz, Trebor, and Liu, Laura. *From Mobile Playgrounds to Sweatshop City.* The Architectural League of New York, 2010. Web. May 14, 2012. Situated Technologies Pamphlets 7.

Scholz, Trebor, and Geert Lovink, eds. *The Art of Free Cooperation.* Pap/DVD. Autonomedia/Institute for Distributed Creativity, 2007. Print.

Sennett, Richard. *The Craftsman.* 1st ed. Yale University Press, 2009. Print.

Shirky, Clay. *Cognitive Surplus: Creativity and Generosity in a Connected Age.* Penguin Press HC, 2010. Print.

Shirky, Clay. *Here Comes Everybody: The Power of Organizing Without Organizations.* Reprint. Penguin (Non-Classics), 2009. Print.

Shirky, Clay. "Shirky: Who Are You Paying When You're Paying Attention?" *Clay Shirky's Writings About the Internet.* Web. May 14, 2012.

Solove, Daniel J. *Nothing to Hide: The False Tradeoff Between Privacy and Security.* Yale University Press, 2011. Print.

Standing, Guy. *The Precariat: The New Dangerous Class.* Bloomsbury USA, 2011. Print.

Stiegler, Bernard. *For a New Critique of Political Economy.* 1st ed. Trans. Daniel Ross. Polity, 2010. Print.

Terranova, Tiziana. *Network Culture: Politics for the Information Age.* Pluto Press, 2004. Print.

Thrift, Nigel. *Knowing Capitalism.* 1st ed. Sage Publications Ltd, 2005. Print.

Toffler, Alvin. *Future Shock.* PAN, 1971. Print.

Translated, Georg Simmel et al. *Sociology: Inquiries into the Construction of Social Forms, 2 Volume Set.* Ed. Anthony J. Blasi, Anton K. Jacobs, & Mathew Kanjirathinkal. Brill, 2009. Print.

Turner, Fred. *From Counterculture to Cyberculture: Stewart Brand, the Whole Earth Network, and the Rise of Digital Utopianism.* University of Chicago Press, 2008. Print.

Vaidhyanathan, Siva. *The Googlization of Everything:* 1st ed. University of California Press, 2011. Print.

Virno, Paolo. *A Grammar of the Multitude: For an Analysis of Contemporary Forms of Life (Semiotext(e)).* First US ed. Trans. Isabella Bertoletti, James Cascaito, & Andrea Casson. Semiotex(e), 2004. Print.

Virno, Paolo, and Michael Hardt, eds. *Radical Thought in Italy: A Potential Politics.* 1st ed. University of Minnesota Press, 2006. Print.

Wark, McKenzie. *A Hacker Manifesto.* Harvard University Press, 2004. Print.

Wittkower, D. E., ed. *Facebook and Philosophy: What's on Your Mind?* Open Court, 2010. Print.

Zandt, Deanna. *Share This!: How You Will Change the World with Social Networking.* 1st ed. Berrett-Koehler Publishers, 2010. Print.

Zittrain, Jonathan. *The Future of the Internet—And How to Stop It.* Yale University Press, 2009. Print.

CONTRIBUTORS

Mark Andrejevic is a QE II Postdoctoral Researcher at the Centre for Critical and Cultural Studies, University of Queensland. His work focuses on the productive aspect of surveillance and monitoring in the digital era. In particular, he explores the ways in which the capture of detailed information about citizens becomes a source of value creation and generation within the context of the emerging interactive commercial model. He is the author of *Reality TV: The Work of Being Watched* and *iSpy: Surveillance and Power in the Interactive Era,* as well as numerous articles and book chapters on surveillance, popular culture, and digital media.

Ayhan Aytes received his PhD degree in Communication and Cognitive Science from the University of California, San Diego, in 2012. His research interests are related to the cultural history of artificial intelligence in relation to subjectivity, body, autonomy, temporality, religion, and race. His dissertation, *The 'Other' in the Machine: Oriental Automata and the Mechanization of the Mind,* is an inquiry into a long-term cultural relationship between intelligent automata and the Western discourse of Orientalism. His digital media works have been exhibited in various venues, including the Istanbul Museum of the History of Science and Technology in Islam and Aksanat Culture and Arts Center. www.ayhanaytes.net.

Michel Bauwens is a writer, researcher, and speaker on the subjects of technology, culture, and business innovation. He is the founder of the Foundation for Peer-to-Peer Alternatives (www.p2pfoundation.net) and collaborates with a global group of researchers in the exploration of peer production, governance, and property. He has been an analyst for the United States Information Agency, knowledge manager for British Petroleum, e-business strategy manager for Belgacom, and an Internet entrepreneur in his native Belgium. He coproduced the TV documentary *Technocalyps* with Frank Theys and coedited a two-volume book about the anthropology of digital society with Salvino Salvaggio. Bauwens is Primavera Research Fellow at the University of Amsterdam and an external expert for the Pontifical Academy of Social Sciences. He currently lives in Chiang Mai, Thailand. He is a partner with the Commons Strategies Group and serves on the advisory boards of the Union of International Associations (Brussels), *Shareable* magazine (San Francisco), and the Zumbara Timebank (Istanbul).

Jonathan Beller is Professor of Humanities and Media Studies and Critical and Visual Studies at The Pratt Institute. He also directs Pratt's graduate program in media Studies. He is the author of *The Cinematic Mode of Production: Attention Economy and the Society of the Spectacle* (2006) and *Acquiring Eyes: Philippine Visuality, Nationalist Struggle and the World-Media System* (2006). Current book projects include *Present Senses: Aesthetics/Affect/Asia* (with Neferti Tadiar) and *Wagers within the Image*. He is editing a special issue of *The Scholar and Feminist Online* titled *Feminist Media Theory: Iterations of Social Difference*. www.jonathanbeller.wordpress.com.

Patricia Ticineto Clough is Professor of Sociology and Women's Studies at the City University of New York–Queens College and the Graduate Center. She is the author of *Autoaffection: Unconscious Thought in the Age of Teletechnology* (2000), *Feminist Thought: Desire, Power and Academic Discourse* (1994), and *The End(s) of Ethnography: From Realism to Social Criticism* (1998). She is editor of *The Affective Turn: Theorizing the Social* (2007) and, with Craig Willse, editor of *Beyond Biopolitics: Essays on the Governance of Life and Death* (forthcoming).

Sean Cubitt is Professor of Film and Television at Goldsmiths, University of London; Professorial Fellow of the University of Melbourne; and Honorary Professor of the University of Dundee. His publications include *Timeshift: On Video Culture, Videography: Video Media as Art and Culture, Digital Aesthetics, Simulation and Social Theory, The Cinema Effect,* and *EcoMedia.* He is the series editor for Leonardo Books at MIT Press. His current research is on the history and philosophy of visual technologies, on media art history, and on ecocriticism and mediation.

Jodi Dean is Professor of Political Science at Hobart and William Smith Colleges. Her books include *Aliens in America* (1998), *Publicity's Secret* (2002), *Zizek's Politics* (2006), *Democracy and Other Neoliberal Fantasies* (2009), *Blog Theory* (2010), and *The Communist Horizon* (2012). She is coeditor of the international electronic journal of critical political and cultural theory, *Theory & Event.*

Abigail De Kosnik is Assistant Professor at the University of California–Berkeley, at the Berkeley Center for New Media and the Department of Theater, Dance and Performance Studies. www.twitter.com/De_Kosnik.

Christian Fuchs is Chair Professor in Media and Communication Studies at Uppsala University. His main research interests are critical social theory; media and society; critical political economy of media; and communication, digital media, and society. He is chair of the European Sociological Association's Research Network 18—Sociology of Communications and Media Research, cofounder of the ICTs and Society Network (www.icts-and-society.net) and editor of *tripleC—Open Access Journal for a Global Sustainable Information Society* (www.triple-c.at). He is author of the books *Internet and Society: Social Theory in the Information Age* (2008), *Foundations of Critical Media and Information Studies* (2011), and *Social Media: A Critical Introduction* (forthcoming). And he is coeditor of *Internet and Surveillance. The Challenges of Web 2.0 and Social Media* (2012). His website is www.fuchs.uti.at.

Lisa Nakamura is the Director of the Asian American Studies Program, Professor in the Institute of Communication Research and Media Studies program, and Professor of Asian American Studies at the University of Illinois at Urbana-Champaign. She is the author of *Digitizing Race: Visual Cultures of the Internet* (2008) and *Cybertypes: Race, Ethnicity and Identity on the Internet* (2002), and she is coeditor of *Race in Cyberspace* (2000) and *Race After the Internet* (2011). She has published articles in *PMLA, Cinema Journal, Women's Review of Books, Camera Obscura,* and the *Iowa Journal of Cultural Studies.* Her research focuses on race and gender in online social spaces such as massively multiplayer online role-playing games, and she is currently investigating the racializaton of labor in transnational contexts and avatarial operations in a postracial world.

Andrew Ross is a Professor of Social and Cultural Analysis at New York University. He is a contributor to *The Nation,* the *Village Voice, New York Times,* and *Artforum,* and he is the author of many books, including, most recently, *Bird on Fire: Lessons from the World's Least Sustainable City; Nice Work If You Can Get It: Life and Labor in Precarious Times; Fast Boat to China—Lessons from Shanghai; Low Pay, High Profile: The Global Push for Fair Labor; No-Collar: The Humane Workplace and Its Hidden Costs;* and *The Celebration Chronicles: Life, Liberty and the Pursuit of Property Value in Disney's New Town.*

Ned Rossiter is an Australian media theorist and author of *Organized Networks: Media Theory, Creative Labour, New Institutions* (2006). He was based in Perth, Melbourne, Ulster, Beijing, Shanghai, and Ningbo before taking up an appointment as Professor of Communication in 2011 in the School of Humanities and Communication Arts at the University of Western Sydney, where he is also a member of the Institute for Culture and Society. Rossiter is also an Honorary Research Fellow at the Centre for Creative Industries, Beida (Peking) University. He is a core-searcher on Transit Labour: Circuits, Regions, Borders (www.transitlabour.asia).

Trebor Scholz is an artist, writer, catalyst, and chair of the conference series The Politics of Digital Culture at The New School in New York City, where he is an Associate Professor of Culture and Media. His forthcoming monograph with

Polity Press offers a history of the social web and its Orwellian economies. In 2011, he coauthored (with Laura Y. Liu) *From Mobile Playgrounds to Sweatshop City*. Scholz is the editor of two collections of essays, *Learning Through Digital Media* (2011), and a volume on digital labor (2013). He coedited the Situated Technologies series of nine books and *The Art of Free Cooperation* (2007). Recent book chapters include "Facebook as Playground and Factory," and "Cheaper by the Dozen: An Introduction to Crowdsourcing." He also founded the Institute for Distributed Creativity, which is widely known for its online discussions of critical network culture. Scholz holds a grant from the John D. and Catherine T. MacArthur Foundation. He chaired seven major conferences including the MobilityShifts summit in 2011. www.digitallabor.org.

Tiziana Terranova is Associate Professor in the Sociology of Communications at the Dipartimento di Scienze Umane e Sociali, Università degli Studi di Napoli "L'Orientale." Her research interests lie in the area of the culture, science, technology, and political economy of new media. She is the author of *Corpi Nella Rete* (1996), *Network Culture: Politics for the Information Age* (2004), and numerous essays on new media published in journals such as *Derive e Approdi, New Formations, Ctheory, Angelaki, Social Text, Theory Culture and Society,* and *Transversal*. She is a member of the editorial board of the journal *Studi Culturali* (Il Mulino); associate editor of the journal *Theory, Culture and Society;* and a member of the Italian free university network UniNomade (www.uninomade.org). She occasionally also writes on matters of new media for the Italian newspaper *Il Manifesto*.

McKenzie Wark is the author of *A Hacker Manifesto* (2004), *Gamer Theory* (2007), and various other works. He is Professor of Culture and Media at Eugene Lang College, The New School for Liberal Arts. www.en.wikipedia.org/wiki/McKenzie_Wark.

Soenke Zehle is Lecturer in Media Art and Design and has a long-time involvement in the collaborative conceptualization and implementation of transnational net.cultural art and research projects. Soenke is director of XMLab—Experimental Media Lab at the Academy of Fine Arts Saar, Ö Saarbrücken, Germany. For more information on her projects and publications, see www.xmlab.org.

INDEX